When I Go Home

An Alzheimer's Caregiver Story of Love

Bill Galea

Pacific Book Review
(5 Star Review)

When I Go Home is truly a special kind of love story. It is a poignant memoir that takes readers into the world of Alzheimer's disease and offers an insightful perspective from a devoted son who knew no bounds in providing compassion and care for his beloved mother who suffered with this illness.

Bill Galea's mom was the heart and soul of her family. Beautiful, kind, and generous, her glowing personality would light up a room. In 1999, short-term memory issues and the incident of leaving a tea kettle boiling on the stove brought her to a neurologist where she was diagnosed with MCI (Mild Cognitive Impairment), a precursor to Alzheimer's disease. Medication slowed its progression, but ultimately her subsequent wanderings led the family to decide the best option was to place her in a nursing facility.

It was a heart-wrenching necessity that Bill likened to "an emotional tsunami." At the same time, Bill was dealing with his father's recurring cancer, then sadly, his passing shortly thereafter. Clearly these events exemplified the old adage of "when it rains, it pours." For anyone who has dealt with an ailing loved one, it is hard not to be touched by Bill's moving biographical account. The main focus of this book is specifically on the challenges of Alzheimer's, a disease that attacks the brain and robs an individual of their memory, physicality, identity, and dignity. Readers dealing with any type of long-term caregiving situation should find value in Bill's shared experience, personal insights, and diligent observations. His near daily visits with his mother led to extensive journaling that he openly incorporates into this book. Here readers will witness the tender moments of hugs, laughter, and tears between a mother and her adult child, as well as glimpse the harsh realities of dealing with inadequate health care facilities. Readers will feel the stress of coping with financial issues and realize the major toll this devastating illness takes on both the patient and family members.

When Bill heard his mom use the phrase "When I Go Home" while she was conversing with an aide, though he felt this may be an impossibility, his mother's sense of hope inspired him to use it as the title of this book. For the Alzheimer's patient we learn that the word "home" is often just a concept or idea of being in a loving place, surrounded by family. While the decline of a loved one is always sad, any humorous light amidst a serious prognosis should always be treasured. One such highlight occurred as Bill pointed out a 100-year-old fellow patient to his mom. He stated, "Mom, this woman is almost 100 years old. Can you believe it?" Her response was a quick and snappy "She looks it!" Laughter is always good medicine. The book also includes several black and white images that help put a face to his family. From childhood snapshots to wedding photos and a lovely 50th Anniversary portrait of his parents, all seem bittersweet reminders of happier and healthier times.

Bill also makes an important analogy when he likens Alzheimer's patients to delicate flowers needing water, nutrients, sunshine, care, love, and attention. These are not merely elements for survival, but rather key components for a patient to thrive and bloom. During such overwhelmingly trying times, he wisely stresses that caregivers also need to treat themselves with delicate and purposeful care. Under the mountain of stress that a situation like this brings upon you, caring for yourself is a necessary indulgence.

At the heart of this story is a powerful lesson about being the best possible advocate for any loved one afflicted with this terrible disease. Reading this emotionally charged book is a humbling experience that will leave you with no regrets. There is real gratitude for the moments of living life with those you love that are so important to cherish; as the memory and legacy of those encounters are all that truly remain years afterward.

Everyone needs to read When I Go Home: An Alzheimer's Caregiver Story of Love. This book is not only for those who are faced with Alzheimer's or dementia in their lives, but also for anyone who has ever cared for another human being afflicted with any type of illness, because sooner or later most people will face this in his or her life.

Contents

Preface

My mom has Alzheimer's disease. It is in our family. In addition to my mom, her mom had it, her grandma had it, and her great-grandma had it. Therefore, I care very deeply about Alzheimer's disease and its impact on people, as well as how it affects their loved ones. This story is about a son's unwavering love and devotion to his mom.

The original idea for this book came from the many hours that I have spent visiting with and caring for my mom, especially after she had to go into a nursing home. During this period, I have had many wonderful times and conversations with her. Every moment that I spend with Mom is precious. After visiting Mom for the first two years in the nursing home, I decided that it would be a good idea to keep a journal of our conversations and other noteworthy things that happened. This was the genesis of my book.

I've always been a sensitive and compassionate person. I care so deeply about this issue because it affects my mom, the most important person in my life. I believe that I bring a unique perspective and contribution to the Alzheimer's movement.

Acknowledgments

∞

I would like to thank the following people who have been helpful to me in the process of writing this book. If I forgot to mention someone, it certainly was not intentional.

First and foremost, I want to thank my mom for being the most wonderful, precious, and special person that I have ever known in my life. Your daily strength, grace, and dignity in dealing with your disease will always will be the most incredible source of pride and inspiration to me. I love you, Mom. This book is dedicated to you.

I want to thank my dad (rest in peace). Although our dad is no longer with us, I know that he's watching over Mom and the rest of us from heaven. Thank you, Dad, for all your love, strength, wisdom, guidance, and support over the years. I love you, Dad.

I would like to thank my sister, Mary, for serving alongside me as the main caregivers to our mom. Thank you to my brothers, Andy and John, for their caring efforts and their shared burden of love and concern for Mom.

I want to thank all the other caregivers who are going through or have gone through what I go through on a daily basis. You have my understanding, support, and love.

I want to thank the professionals in the field of human potential for their passion, wisdom, guidance and support in helping me and others to really step out into the world and contribute to it in a meaningful way.

I also want to thank all of my friends who have believed in me and supported me over many years. You have my utmost gratitude.

Introduction

It wasn't supposed to be this way.

When I was four years old, everything seemed so simple. I used to lie down on the grass and look up at the beautiful blue summer sky, watching the clouds drift by. I would just lie there and gaze at the sky for what seemed to be forever. By the time I was five years old, we had moved to another town in New Jersey, and I would sometimes go down the block to lie on the grass next to a stream. I would look up at the sky and watch all the clouds rolling by, as if they were parading on for my benefit. It was all so simple back then.

In the midst of all my childhood reverie, I never saw the storm clouds approaching far off in the distance. How could I have? However, they were marching on in their inexorable way. There was nothing that I could do to stop them.

Many years later, in the middle to late part of 1999, my siblings and I began to notice that our mom's memory wasn't working as well as usual. She was becoming forgetful about different things. In the beginning, Mom would make light of it. It seemed to be her way of dealing with it.

When we brought it to the attention of our dad, he first thought it was just a part of the aging process. But we continued to bring it up periodically, and within approximately three to six months' time, Dad took Mom to see a neurologist. After the examination, the doctor said that Mom had mild cognitive impairment (MCI), a precursor to Alzheimer's disease. We were all very saddened and fearful about this diagnosis. We now know that Alzheimer's disease begins before there's even a diagnosis. Mom's disease most likely began prior to the year 2000. Although there is a family history of the disease, we never really expected her to get it.

Everyone knows about the danger of heart attacks, but Alzheimer's disease is a brain attack. It causes brain damage. It is a progressive disease, and it has no cure. The medications available today can only slow down its progression. If there is any good news here, it is that the disease progresses more slowly as the patient ages.

In the landscape of a person's emotional life, Alzheimer's disease brings complete devastation. My heart breaks each and every day over what is happening to Mom. I feel this way seven days a week, fifty-two weeks a year. I never get a day off from that feeling, and it adds a lot of stress to my life.

I would not want anyone to get Alzheimer's disease. I continue to question why someone as loving, special, and wonderful as my mom has come down with it. After all that she has done for our family, after all her hard work and the sacrifices that she has made, this is no way for her to spend her golden years, living with Alzheimer's and requiring twenty-four hour care in a nursing home.

I'm not angry at my mom because she has this disease. I'm angry at the disease, I'm angry at God, and I'm angry that this hurts not only Mom but our entire family. It takes a tremendous emotional toll on all of us, especially our Mom. There's a feeling of being powerless over this disease, especially because there is no known cure at this time.

My message to Alzheimer's disease is that when you picked on my mom, you picked on the wrong person. Now that I'm in the fight, I can assure you that I will never, ever give up. I will never give in. I will be relentless in my pursuit for awareness, sensitivity, funding, and a cure.

I will continue to speak clearly, profoundly, and with conviction in the righteousness of this cause. I speak for those who can no longer speak for themselves, the people who suffer from Alzheimer's disease. I also want to speak out for those caregivers who spend every day of their lives worrying about, caring for and advocating on behalf of their loved ones. I want to share my experiences. It is my hope that other caregivers will relate and gain strength and inspiration from our story. I also hope that it will inspire the Alzheimer's movement to push even harder for funding and for a cure.

Now is the time to bring this disease all the attention, focus, and commitment that it deserves. As I hear the trumpeting for a call to action, I'm here to answer it.

Mom, for all the wonderful things that you have done for me in my life, for all the love that you have shown me, I can never, ever fully repay you. But at least now I can try.

This book is dedicated to you, Mom. You mean everything in the world to me. You are the most amazing, special, and wonderful person that I have ever known. You are my precious angel.

You know, it really wasn't supposed to be this way.

1

Let Me Tell You about My Mom

I WANT TO TELL you a little bit about my mom so you can understand who she is and why she means so much to us.

When I talk about my mom, I'm talking about the person who has always been the most special and wonderful person in my life. She was always there for me, from the youngest age that I can remember. I always felt closest to her in our family. I still feel that way.

Mom was born and raised in Massachusetts. Her parents got divorced when she was very young. Due to the Great Depression, her mother needed to work full-time. Since her Mom couldn't simultaneously work and take care of her, Mom went to live with her paternal grandparents from the age of four until she was fourteen years old. My mom really loved her grandma and was extremely close to her. For all intents and purposes, Mom's grandmother was really her mom when she was growing up.

During her high school years, Mom moved to Bayside, New York, and lived with her half-sister and her stepdad. While living there, she attended and graduated from Bayside High School. She went back to her hometown of Lowell, Massachusetts, during her summers off every year to live with her grandparents. After graduating from Bayside High School, Mom eventually moved to Englewood, New Jersey, to live with her mom and her new stepdad. This is where our mom and dad first met. One day, Mom went into the grocery store where my dad was working before he started college. She bought some things and then left. Dad recognized her as the new girl who had moved in across the street and a few houses down. One day, my dad's sister noticed that my mom went to a particular mass at church, so Dad made sure to be there the next time she went. And that's when they met.

They dated for a few years, got engaged, and then got married. Mom and Dad raised four children—three boys and one girl. We grew up in a middle-class neighborhood in suburban Bergen County, New Jersey.

Mom was a great stay-at-home mom. She also did volunteer work, mainly community and church-based work, while she was raising us. Her volunteer work included working for the church and the school, being a Girl Scout leader, helping out at the concession stand at my baseball games, and helping many of our neighbors in need. She worked very hard all of her life. She also took a full- or part-time job outside of the house when she could.

Mom used to prepare care packages for an elderly woman who lived alone at the end of our street. She would make a nice homemade meal and dessert for her on each of the holidays, and I would take the meal to her house. I still have a note that this woman wrote to my mom, thanking her for the wonderful meal.

Also, when I was a young boy, I had a friend who had a tumor removed from his head. As a result of the surgery, he became blind and partially paralyzed. Mom used to go over to his house to read to him, but she never told me about this. I only found out many years later when his mom told me about it. That's how wonderful my mom was. She did things straight from her heart and never asked for anything in return. She never bragged about it or told anyone. She just did it out of the goodness and kindness of her heart. She was always ready, willing, and able to help out those in need. She is the most compassionate person that I've ever known.

Of course, the things that I've just mentioned are only a few of the things that I actually remember about the charity and giving that was so strong within her. I'm sure that there were many other acts of kindness and generosity that Mom did for other people without anyone else ever knowing about them, including me.

Mom was also a very religious woman. She used to go to the church practically every day and always on Sundays. She went so often that I said that Mom was at church because it was an "Every Day of Obligation," a play on words regarding the observance of the Holy Day of Obligation.

Mom firmly believed in the value of a good education. I remember how happy and proud she was of all her children whenever we graduated from the school that we were attending. I also remember my whole family, including my mom, being there for me when I graduated from college. It meant the world for me to have all my family there to help me celebrate that special event.

One of the other things I remember about Mom was that she enjoyed sitting with me at the kitchen table, having a cup of coffee or tea, and just having a nice, pleasant conversation. Mom really loved people, and people really loved her.

Mom did so many wonderful things for me. I was sick a lot as a kid. When I was a little baby, I had pyloric stenosis that required surgery. I was six months old and had to be in an oxygen tent because of a severe asthma attack. I've had asthma all my life. When I was about six years old, I developed allergies to many things, such as certain types of foods, mold, pollen, fall leaves, and animals, and I received several thousand shots, including the old style allergy testing shots over the course of many years of my childhood. My asthma was triggered not only by certain substances but also by overexertion, so I couldn't always keep up with the kids when we were playing. I would sometimes get an attack and have to stop. I felt as if I was allergic to life. I also had other medical issues of a more personal nature that I had to deal with while growing up.

I remember sitting in the living room, suffering from allergies and asthma. Mom made soup for me and made sure that I took my medicine and drank lots of fluids. I read many books while growing up, especially when I was home sick. Mom had instilled a love of reading in me. She used to go to the library to get books for both of us to read. I read many different types of books. They opened up a whole new and exciting world for me.

Mom was the heart and soul of our family. Whenever I needed her, she was there for me. She always took care of me, especially when I was sick, and nurtured me back to health.

Mom taught me to love and enjoy life, to respect all people, and to value hard work and sacrifice. She taught me how to live a good life and how to be a really good person. Maybe I'm being partial because she's my mom, but she is the best person I have ever known in my whole life. I say this because she has so much incredible goodness in her. She has an abundance of wonderful qualities. Mom always knew the right thing to do in any situation. She lived her life that way and expected us to do the same.

Mom also has a wonderful personality and a great sense of humor. She could be the life of the party, walking into a room and lighting it up with her presence. For example, early in 2011, I was talking to my mom's cousin Virginia over the phone. She told me that when Mom was a young lady living in Massachusetts, Virginia and all of Mom's relatives would get excited whenever they knew Mom was coming to visit them. This is because Mom was such a special, wonderful, and lively person. She was also a very good person. She is beautiful inside and out. She was attractive and glamorous enough to be a movie star in Hollywood. However, I'm really glad that she was my mom and not a Hollywood movie star.

Dad was also a big help to me. He was the breadwinner of the household and also the rock of the family. He worked hard all of his life. Besides putting food on the table and paying the bills, he paid for all my medical and dental bills when I was a kid, along with those of the rest of the family. While growing up, Mom occasionally got jobs outside of the house, but she still ran the house and raised the children while Dad was working.

I was never a parent. I understand that even though it has its share of rewards, it's also the toughest job in the world. We were raised in a traditional environment. Although we had many fun times and laughs together, things could also be tough at times. Mom and Dad could be strict with us.

I want to share a little bit more about my mom by listing some of her favorite expressions. I think that it gives some additional insight into her personality and how much fun she was. Although this list is not all-inclusive, I have included as many of them as I can remember. Some of her expressions are also included in other parts of this book. I have listed them by category to keep them in a particular order.

Funny Expressions

- Kryminaltees! (spelled phonetically)—Mom said this to express surprise at something.
- Let's not and say we did.
- The funny thing is . . .
- For heaven sakes!
- For crying out loud!
- If you say so.
- Oh, my goodness!
- Oh, for goodness sakes!
- Isn't that something?
- Isn't that the funniest thing?
- You're a sketch (or "that's a sketch" or "isn't that a sketch").
- Wow, that's something!
- Not that I know of.
- Are you kidding me?
- You're kidding!
- I'm telling you!
- It's for the birds!

Cute Expressions

- You bet!
- Oh, drat!
- As a matter of fact . . .
- It's true.
- Really and truly.
- She's so cute.
- That's cute.
- How wonderful.
- That's wonderful.
- That's lovely.

- The little darling(s) . . .
- Oh, God, yes!
- Honest to God.
- Honest to goodness.
- For God's sake.
- Too much!
- That's all right.
- That's quite all right.
- Jesus, Mary, and Joseph!
- That's grand!
- Oh, my good God!
- That's nice.
- Yup!
- Okay, then.
- Yah, yah (pronounced "yeah, yeah" in New Jersey).

My favorite expression that Mom would say when she was mad at us was, "You'd have to get up pretty early in the morning, before the birds get up, to fool me!" Of course, it wasn't a fun moment if she was saying it directly to me or one of my siblings.

When I look back on the time growing up at home with Mom and Dad, it's amazing to me how quickly time has passed. It seems like yesterday that we were kids and Mom and Dad were taking us out for the weekend together.

Mom wants all of her children to be the best possible people that we can be in this world. She wants us all to be happy and successful in whatever we choose to do in life.

There is so much more that I could say about my mom. That would be a whole new book in itself.

2

Diagnosis and Emotional Fallout

AS WITH ALL OTHER patients who develop Alzheimer's disease, Mom exhibited warning signs. Sometime in mid to late 1999, we began to notice that Mom was having trouble remembering things. She would forget things that she had told us a half-hour earlier. She was forgetting things that were related to short-term memory.

One time, when Mom was boiling water for tea, she went downstairs to the basement to do some laundry. No one else was in the house at the time. Although she didn't realize it, the water in the kettle boiled to the point of evaporation while she was in the basement. The kettle did not have a whistle feature on it, and it started burning on the stove. Dad got home just in time and turned off the stove. The kettle had been badly burned by the flames of the stove and was no longer usable. All that time that my mom was in the basement doing the laundry, she forgot that she had put water on for tea. There was no way for her to tell that the water was boiling unless she was standing there watching it.

Thank God nothing more serious happened. The house could have caught on fire. At that point, we knew that we could not take anything for granted. We had to watch Mom very closely and make sure that she was never left alone in the house.

Around that time, people would call and ask to speak to Dad or to my sister Mary. My parents didn't use an answering machine, so whoever answered the phone had to take messages. If a call came in for Dad or Mary and they weren't home, Mom would forget to give them the message. Dad or Mary would find out only if the person called back and got them on the phone. They would say that they had already left a message with Mom.

We made a point of mentioning our concerns to Dad on several different occasions. In the beginning, he reasoned that it was part of the normal aging process. A short while later, Mary spoke to Dad again about it, and Dad decided to take Mom to see the neurologist, who examined Mom and determined that she had mild cognitive impairment (MCI). She was placed on Aricept, which helped. It helped slow the progression of the MCI for a number of years.

We knew that MCI was the first stage of Alzheimer's disease. We also knew that Mom's family had a history of Alzheimer's. Her mother, grandmother, and great-grandmother had all suffered from it. Needless to say, we were all very upset when we heard the news.

After the initial diagnosis of MCI, we knew that we had to prepare for the worst. We knew how difficult Alzheimer's disease could be on the patient and on their loved ones. We had experienced it firsthand when our grandmother (Mom's mother) developed it.

Eventually, Grandma had to be put into a nursing home, which she did not like at all. She'd always been an extremely independent person. If

Grandma had never gotten Alzheimer's disease, she would have lived in her own apartment for the rest of her life.

My mom didn't enjoy a close relationship with her mom for a good period of their lives together. This was probably due to some things that happened in her childhood, like being raised by her grandparents from age four through fourteen. As I mentioned earlier, her parents were divorced. Her mom felt that she couldn't take care of Mom and work full-time at the same time. This was during and shortly after the Great Depression.

However, my mom was absolutely fantastic in taking care of Grandma when she had to go into the nursing home. Mom used to visit her several times a week even though she never drove a car. If Dad wasn't available to drive her there and pick her up later on, Mom would take a bus there and back. She washed Grandma's clothes and was her main caregiver. I'm sure that this added a lot of stress to Mom's life. She not only had her own family to worry about but also had to worry about the care and well-being of her own mom in the nursing home.

We saw how loving, caring, and wonderful our mom was with her mom when Grandma was in the nursing home, so we knew a little bit about what to expect when it actually happened to us. However, you're never prepared for that moment.

I knew after Mom was diagnosed with MCI that my life would never be the same again. Ever since the diagnosis, I have worried about her every single day. It is always with me, always present in my everyday life and in everything that I say and do. If it's not at the front of my mind, it's in the back of my mind. Needless to say, I'm more cautious about how I live my life because I want to be here to help take care of my mom.

After the initial diagnosis, things progressed slowly but surely. It got to the point that Mom would leave the house without telling anyone where she was going. Luckily, in those moments at the beginning of the disease, she mostly ended up walking back to the house. Otherwise, my dad or my sister went out in the car to find her and bring her back home.

There were a few times in the 2005 to 2006 time frame that Mom would still leave the house and not tell anyone. Dad wouldn't know where she was. Then he would get a call from the local police station telling him that Mom was there. When she was a Girl Scout leader, she had taken her troop up there for trips. She had accessed her long-term memory to remember how to get there.

On at least one occasion, according to a story that my dad told me, Mom and Dad had an argument, and Mom got upset and left the house. Dad followed her in his car. By the time she crossed over the railroad tracks, Dad was able to convince her to get in the car so that he could take her home.

These were very scary times indeed. Not only did Mom have to be watched, but my sister and my dad had to make sure that she didn't try to leave the house without their knowledge.

This problem is common for many families who are dealing with a loved one in the beginning stages of Alzheimer's disease. It is not only devastating to the person but is also devastating to the loved ones, who must be constantly on alert and hope every day that nothing bad will happen to their loved one.

I've always wondered what goes through the minds of people who have Alzheimer's disease. What happens when they realize that they're not in control of their minds or their lives like they used to be? I wonder what Mom's thoughts were and how she felt as she was going through the beginning stages of the disease. How did she feel when the disease was progressing and she knew that she was getting worse? It must have been unbelievably frightening for Mom to deal with the impact of this disease on her mind, heart, and spirit.

When Mom's Alzheimer's disease progressed, it helped us to become even more aware of her plight and to take every necessary precaution to ensure her overall safety and well-being. My Mom has told me on many different occasions, even as recently as 2013, that she is scared. Sometimes when she starts to get agitated, I ask her if she is scared, and many times she will say yes. It always makes me feel bad. In those moments, I always reassure her. I tell her that I'm also scared for her but that I will be with her all the way and never leave her side. She won't have to go through this alone.

One day during the winter of 2006, I went over to the house to visit Mom and Dad and Mary. As I pulled up in my Volkswagen Passat, Mom came running out of the house and right up to the car with her coat on. She opened the door and got in, saying that she wanted to go for ice cream. I asked her if she had told Dad and Mary that she was coming out to my car, and she said yes. But I found out just a minute or two later that Mom hadn't told either of them that she was leaving the house. Mary called me on my cell phone and wanted to know where Mom was. I told her what had happened, and she was annoyed. She scolded me for not calling the house and telling them right away what was happening.

A little while later, Mary called me back and apologized for the way she had talked to me. I appreciated that. I told her that I was sorry that I hadn't called; I had believed what Mom told me. I hadn't had any experience up to that time with my mom telling me something that wasn't true. In fact, Mom may have even thought that she had told Dad or Mary that she was going out even though she actually hadn't told anyone. I resolved to never let it happen again.

Mom and I ended up going to an ice cream parlor in Teaneck, New Jersey, and had a wonderful time. I asked the owners of the store to please keep an eye on her while I used the bathroom for a few minutes, and I explained to them why I needed them to do that for me. They were more than happy to assist me. I thanked them several times. Later, Mom went over to a family that was sitting together, ordering their food. She liked the kids because they were cute; one or two of them had red hair. When the father looked over at me, I explained to them in a way that Mom couldn't hear that she had Alzheimer's disease and that she loved kids. I could tell by the looks on the parents' faces that they understood. After a minute or two of Mom talking to the family and the kids, I got her to sit back at our table so that we could enjoy our ice cream.

Sometime in 2006 to 2007, I noticed that my mom had stopped calling me on the phone. In the good old days, Mom and I used to talk several times a week. Sometimes we talked almost every day. Mom seemed to call me more often than I initiated the call to her, but I did call her periodically.

Eventually, I realized that the reason Mom had stopped calling me was because she couldn't remember my phone number or where to look to get it. I felt terrible once I had figured it out. I endeavored to call her and to visit with her as much as possible. During this time, Mom wanted me to come over more often and to see her as much as possible. I understood where she was coming from, and I did my best to oblige her.

On one occasion around this time, Mom and Dad were arguing when I was visiting. Dad was factually correct in what he was saying, but I could tell that Mom was getting angrier and more frustrated as the argument went on. I leaned over to Dad and said, "Dad, let her win. She doesn't know that what she's saying isn't factual. She thinks it is. It's because of what she has. She can't help it. It's best to agree with her." Dad understood and let Mom win the argument. I was happy to have made a positive impact. I hoped that Dad would utilize that information if it ever happened again.

Another time, Dad was sitting in the living room and Mom was in the kitchen. Mom did something that bothered Dad, and he scolded her. I knew that whatever it was that she had done, she couldn't help it because of her disease. I went into the kitchen to check on her and see how she was doing. I found her standing behind the kitchen table with her head down. Her feelings were hurt. It made me angry that Dad would speak to her like that, so I decided that I had to say something to him about it. I walked from the kitchen toward the living room, where Dad was sitting on the sofa. I could tell from the look on Dad's face that he was surprised that I was coming over to talk to him about it. He wasn't used to me approaching him this way. I understood that it was frustrating and annoying for him at times and that it tested his patience. I thought about what I would say to him before I said it, and I ended up saying something like, "Dad, I know that it must be frustrating for you at times because you live with Mom. I know that it must be difficult for you. Mom can't help it. She didn't do it on purpose. I could tell that her feelings were hurt. Please be as patient and kind with her as you can."

I was glad that I spoke up for Mom on her behalf. If I hadn't said anything to Dad at that time, Mom probably wouldn't have said anything either. She may not have spoken up out of fear of what might happen to her. Would Dad put her in a nursing home? Would he continue, at times, to be impatient with her and come across as insensitive to what she was going through? I don't know what Mom was thinking at that time, but I wouldn't be surprised if she felt trapped emotionally because of her condition. I fervently hoped that Dad would understand and honor my request when I wasn't there.

At one point in August 2007, Mary was alone in the house with Mom. Mary was upstairs and told Mom that she would be right down. When she went downstairs, she found the front door open. Mom had taken off. Mary was very upset. First, she looked all around for Mom and couldn't find her anywhere. She then realized that Mom may have gone to the police station again, so she called. The police said that they hadn't seen her but that they would go out and look for her. Eventually, Mom did show up at the police station, and the police called Mary so she could pick Mom up. Unfortunately, people who have Alzheimer's disease tend to wander. They don't understand that they are putting their safety and their lives on the line whenever they do so. They can't fully understand the potential consequences because of their condition.

Mom had stopped cooking in the late 1990s, but Mary said that as Mom's disease progressed, she developed a fascination with the stove. She liked to go to the stove—a gas stove—and turn it on, even if she wasn't cooking. Mary said that it was quite scary. Dad and Mary had to keep an eye on Mom to make sure that she didn't turn the stove on.

In late October or early November 2007, Mary had woken up early one particular morning. Mom had awoken right before her. Mom was walking down the stairs around six o'clock, and Mary followed her. Mom went into the kitchen, turned on the light, and tried to turn on the stove, but Mary prevented her from doing it. A big argument ensued. Mom wanted to turn on the stove, and she couldn't understand why Mary wouldn't let her. Mary told Mom that it was dangerous because she wasn't cooking. Mary also told her that the stove is not safe, that you're only supposed to turn it on when you're cooking. Mom got quite upset with that. She didn't understand.

3

Losing Dad: Mom Goes into Nursing Home

DAD WAS ALWAYS A very strong man, in every good sense of the word. He was first diagnosed with prostate cancer in November 1997. He also had a heart condition, so his doctor recommended that he receive radiation on his prostate gland instead of undergoing surgery to remove it. In early 2007, the doctor found that Dad's cancer had come back and had metastasized in his spine. He had to receive more radiation treatments. After the treatments, the cancer went away at that time. But as we approached the summer of 2007, my siblings and I noticed that our dad wasn't feeling as well as he normally did. He looked weaker than he had looked in a while, and he became fatigued quickly.

On August 22, 2007, Dad called and asked me if I could take him to the hospital for a doctor's appointment, explaining that he hadn't been feeling well. I was happy to help my dad in any way that I could. I took some of my vacation time from work so that I could help him out. I picked Dad up at his house, took him to his appointment, and then took him back home. On the way home, we stopped at a diner to have lunch. Dad got out of my car gingerly and walked into the diner (there were brick steps leading in) very slowly and carefully. At that time, I thought that it was his arthritis acting up. I asked him what was wrong, and he said something to the effect that he was having some problems walking. After lunch, we were walking back to the car. Dad had to go slowly again down the front steps of the diner. I still thought it was due to his arthritis acting up.

When Dad got to my car, he asked if he could sit in the back. I said, "Sure, Dad." It was just as easy to get Dad in the back of my car as the front because I was driving a four-door car at that time. He got in, and I made sure that he was securely buckled in. When I was getting ready to close the door, Dad made a kissing sound to me. I wasn't expecting it. It really touched me that he would do that. He normally didn't display his emotions like that. Dad was telling me that he appreciated all that I was doing for him. I would absolutely do anything for him, just like I would for my mom.

I had already arranged with Dad for me to go down to Point Pleasant, New Jersey, the next day. He wanted me to spend a few days at the hotel where Mom and Mary were staying for a little vacation. Dad wanted me to go on his behalf because he didn't feel well enough to join them.

I left early on the morning of August 23, 2007, and drove down to Point Pleasant to be with Mom and Mary. Little did I know that a dramatic sequence of events was about to transpire. As soon as I arrived in the parking lot of the hotel and was parking my car, I got a call from Dad on my cell phone. At the same time, Mary had seen me pull into the lot and was coming out to greet me. I put my hand up to let Mary know that I couldn't talk right then. I told her that it was an important call from Dad.

He told me that he was sitting in a chair in the living room and that he wasn't able to stand up. As we talked, he told me that he noticed that he had a walking cane hanging from the doorknob of the door that led into the kitchen. He was able to reach over, grab the cane, and lift himself up from the chair. Once he was standing up, he used the cane to keep from falling. I told him that I could turn right around and drive back to the house to help him out if he wanted me to. He said that he wanted me to stay with Mom and Mary and that my brother John would help him.

I was glad that John would be helping Dad. It also gave me a good opportunity to spend time with Mom and Mary. I was able to help Mary take care of Mom while they were away together on vacation. Mom needed to be looked after all the time. Being there with Mary was helpful to both her and to Mom.

The entire time that I was down at the Jersey shore with Mom and Mary, I was very concerned about Dad. I didn't know what was actually happening to him, but I knew that it was serious. I was constantly thinking about Dad while I was down in Point Pleasant with Mom and Mary.

The first night that I spent in the hotel room with Mom and Mary was very interesting. The room had two separate beds. Mom and Mary slept in one bed while I was in the other. I lay on the bed before we had all changed and went to sleep that night. Mom was lying on her bed and talking to me. Since it was at night, Mom wasn't functioning as highly as she does during the day. At some point, she didn't even recognize me, asking me questions about who I was. I was answering her in a very kind, loving, and patient way.

For example, when Mom would ask me who I was, I would say, "Mom, I'm your son, Bill. I'm the second of your four children." Mom would reply, "Oh, really?" I went on to talk about her life growing up, all of her relatives, and different things about the past that we shared together.

She kept replying with statements like "Oh, really?" This conversation continued for about an hour and a half before we all went to sleep for the night.

The very next morning, Mom woke up and got out of bed to use the bathroom. She walked past me and saw me lying in bed. She said, "Oh, hi, Bill." This caught me completely by surprise. I knew that Mom hadn't fully understood who I was the night before. However, that morning when she first got out of bed, she was able to recognize me right away and to greet me. Her mind was fresh and rejuvenated from a good night's sleep.

Mary told me later that same day that she thought it was really sweet the way I was responding to Mom's questions in such a patient and loving way the night before. I told Mary that it was my pleasure. I'll do anything for Mom.

Later that day, Mom, Mary, and I were walking together down the board-walk in Point Pleasant. It was a little cool, windy, and overcast that day at the beach. Mom was fully dressed and wearing an overcoat. I was holding Mom's hand, and Mary was walking on the other side of her.

As we continued walking down the boardwalk, I noticed two men who looked to be in their mid-forties or early fifties talking with each other up ahead. They were staring at me holding my mom's hand. They would talk to each other for a few moments and then look back at us. I sensed that they thought it looked odd for a middle-aged man to be holding an elderly woman's hand while walking down the boardwalk with another woman at her side, but I knew that I wasn't doing anything wrong. I was holding my mom's hand. She needed help. If I could have that moment over again, I would have told them that I wasn't sure what they were concerned about, but this woman was my mom and she has Alzheimer's disease. I would have said it to them in a way that Mom couldn't hear me and hope that they would understand and maybe apologize for being insensitive and making an incorrect assumption.

Unbelievably, when Mom, Mary, and I went to a movie the next afternoon, something else happened. I knew that Mom wouldn't like the movie because of the subject matter. It was also hard to make her sit still for any length of time if she wanted to get up and do something. When Mom wants to do something like get up and walk around, you have to go along with her. She wouldn't understand and she probably wouldn't cooperate if I tried to talk her out of leaving.

Suddenly, Mom got up to leave. I told Mary that we would be waiting out in the upstairs lobby for her until the movie was over. While we were there, I sat next to Mom on a small sofa and talked to her. A man and a woman, who appeared to be in their late sixties or early seventies, came out into the upstairs lobby area. The woman was staring at Mom and me sitting together for about ten minutes. Then, she and her husband walked down the stairs to the first landing. The woman stood there with her husband standing next to her and stared up at us for what seemed to be almost a half hour. It was really starting to annoy me. I was getting the impression that she didn't understand why a middle-aged man was sitting next to an elderly woman in the upstairs lobby of a movie theater. Again, if I could have that moment back, I would have asked her if there was something wrong. No matter what her response was, I would have told her that this woman was my mom, that she has Alzheimer's disease, and that I was looking after her until my sister came out of the movie theatre.

It was really none of her business. I was offended by her staring and not wanting to leave. It made me very uncomfortable. There was no reason for her behavior. If she was so concerned about my mom, all she had to do was walk up and ask us if everything was okay. I would have told her that it was and then introduced my mom to her and to her husband.

After Mom, Mary, and I got back home from Point Pleasant, we found out what was going on with Dad. It was the worst possible news. His cancer had returned.

Dad had to be transferred directly from the hospital to a nursing home because he could no longer take care of himself. Around this same time, we also had to place Mom in the same nursing home. With Dad sick, he could no longer care for Mom. We needed professional nursing care for both of them. Mary couldn't take care of Mom at home by herself, and even though I helped out as much as possible, I was working full-time and Mary was getting ready to go back to teaching school two weeks later.

In addition to Dad's cancer returning, he also had a condition that was caused by the radiation treatments that he had received. It first developed sometime after Dad had received his first dosages of radiation ten years earlier. He had opted for radiation treatments for his cancer instead of having it surgically removed because he also had a heart condition. At that time, Dad's doctor recommended against surgery because of Dad's age and his medical condition. According to what my sister Mary told me as recently as 2013, Dad actually did get a second opinion regarding whether or not he should have surgery instead of radiation treatments on his prostate gland. The doctor who gave the second opinion confirmed what Dad's first doctor had stated. So, Dad opted for radiation treatments for his prostate. That may have been the medically prudent thing to do. However, I'm not sure whether or not each doctor's decision was purely medical in nature. Did they also have concerns over potential legal issues in the event that either the surgery was unsuccessful or that Dad might pass away during or shortly after the surgery due to his heart condition? I'll never know. I wish that I could change what ended up happening to Dad.

Dad had been diagnosed with a certain type of anemia as a side effect of his radiation treatments. At the time of the diagnosis, Dad would visit his physicians to get the injections that he needed for the anemia. However, when he was incapacitated because of his cancer in August 2007, he could no longer go to the doctor's office to get these injections. The doctors would not administer the injections to Dad in either the nursing home or in the hospital. Therefore, Dad had to be sent back and forth to the hospital to receive blood transfusions, whenever needed, in lieu of these injections. I believe that Dad received at least twelve pints of blood (and possibly more) over the last two months of his life. On more than one occasion, he received two pints of blood in a row.

Mom, Mary, and I visited Dad again in the hospital on Monday, August 27, 2007. We were all inside Dad's room when his primary physician came in to see him, and we talked for a little while. When the doctor was leaving, I followed him outside the hospital room and asked if I could speak to him for a minute. I asked him how much time my dad had left to live. He launched into a long medical explanation. I had a little trouble following everything that he was saying. He ended by saying that Dad had about two to three months left to live, based on the statistics of other people who have had a similar condition and the progression of the disease that Dad had.

I was stunned. I thought that Dad had more time than that to live. A minute or so later, Mary came out of the room to talk to the doctor. After that, the doctor had to leave, and I thanked him again for his time.

Right after the doctor left, Mary turned to me and asked me how long the doctor had said that Dad had to live. It might have been intuition on her part. As I was preparing to answer that question, I understood the very close relationship that Mary had with Dad. I knew I had to lie to her. If I told her what the doctor had just told me, she wouldn't have been able to handle it. The best thing to do in that situation was to lie. I knew in my heart that the truth would have been much too painful for her to take at that time.

So, I told Mary that the doctor said that the next three to six months would be very critical for Dad. If he could make it through that time period, there was a good chance that he could live six months to one year or even for a couple of more years. I told her that we just had to do the best that we could for Dad and help him get through this period of time. We had to wait and see how he was doing, especially during the next three months. The whole time, unfortunately, I knew it was a lie. It was a lie that I had to tell.

When Dad went back into the nursing home, I visited him and Mom as much as possible. During one visit, the physical therapist had to take Dad to exercise. He was trying to help him become stronger and more physically able to do things. I had been with Dad while he was doing his physical therapy on at least one other occasion, and he asked me if I could join him again that day. I told him that I didn't think that I could because I had to leave soon to get some things done. The physical therapist wheeled Dad into the physical therapy room, and I thought about it for a minute. I decided to put off what I had to do so that I could spend more time with Dad. As I walked down the hallway leading into the physical therapy area, Dad turned and looked at me. When he saw me, a big smile came across his face. It meant everything in the world to me to see Dad smile like that. I'll never forget it. It was a moment that I'll remember for the rest of my life. While I was with Dad, I saw that he was struggling with the physical therapy, especially pedaling on the stationary bicycle. I felt so bad for him. He had become so weakened by his cancer. I wished that I could give him all of the strength that I had in my body so he could get back to being himself again.

Dad still had to be taken back and forth to the hospital for blood transfusions. As I stated before, on several occasions, he had to get two pints of blood, one right after the other. I began to donate my own blood to the blood bank to help pay for the blood that Dad was using and to honor him by giving blood in his name.

There were many instances when Dad had to stay more than one day at the hospital. All of the rooms at this nursing home were shared rooms. In those cases, Mom had to be moved from the room that she shared with Dad into a room with another woman. At night, after Mom went to bed, she would sometimes get up in the middle of the night and start looking for Dad, forgetting that he was in the hospital. She would wander in and out of people's rooms searching for Dad and get confused and frightened when she wasn't able to find him. The staff would tell me about Mom's activities the next day. For some reason, they hadn't attached a bed alarm to Mom's bed, which would have gone off every time she got out of bed, notifying them that she was out and about. They could have found her right away and put her back to bed. I'm still not sure why they didn't have a bed alarm attached to my Mom's bed.

I felt such love and compassion for Mom. I wish that Mary or I could have been able to stay with her every night. Imagine how scared Mom was because of her Alzheimer's disease. She would wake up in the night and see that Dad wasn't in the room with her. It must have been so frightening for her to not know where Dad was or what had happened to him. Also, the nursing home was a strange place filled with a lot of unfamiliar people.

After the incidents involving Mom's wandering in and out of rooms during the night on several different occasions, the administrator of the nursing home recommended that we place Mom in a more secure lockdown facility as a temporary measure. At this time, Dad was so sick that he had to stay in the hospital. Whenever it was required, he was being sent back and forth from his hospital room to the intensive care unit. Reluctantly, I agreed with the administrator to place Mom in another nursing home that was more secure. I felt as if I had no choice other than to agree to it.

It was Saturday, October 13, 2007. Mary went to visit Mom at the nursing home after Mom had her lunch. She was going to take Mom to visit Dad at the hospital. However, the administrator said that Mary couldn't take Mom because she was being transferred later that day to the new nursing home. Even if this nursing home had known about the transfer that morning, no one on their staff had bothered to contact me or my sister Mary about it. If I had known ahead of time that Mom was being transferred, I would have also been there for her. I thought that the nursing home had complicated matters either through administrative bungling or their insensitivity to our legitimate needs and concerns as Mom's caregivers.

Mary ended up having to wait about seven hours before the actual transfer was initiated. Mary followed the ambulette that transported Mom to the new facility and then stayed with Mom for another six hours.

Thank God that Mary was there. The transport people brought Mom into the activity room section of the new nursing home. Mary said that she felt uncomfortable leaving Mom in that room with people who seemed a bit off. The transport people told Mary on the way out, "Your mom doesn't belong in that unit."

So Mary went to the nursing home administrators and insisted that Mom be put in the other unit, which seemed safer. Mary got Mom out of the room and said that she wasn't leaving until Mom was placed in a safe area. Mary said that she fought like a lioness protecting her cub to make sure that Mom was in a safe place for the night. Eventually, the nurses placed Mom in a secure room right next to the nurse's station. No one would be able to bother Mom while she was in there for the evening. Also, the staff was right there just in case Mom needed anything. Mary ended up staying with Mom for over thirteen hours that day. I really appreciated hearing that and knowing that Mary had been there to care for and to protect Mom.

Mary called the facility early the next morning to make sure that Mom would be put on the other side of the unit with the higher-functioning people. The nursing home had promised that they would do it, and they kept their word. The transfer occurred early that same day.

While Mom was at the new facility, I tried to visit her every day. It was difficult because I was working full-time and also checking on Dad during the day. I was lucky enough to be working in the marketing department of the hospital that Dad was staying at, which also enabled me to advocate on his behalf whenever necessary. I spoke directly to the necessary people about things that happened that concerned me. Depending on the situation or their response, I sometimes reported their behavior concerning the care of my dad to their supervisors.

One day, the nurse manager of my department said that people were complaining that I was going to their supervisors concerning my dad. She said that I was getting a reputation for doing this sort of thing. I responded by saying that I spoke up on my dad's behalf whenever I thought that it was necessary. I also said that I would do the same thing whether I was working there or not. I ended by stating that I didn't want to be made the scapegoat for the problems of the hospital and that if the people involved would just do their jobs and complete them in an appropriate and professional way, then they wouldn't hear anything from me.

There were more than a few occasions when I had to speak up for my dad. For example, one morning I went over to check on him to see how he was doing. His breakfast was on a tray in his room. I couldn't find anyone to help me pick Dad up a little more and adjust him in his bed, so I did it by myself to the best of my ability. When I was feeding Dad his breakfast, an aide walked into the room and commented on what I was doing. She asked if I would like to eat my breakfast that way. She repeated this comment to me at least once or twice more. I told her that I had tried to find someone to help me but that no one was available. I also felt at the time that Dad was still in a position to eat, although it may not have been the best position for him. She ended up helping me to shift Dad a little more in his bed.

After she left, I went and complained to her supervisor about it. I thought that it was immature and unprofessional of her to talk to me like that. Instead of assuming that I hadn't already tried to reposition Dad in his bed or looked for someone to help me with it, she could have just said something like, "Your dad isn't in the best position to eat his breakfast. Let me help you get him into a better position." I also didn't appreciate it because I was under so much stress already with what was going on simultaneously with Dad and Mom. Although I didn't expect her to know that, she should have just used common sense and adopted a more professional attitude in dealing with the loved one of a parent who was very sick. She apologized to me the next time that she saw me in the hospital. I'm sure that something had been said to her. I'm glad that I spoke up when I did.

On another occasion, while Dad was still in the hospital, he had to get surgery for an old injury that was still bothering him. He had a torn rotator cuff in his right shoulder. I spoke to the nurse manager of the unit that Dad was stationed in before his surgery. I told her that when she talked to him, she needed to keep in mind that he sometimes gets forgetful. I explained that I didn't know whether or not this had to do with all his medications, including the medicine that they gave him to relax him before his surgery, or with his age. I also didn't know if his cancer was adversely affecting his memory.

When the nurse manager and I went back to the room to check on my dad, he asked her what time his surgery was scheduled for. She said it would be at one o'clock that afternoon. About five or ten minutes later, he asked her the same question again. Either he had forgotten that he had already asked her or he was just anxious about it. The nurse manager said in a cold and mean way, "I said that it's one o'clock!" My dad didn't say anything. If he had been his old self, I'm sure that he would have said something like, "Hey, don't you talk to me that way! I'm allowed to ask if I need to." I wish that I had spoken up to her in that moment. I may not have because I was already getting into "hot water" for fighting on Dad's behalf while working at the hospital that he was staying at. I later regretted not saying anything to her right then and there. After she left the room, I stayed with Dad for a little while longer.

I was determined to speak to her on the way out of my dad's hospital room. I wasn't going to let her get away with speaking to my dad like that. So, on my way out, I stopped and talked to her again. I spoke calmly to her. I stated that the conversation she had had earlier with my dad in his room was evidence that he had a hard time remembering things, and that's why he had asked her again about the time of his surgery. She listened to me but didn't say anything in response. I was expecting her to apologize. I really wanted her to apologize to my dad, not to me. However, she never bothered to apologize for talking to my dad like that in his condition and in his time of need. She really should have been ashamed of herself. I was thinking about complaining about it to her supervisor. I actually knew who her supervisor was, but I ended up not going to her supervisor. In hindsight, I wish that I had in spite of the reputation that I was getting in the hospital. It's just too bad that the "powers that be" don't like it when I stand up for my dad in any situation where it's called for. Maybe the hospital should hire better people or train their current staff better in how to act and to communicate in the most caring and professional way to their patients and the patient's loved ones.

There were many other occasions during Dad's hospital stay when things were said or done that bothered me. One time, I received a call from a doctor in the middle of the night. Even though my cell phone was on, I was not awakened by the call. I saw the message when I got up early that morning. I called the doctor back right away. The doctor said that my dad was aspirating and needed to be put in the intensive care unit with a ventilator to help him breathe. The doctor then asked me if Dad had an advanced directive, which is a legal document that states what to do in the event that a loved one is in critical condition and needs to be kept alive. It states what the person actually wants to be done and not to be done on his or her behalf to help keep him alive.

Dad's advanced directive stated that he didn't want to be kept alive by artificial means, including the use of a ventilator. When I relayed this to the doctor, he said in an angry manner something like, "Then why the hell do we have him on a ventilator?" I was taken aback. I was really offended by what he said and how he said it to me. I stated calmly that I didn't know that my dad had been put on a ventilator during the middle of the night in response to his aspirating and that I had only found out about it from him. I considered finding out who the doctor's superior was and talking to him about the way he spoke to me. However, I never said anything about it to the hospital administration. Although I was standing up for my dad whenever I thought it was necessary, I may not have said anything on this particular occasion because I was already under so much stress. After some thought and contemplation, I decided to let this incident with the doctor go. It was yet another example of a medical professional, in this case a doctor, either not knowing or caring about how he spoke to me concerning the care of my dad. Again, shame on him! If the roles were reversed, I'm quite sure that he wouldn't want me to talk to him like that concerning the care and treatment of his dad.

Another incident occurred when my dad was staying for a few consecutive nights in one of the hospital units. The nurse supervisor told me that they wanted approval to give a certain medication to my dad. However, my dad didn't want to take it. He said he knew that it had polystyrene in it. Since my dad had worked for many years in the plastics industry, he knew that polystyrene was not good to ingest, even if it was in pill form. I went back and talked to the nursing supervisor about it, but she insisted on giving it to him. I told her no and explained why. She and I went back and forth for about ten minutes or so. Eventually, she conceded that she couldn't administer the medication at that time because my dad had refused to take it and I had backed him up. A few days later, I saw her as I was walking into my department. She had an office down the hall from where I worked. She saw me when she was looking through the glass window of the purchasing department. She gave me a really dirty look and started staring me down. I looked back at her for a second and then looked away. I was hurt and angry at her for trying to intimidate me because she didn't get her way about the medication that she wanted to administer to my dad. I told my dad about it a few days later. He told me to give her a dirty look back the next time that I saw her. God bless Dad! Since I didn't want to get into a long and protracted conflict over it, I didn't give her a dirty look. Her behavior toward me was extremely mean-spirited and unprofessional. Again, it's just too bad. I did the right thing by my dad. I honored his wishes. If the nurse manager or anyone else doesn't like me for doing the right thing or chooses to retaliate against me for it in some way, I'm just not going to lose any sleep over it!

We were now entering uncharted territory. Events started to unfold quickly. On Tuesday, October 23, 2007, I had taken a half day off from work by using my vacation time. I had to go to the nursing home that Mom was at to participate in her psychiatric evaluation. The previous week, I had been trying to get in touch with the psychiatrist who was in charge of Mom at the nursing home so that I could take Mom out for part of a day. I wanted Mom to visit Dad while he was in intensive care. I knew that Dad didn't have much longer to live. For whatever reason, the psychiatrist wouldn't call me back, despite my having left several messages. I had left two to three messages the previous week and another message the day before, on Monday, October 22.

What happened on October 23 was so incredibly dramatic that it could have been the pivotal scene in a movie. I was driving out to the nursing home to see Mom and to participate in her psychiatric evaluation. Just as I was approaching the actual exit off of the highway to Mom's nursing home, I received a call from the doctor who was taking care of Dad. The doctor told me that Dad looked worse than he had the day before. She said that the color in his face was bad and that he was unresponsive. I knew right away that this was it. This was the day that my dad was going to die. I started to cry on the phone while I was talking to the doctor. The doctor knew that I was on my way to the psychiatric evaluation for my mom. I asked her if I should go through with it for Mom or turn around right away and head back to the hospital. She said I should come back to the hospital but not to rush. I thanked her for the call and got off the phone. After exiting, I had to make a U-turn and head back to the hospital. I called the nursing home right away to tell them that I couldn't make the psychiatric evaluation. I told them that I was sorry but that I had to get back to the hospital for my dad because it was a medical emergency. They understood.

In hindsight, if I had known that I had a little more time, I would have driven to the nursing home and tried to get my mom out right away to see my dad before he passed away. Given the nature of the emergency and not knowing how much time that my dad had left, along with my experiences of the past week in trying to get my mom released for part of the day to visit my dad, I decided to take the doctor's advice and head right back to the hospital. We were ultimately unable to get Mom out of the nursing home in time to be with Dad when he passed away.

After I got off the phone with the nursing home, I immediately called my sister at work, calling her classroom phone. I felt like I was a 9-1-1 operator, being on all these emergency calls in a very short period of time. When I got Mary on the phone, she said, "Hi, Bill. How are you doing?" I said, "Not good, Mary. I just got a call from the doctor at the hospital. She said that Dad looked worse than yesterday and that he was unresponsive. You need to get over to the hospital right away." Mary pulled the phone away from her face and screamed, "No!" I felt so bad for her. She told me that she was on her way. I didn't realize at the time that Mary was much too upset and overwhelmed to drive on her own. One of her friends from school drove her over to the hospital.

Right after that, I called my brothers. My younger brother is in sales and is on the road a lot, but he happened to be in the area and said that he would come right over. When I called my other brother, he said that he was the only one running the car dealership that day, so he didn't know whether or not he could get a replacement. I told him something along the lines of, "I think that this is it for Dad. This is his last day. It's up to you. I highly recommend that you do whatever it takes to get someone to replace you so that you can come see Dad in the hospital." He said that he would call his boss to come in and take over.

I then decided to call my dad's two brothers. With my first call, I got Aunt Mary on the phone, and she said that she and Uncle Fred (my dad's older brother) would be on their way over to the hospital. She also said that she would contact my dad's other brother, Phil (my dad's younger brother), to let him know so he could also try to be there. Uncle Phil was working in New York City.

I was the first to arrive at the hospital. When I went into Dad's room, he was lying in bed with an oxygen mask on his face to help him breathe. I went over to the side of the bed and kissed him on his head. I grabbed his hand and held it, but he wasn't able to squeeze my hand at all. His hand was lifeless. It was as if the life was draining out of him. I leaned over to talk to him. I knew that he wasn't able to communicate with me and was unresponsive, but I also knew in my heart that he could hear my voice. I started talking to him quietly in his ear. I said things like, "It's Bill, Dad. I'm here. I know that you can hear me. I love you. I've always loved you and always will. Andy, Mary, and John are on their way. They should be here soon. I'll let you know when they arrive. I'm sorry, but I couldn't get Mom out of the nursing home in time. When I got the call, I had to come right over to see you. Hang in there, Dad. I'm here for you."

About ten minutes later, John arrived. He kissed Dad and spoke to him for a few minutes. Then, about ten minutes later, Andy arrived and did the same. Mary came in about five to ten minutes after that and followed suit. Although Dad was unresponsive and breathing with the help of an oxygen mask, we all had the opportunity to connect with him one-on-one.

I had also called my nurse manager and asked if she could get our boss, Joan, the vice president of marketing, to come to my dad's room. I asked for Joan because she is also an ordained minister. Joan showed up within ten minutes' time. In Dad's room, we had Andy, Mary, John, Joan, and me. I talked to Joan in the room and looked back at my dad to check on him every few minutes. About five minutes after Mary had arrived and talked to Dad, I turned to look back at him. At this time, Mary was in another area of the room talking to our brother John. Dad had the oxygen mask on his face, but he had stopped breathing. I said out loud, "He's not breathing!"

I started crying, loudly, along with my siblings. One of my brothers came over to me and asked me to keep it down. I guess that he felt like he could tell me how to grieve my dad. I immediately replied to him that I would grieve Dad the way that I wanted to grieve him. I told my brother either later that day or on another day that the reason that I was so emotional (not that I should have had to explain it to him or to anyone) was because I had been caring and fighting for Dad for the last two months of his life. I did everything that I possibly could to keep him alive as long as possible. When he passed away, not only was

I overwhelmed with grief, but all the pent-up emotions that came with trying my very best to keep him alive during that time were released.

Someone went out right away to get the nurse, and she came in and checked on Dad. We were waiting for the doctor to come in and make it official. A few minutes later, the doctor came in the room and checked Dad's vital signs. When he didn't find anything, he confirmed what we already knew. He made it official by saying in effect, "He has passed away. I'm sorry for your loss."

I started to cry again. A few minutes later, we got the priest in the room to say some prayers for our dad. Around this time, Uncle Fred and Aunt Mary showed up. I wasn't sure if Uncle Fred knew that my dad had just passed away. I said, "Uncle Fred, Dad has passed away." Although he didn't cry, I could tell that he was shaken by the news. All of us in the room held hands as we followed the priest in saying prayers for Dad. The priest told me before I left that I could call him at any time. I thanked him again for his service and for his kind offer.

When Dad had gone back to the hospital on August 23, 2007, he was told then that his cancer had returned. He ended up passing away from that cancer on October 23, 2007, exactly two months later.

We were allowed to stay with Dad for another one to two hours before the funeral director came over to take his body over to the funeral home. Dad's body was becoming cold. His face was losing its color, and he started to develop an ashen look. I kissed him on the head several times and told him that I had always loved him and I always would. I told him that I would take care of everything for him.

On the day that Dad passed away, we were finally able to get Mom out of the nursing home. I was angry with the nursing home administrators. I had tried on at least three different occasions within the week before Dad passed away to get Mom out to visit him for a few hours, but the psychiatrist who had the authority to permit it didn't return any of my calls.

When Dad passed away, Mary took two weeks off from work. She got the first week off for bereavement leave, and she took the additional week so that she could be with Mom and we could find a new nursing home to put Mom into. We didn't like the nursing home that Mom had just come out of for several reasons. Also, we had tried several different times to have a live-in aide at the house, but it hadn't worked out for us.

During the period of Dad's wake and funeral, we had Mom back home for a few weeks. Mom and Mary were living in the house together, and I know that Mary was having a difficult time. We had just lost Dad, and then she was looking after Mom in the house. I was also having a very difficult time. Besides dealing with the loss of my dad, I was involved in all of the arrangements, along with Mary, for the wake and the funeral. I was also involved in all the paperwork as the executor of Dad's estate and as one of the people with power of attorney, along with Mary, for my mom. The two of us also had power of attorney for Dad when he was still alive.

Mary and I eulogized our dad at the end of his funeral mass. My brothers, Andy and John, chose not to speak. Mary and I were each up on the altar for about five minutes. I went first, and I talked about Dad and all that he meant to me. I talked about how strong of a person he was and said that Dad always knew right from wrong. I also mentioned that Dad had a way of putting people in their place better than anyone I had ever known in my life. When I was done, many people in the church applauded. I wasn't expecting it, but it was comforting to hear. In fact, one of my brother's friends looked impressed. He told me later that I had spoken very well. I was happy to hear that because he has a very successful business career and is the chief executive of his own company. Mary's eulogy was very touching, also.

When the funeral mass ended, I walked directly behind my dad's casket like the loyal son that I am. I felt like a soldier honoring my dad. Dad was a US Army veteran of World War II, and it was great to see him honored by the US Army Honor Guard. His casket was draped with the American flag. After the casket was taken to the cemetery, the flag was taken off by the Honor Guard, folded according to military tradition, and presented to my mom. It was a beautiful, dignified, and ennobling moment.

For the repast luncheon after Dad's funeral, our family, relatives, and some family friends gathered in a restaurant. Mom sat at a table with our relatives who were in her age group. I sat at another table with my two brothers, my sister, and other relatives and friends. I was told later on during the luncheon that Mom had asked the people at her table where Dad was. This is one of the tragic aspects of Mom's disease. Even if she understood when we were at the funeral home and during the funeral mass that Dad had passed, she forgot later on. I'm sure that our relatives reminded her in a kind, compassionate, and loving way.

A day or so after the funeral, I finally received a call back from the psychiatrist who was in charge of Mom while Mom was spending almost two weeks in the nursing home with the lockdown facility before Dad passed away. We first exchanged pleasantries, and then I asked her why she hadn't returned my phone calls. In all of the messages, I had left information about wanting to get my mom out for part of the day in order to visit Dad before he passed away. She said that because Mom had been in the lockdown facility and was on Medicare, it wasn't that easy to release her to visit someone. She went on to say, "She wouldn't have remembered anyway." I was completely stunned and offended that she would say something like that, especially considering that she was a psychiatrist who works with elderly people and people with dementia.

I responded by saying something like, "It doesn't matter. What matters is that Mom would have gotten to see my dad before he passed away. Even if she would not have remembered, we would have remembered, and we all would have appreciated having Mom there before Dad passed away. I'm sure that my dad would have appreciated it also."

She told me that she was sorry, but that wasn't good enough for me. I was still so angry at her. I asked the estate lawyer if I could sue her for negligence. I told the lawyer that I had left at least three and maybe four or five messages with her about letting my mom out for part of the day to see Dad because he was in critical condition and near death. Our lawyer was very sympathetic. However, she told me that we couldn't sue because I would have to prove that it was intentional. I was glad that I asked. I'm not someone who likes to sue, but I was absolutely infuriated by the psychiatrist's failure to return my calls in a timely manner along with her attitude when she finally did call. I bet that if the shoe had been on the other foot and it was *her* mom who needed to be released for part of the day to see her dad who was dying, it would have happened, regardless of whether or not her mom would have remembered.

Mom stayed home with Mary and me for those two weeks around Dad's wake and funeral. Mary and I visited many different nursing homes until we found one that we felt was best for Mom. The only problem was that it wasn't considered a lockdown facility. There were locks on the two sets of doors leading out of the facility, and a square button on the wall had to be pushed in order for the electronic doors to open. The staff said they would make sure to keep a vigilant eye out for Mom to make sure that she didn't try to leave.

On the Thursday or Friday before Mary had to get back to her class on the following Monday, and after I got all the paperwork completed and the checks written for the security deposit and the first month's rent, we took Mom into the nursing home. Mary and I stayed with her for at least five hours that day. I knew that we were going to have to leave Mom there when we left for the day, and I had a feeling at that time that Mom would never be able to come back home again. I knew that at least for the short term, we would have to keep her in a nursing home.

When we were getting ready to leave, Mary and I said good-bye to Mom. I think that Mom was confused about why we were leaving. Each time we tried to walk away, she would start to follow us out the door. This is totally normal behavior for someone with dementia. I'm sure that Mom didn't understand why we were leaving her there. I didn't want to do it. I had to fight with every fiber of my being to leave. Although I knew that Mom would be okay there, it was the most difficult thing that I ever had to do in my life.

Eventually, we had to get help from the staff to distract Mom long enough to enable us to leave her there. After a few attempts, they were able to get Mom to stay when one of the aides started to play a little game with her. Mary and I then walked down the long hallway toward the main entrance to leave. When we got outside, it was dark. As Mary and I got into her car and buckled up to leave, Mary put the car into reverse, and I started crying my eyes out. I cried out loud for a good ten minutes or so. I felt completely horrible about what had just happened. I felt so incredibly bad for Mom. Even though this was the best possible solution for Mom based on the circumstances at that time, I felt as if I was abandoning her. I was taking the person that I love, respect, and adore the most in the world and leaving her in a nursing home. After all that she had done for me in my life, I felt as if I was not only abandoning her but betraying her. Although this wasn't the case, it was definitely how it felt to me.

I knew Mom's personal history, and it added to my terrible feelings of guilt and anxiety about leaving her in a nursing home. Because her parents had gotten divorced when she was a young girl and she was raised by her grandparents for ten years from the age of four, she more than likely had some abandonment issues from that experience. Leaving her alone in the nursing home made me feel that she was being abandoned again. It broke my heart into a million pieces.

It was also unbelievable to me that the two hardest and most excruciating days of my life had occurred within a two-week span of each other—the day that Dad passed away and the day that we had to put Mom back into the nursing home to stay. How much pain and suffering can a person bear? My heart was more than broken; I felt that it had been ripped out of my body. I felt completely empty inside. I was drained from the entire ordeal. I still don't know how I was able to survive and get through that period of my life.

I went to visit Mom every day in her new nursing home. Although I was working full-time, I made a point of seeing her seven days a week for the first two to three months of her stay there. I felt so terrible. I had to see her every day in order to help her adjust to her new life. I was also doing all the paperwork for my dad's estate and for my mom, along with my own paperwork and housework, and I helped Mary out as much as I possibly could with things that needed to be done at my parents' house. It was wearing me down, and some people were noticing. They told me that I should take some time for myself because if I didn't, I would burn out. And then I might not be in any position to help anyone.

This was my emotional tsunami. It was the overall effect of seeing Dad's cancer come back and losing him within two months, having to place Mom in a nursing home, and dealing with all of the other numerous family and personal obligations. I had to handle all these things while I was working full-time. It was a perfect storm of pain, suffering, and chaos, and just surviving the onslaught of problems and concerns was a daily struggle for me.

Around Christmas 2007, Mary went into a down period. She had felt down for quite a long time with Dad having just passed away, Mom being placed back in the nursing home, and Mary living in their house by herself. I would go over once a week, usually on Saturdays, and spend the day with Mary, helping out around the house and keeping her company. A lot of what needed to be done involved working around the house and maintaining the yard. I would also spend the night there so that Mary could have another family member sleeping over at the house at least once a week.

I had to be there for my sister when she was feeling down even though all these events were also taking their toll on me. Not only was I under a lot of pressure at work, but I also needed to help my sister.

Mary asked me on several different occasions if I would be willing to move back home and help her with the house. I told her that the only way I would feel comfortable doing that was if we could take Mom back home and get a home aide for her. Mary agreed that we could do that at a later date.

Eventually, in March 2009, I was laid off from my job. All these unfortunate events took place within less than a year and a half. Without employment, I felt like the biblical Job without a job. While I was laid off, in addition to looking for suitable work, I did all the paperwork to get Mom approved for Medicaid. Mom's original and agreed upon Medicaid eligibility date was February 2009. When Mom finally was approved for Medicaid, Medicaid had changed the eligibility date to March 2009, so I had to get her eligibility date changed back to the original date. If I didn't do it, we would have had to pay approximately $8,500 extra for the month of February 2009. This represented the difference between what we paid per month for Mom's nursing home stay versus what we would pay under Medicaid for that particular month. There was a tremendous amount of paperwork and detail involved in getting all of this accomplished. I also went to computer training for five months. After graduating with a 4.0 GPA, I studied for and passed the tests and became a Microsoft Office Specialist in Word, Excel, and PowerPoint. Another good thing about having the extra time was that it gave me more time to be with Mom and to advocate on her behalf, along with writing about our journey together.

4

Mom Gets Moved Around

I WAS TRYING TO keep everything together for the family in the midst of all the chaos.

As I stated before, we finally found a nursing home that we thought was the best place for Mom at that time. It wasn't a lockdown facility, but people had to be buzzed in and a button had to be pushed to leave.

Mom was very clever. She was always looking for an opportunity to get out of the nursing home. This is actually normal behavior for people with Alzheimer's, especially when they are first placed into a nursing home environment. I found out later that Mom almost got out through the facility's front door by following some people out. I was told two versions of the story. One stated that she got through the first set of double doors but was unable to get through the second set before the staff retrieved her. The other version said that she got through both sets of double doors and was actually walking out of the front of the building toward the parking lot. She was stopped just outside the facility and brought back in.

On another occasion, Mom had somehow gotten into the backyard of the facility. She was in the backyard and tapping on a window. She was showing off the flowers that she had just picked. I believe that she was getting the flowers to give to someone in the facility because she's such a wonderful, giving person. The staff came to the conclusion that she must have slipped through the back kitchen door to the backyard. The backyard was fenced in, although I'm not sure if it was totally enclosed.

These events were of great concern to our family. Mom was doing what most, if not all, people would do in her situation. The biggest problem is that she has Alzheimer's disease. She doesn't realize that her life would be in grave danger if she ever got out and no one knew that she was gone for a while. People with Alzheimer's disease aren't able to use proper judgment. Thank God that nothing ever happened to Mom in her attempts to leave the facility.

After Mom had been there for a while, the staff told us that we had to find a place for her that had a lockdown unit. I found one that I thought was okay based on a recommendation from someone on the staff at the nursing home, so my brothers, my sister, and I took a look. Although it was a nursing home-type facility, it was actually a big house on a fenced-in property with separate rooms for the patients. There was something about this place that rubbed me the wrong way. I didn't feel that they would have enough activities for Mom, and I wasn't totally convinced that it was the best place or even a safe enough place for her.

We ended up putting her in a nursing home that was less than two miles away from the nursing home that we were moving her from. I discovered it somehow, and we all really liked it. It was a relatively new building, having been built only a year or so earlier, and it had a lockdown unit for people with Alzheimer's disease. This is where we took Mom to live.

The day that I was taking Mom out of the previous nursing home to the new one, we had gotten her to say good-bye to some of the residents and staff there. I told her that I was taking her for a ride. When we were leaving, Mom turned to me and said something like, "Tell everyone that I said good-bye." I was stunned. Mom knew that I was taking her somewhere else. She had figured it out for herself. I hadn't wanted to tell her because I didn't want her to be afraid or upset.

She had her own beautiful room at the new facility. The food there was very good, and we felt that the staff did a very good job in that unit. Unfortunately, as part of the progression of my mom's Alzheimer's disease, she eventually lost her ability to walk and became confined to a wheelchair. Around this time, I was asked to take Mom to a neurologist to have her checked out. So on August 28, 2008, I met her at the neurologist's office after leaving work. I was still working at the hospital at that time. Mom had been brought to the neurologist's office by an ambulette. When Mom first saw me as she was being lowered off of the ambulette in her wheelchair, she said, "Billy! For crying out loud!" It made me feel so good that she recognized me right away and that she was so happy to see me. I am always happy to see Mom. I also love this expression of hers. I'll never forget that moment. It was an adorable thing for her to say to me. I only wish that I had a video recording of it for posterity. It will always be in my heart and mind.

After the neurologist examined Mom, he determined that she had symptoms of Parkinson's disease but that she did not actually have it. He recommended against giving her medication for Parkinson's because the side effects would outweigh the benefits. I agreed with him.

Shortly thereafter, the nursing home staff requested a meeting about Mom. I was concerned about what it might entail. My sister and I were told that because Mom was confined to a wheelchair, she would have to be moved to a nursing home that could provide a greater level of nursing care. I started to tear up and cry a little. I really liked the place that Mom was currently in, and it bothered me that we had to move her again when she seemed to have adjusted to being there.

Her current home at that time was actually an assisted-living facility. The staff told Mary and me that they would keep Mom there until we could find a suitable place for her. They recommended a sister facility that was nearby in Bergen County. When a bed finally opened up there, we had Mom taken over there. This is where Mom has lived since then. We felt lucky to get her into this facility because it has a very good reputation statewide. Also, my mom had gone to the day-care facility on the same campus a few years before as part of the process of helping her while she was dealing with her Alzheimer's disease. Dad was alive at that time. This gave Dad the ability to leave the house while Mom was at the day-care facility, so he could go shopping, run errands, or go to doctor's appointments for himself. It was fortunate that Mom ended up on the same campus as the place she had initially gone for her day-care.

It always takes the patient time to adjust to a new facility and a new environment. As we discovered, it also takes time for the family to adjust to it. Mom did eventually adjust to being there, as did we. However, to this day, Mom will occasionally say that she wants to go home. Sometimes, she'll just look at us and say, "Let's go!" It breaks my heart every time. In those moments, I always tell her what is going on and why she needs to be in a nursing home. I also tell her that if I can make a lot of money so that I can afford to buy a nice house and bring her home, then I will do that. I tell her that this is the best place for her in the meantime. I also tell her that I am doing the best that I can for her.

You absolutely need to have your loved one in the right nursing home, getting the proper care, and receiving frequent visits from family members who advocate on his or her behalf whenever necessary. It makes a real difference in their quality of life, happiness, and longevity. Ultimately, it changes the outcome from a potentially bad one to one that is as good as it can possibly be. It increases the chances that the patient will live longer and more happily than he or she might have otherwise. I truly believe that it can be the difference between life and death.

5

Nursing Home Abuses

FROM TIME TO TIME, problems have arisen at the different facilities that my mom has lived in. If something happens to a patient as a result of someone's physical or emotional abuse or neglect, many times there's no real way to prove it unless a staff member witnesses it and tells management about it and then management notifies the responsible family member. Otherwise, there's no way for families to find out if they're not there when something happens. Also, if something happens to a person with Alzheimer's disease, the victim won't remember it shortly thereafter. It would be like it never really happened. In this way, it's a nightmare for both the patients and their loved ones.

I don't remember any specific examples of any physical or emotional abuse affecting my mom at the first nursing home. However, I do remember speaking with someone in the administration office regarding my mom's going in and out of other people's rooms in the middle of the night when Dad was in the hospital.

A woman in administration at the first nursing home told me some stories about it and laughed out loud and continuously. I explained to her that although it might seem funny, it wasn't funny to me because it was my mom. I told the top administrative person there about the conversation the next day and how much it annoyed me and made me upset. Talking that way was a very ignorant thing for this woman to do, but I'm not sure if any action was ever taken. However, I do know that a short time after that, she was no longer working at that facility.

As I mentioned earlier, the next facility that Mom was in (just before Dad passed away) gave us some trouble when she was initially placed there. The staff wanted to put Mom in a unit with a lot of unruly residents. Thank God that Mary was there with Mom to protect her and to make sure that Mom got placed in a safe area until she was assigned to a room at the facility. On a different occasion there, one of the staff members was very rude to me when she saw me talking to a resident who was sharing a room with my mom. She told me that I wasn't allowed in the room alone with another resident unless my mom was in there with me. But it wasn't what she told me; it was the way that she said it. She spoke to me in a very mean and condescending way, as if I were a child, which I totally resented.

I explained to her that I was only in the room to look for my mom and that the other resident started speaking to me as I was leaving. If I had known that it was a problem, I wouldn't have entered the room in the first place. I would have told the woman that I was sorry but I couldn't talk to her unless my mom was also in the room.

This is the same facility that prevented me, for whatever reason, from getting Mom out to see Dad in the hospital before Dad passed away. The explanation that I received after Dad's passing had something to do with the Medicare requirements making it difficult to release Mom for part of the day to visit Dad. Even if that was the case, it was never explained to me beforehand. I also believe that I could have gotten Mom out for part of the day while Dad was still alive if only the psychiatrist had returned just one of my calls. Overall, I don't have good memories of my mom's two-week stay there.

The next facility that Mom stayed at was the first new facility that she was at after Dad passed away. Things were relatively okay in the beginning of her stay there. However, I had a problem with one of the nurses who worked in Mom's unit. She was a big, tall woman who had a bullying aspect to her personality. One day, when I went to see my mom after work, I went into her room and noticed that the lights were out. This was unusual. It was starting to get dark outside, and there was always at least one light on in Mom's room during the day. When I turned on the lights, I saw Mom lying on her bed at an angle with her legs hanging off the bed and with her shoes still on. The room looked disheveled. I turned on the other lights in the room and walked over to Mom. She was awake, but she didn't seem to know what was going on. I asked her what had happened, hoping that she could provide some sort of answer. Mom said, "I don't know. I don't know what I did." I knew right away from Mom's comment that something had happened to her. I sensed that she was being punished for some reason.

I went right over to the nurse to talk to her about it. I told her that it seemed that someone had put Mom in her room and turned the lights out on her. The nurse told me that she had done it herself. I then expressed my displeasure at what I had seen and what Mom had told me.

The nurse essentially said that Mom had been acting up. Sometimes the nurses allowed some of the residents in that unit to sit behind the nurse's station with them, and Mom had had a turn earlier that day. Apparently, one of the things that Mom did to annoy the nurse was to stick her hands into the pitcher of water on the cart. The nurse went on to say to me that my mom was "spoiled." She had a lot of nerve saying that to me and treating my mom like she was a bad kid who had done something that she knew she wasn't supposed to do. Mom has Alzheimer's disease; she doesn't know what she's doing. That's why she was staying there in the first place. A nurse who works in a dementia unit should absolutely know better than that. If that is the attitude that she takes with people who suffer from Alzheimer's disease, then she shouldn't be working there.

I said something to the effect that she couldn't punish my mom because Mom couldn't help her behavior. Whatever else transpired between the nurse and me—I don't remember it exactly—I was extremely upset. I ended the conversation by saying, "Well, we'll see about that!"

I went down to complain to the nursing manager. Although I wasn't there when they confronted the nurse over my allegations, I was told later that she denied saying that my mom was spoiled. She actually denied everything, including punishing my mom by taking her into her room, putting her on her bed, and turning out the lights on her when she left the room. When the nursing manager told me that the nurse had denied everything, I said that she was lying. I said that she was just covering up so that she wouldn't look bad or get into trouble for what she did.

Needless to say, the nurse had an attitude toward me after that incident. It doesn't matter to me who I have to go up against to protect and defend my mom. If people don't like me because of what I do on behalf of my mom, then so be it. It may make things uncomfortable for me at times. However, I'm not going to lose any sleep over it.

On another occasion at this same facility, I called the unit to check on something for Mom before Mary and I went to visit her. The first time that I called, no one answered, so I called back about twenty minutes later. When I got the nurse on the phone, I told her that I had called earlier but that she must have been busy at the time. She took it the wrong way. She said in a mean and nasty way something to the effect that she had been on her break, or whatever the reason was that she wasn't at the phone at the time that I called. I told my sister that I was going to talk to the nurse when we got to the nursing home about the way that she had spoken to me.

After we arrived, I saw the nurse and asked to speak to her for a second. I explained that when I had spoken to her on the phone earlier, I wasn't saying that she didn't have a reason to not answer the phone. I said that I understood that they are busy and can't always be by the phone. At first, she got defensive with me, but I maintained my composure. I explained again that I hadn't meant anything negative or anything against her when I said that. I said that I understood that she was busy and was just acknowledging that. She seemed to accept my explanation at that point. It was the truth. She had just misinterpreted what I had said and gotten angry with me for no good reason.

The reason I'm mentioning this incident is because something else happened between this nurse and me about a week after this conversation. I was visiting with my mom again. At one point, Mom did something that I didn't understand, so I went to this nurse and asked her about it. The nurse responded in a nasty and shrill voice, "Her brain is shrinking!" I was absolutely horrified by her response. It was not only extremely unprofessional and inappropriate, but it was cruel and chock full of hostility. I was completely taken aback by her reaction, but I didn't report her comment to administration at that time. I was concerned that she might try to retaliate in some way against my mom when I wasn't there, especially since she had just responded to me in a hostile manner the week before based on her incorrect perception of something that I said to her in a phone call. I believe that she spoke to me that way as retaliation for me clarifying the previous week's phone call. So not only did she not accept responsibility for her unprofessional behavior the week before, but she also had to "get even with me" because I had the courage and decency to speak up about her being abusive toward me.

She should be ashamed of herself for talking to me that way, especially considering the fact that my mom has Alzheimer's disease and that I am her loving and devoted son.

I believe that the fear of retaliation against our loved ones in nursing homes is very common among family members. We may feel inhibited under certain circumstances and choose not to speak up for fear that someone may take out his or her anger and resentment on our loved ones when we're not around. Of course, in any situation where I felt that I really had to speak up and say something, I always did. In this instance, I didn't say anything about it while my mom was still a resident there. However, a few years after Mom had left, I told Mary about it. She said that I should talk to the administration at the facility about it and offered to go with me if I chose to speak to them. I ended up going on my own. I was driving in the area of this nursing home one day, and I decided to go in. I spoke to the top administrator and her aide in a private meeting and retold the story. I explained my reason for not telling them about it at the time that it happened or shortly thereafter, saying that I basically didn't want any type of retaliation against my mom since I wasn't always available to be by her side. The administrator told me that this particular nurse had already retired, but she took notes about what I told her. She seemed to understand why I had waited to tell her about what had happened.

In the next facility that we had our mom in, Mary and I continued to have our share of problems with some of the staff members. This was the new facility that had a lockdown unit for Alzheimer's patients. In some ways, we thought that it was the best place that Mom had been in up to that point. However, some staff members demonstrated a bad attitude to us at times. One of the staff members wheeled Mom out after her dinner very abruptly and quickly. This was right after Mom had yelled at her. This aide should have known better. Mom sometimes yells at my sister and me too. She can't help it; she has Alzheimer's disease. I remember the look on my mom's face upon being removed so hastily. She looked startled, like she didn't know what was going on. I felt so bad for her. After the aide took Mom into the dining room and stationed her in an area there, the aide looked at me and said she was sorry about what she had just done. I explained that Mom hadn't meant anything when she raised her voice.

Another time, when I was coming in to visit Mom, I saw that the same aide had just wheeled Mom into a separate room and left her there alone in the wheelchair. As she was walking away from Mom, she said, "Well, if you want quiet, it's quiet in here!" in a very abrupt and annoyed way. Luckily, I got there just in time to be with my mom and to comfort her. When I got to her side, she was acting very anxious and was saying things that didn't make much sense to me. I gave her a hug and a kiss and told her that everything was all right. I was upset with the aide for speaking to my mom like that, but I didn't say anything to her about it at that time. I surmised that Mom may have gotten agitated about something that was going on in the unit. It may have been too loud for her. I know from personal experience that Mom sometimes gets agitated when things get loud. This was probably the reason for this aide's actions and abrupt tone. People who work in nursing homes and act like this shouldn't be working there in the first place, especially if they can't be patient, loving, compassionate, and understanding with the residents who live there.

When we got Mom to the final nursing home, where she currently lives, we had a little bit of a hard time adjusting to it. For one thing, we noticed that the toileting routine wasn't as smooth or as punctual as it had been at the assisted living facility. Some of the aides seemed to have an attitude about helping Mom go to the bathroom whenever she needed. We sometimes had to wait a half hour to forty-five minutes to get someone to come to the room to help her.

We also started to see unexplained bruises on different parts of her body at this nursing home. I don't recall ever having experienced this in any of the places where Mom had previously stayed. There is a possibility that some of these bruises could be explained. For example, Mom may have hit her arm against the rail on the side of the bed while sleeping or while trying to get up and out of bed sometime during the night. Or she may have been injured by another resident. Also, bruising is more common among the elderly because they bruise more easily. Even injections can cause bruises. However, I don't think that they can explain away every bruise. I saw some bruising on her face on at least one occasion, and I also saw bruising along her entire left forearm. It was so bad that I took pictures of it with my digital camera. I always immediately reported any suspicious-looking bruise to the nursing staff.

I had problems with a number of different aides there. One time, an aide was demonstrating how she helps Mom brush her teeth, and she was trying to get Mom to rinse her mouth again. I could tell that Mom didn't want to do it. As the aide continued, Mom gently pushed her hand away. I reached over and touched the aide's hand to stop her, but she continued to do it. She gave Mom a drink of water that was so abrupt that it forced Mom to gulp it down.

As the aide was leaving the room, I thanked her for helping Mom with her teeth. I also mentioned that I thought she had been too forceful. Apparently, she didn't want to hear anything that I had to say at that point in Mom's defense. I told her that I knew she was doing her job but that she needed to be gentler with my mom. The aide said that it had been my "imagination." Her comment upset me, but I didn't go for the bait. We were going back and forth and arguing in front of my mom. After the aide left, I told Mom something like, "You see, Mom? I stick up for you." A short time later, I noticed that Mom had her hands folded on the table in front of her like she was in the act of praying. I realized then that my discussion with this aide had scared her. Even though I was standing up for her, I'm sure that Mom knew that I wasn't going to be there with her all of the time. She was probably praying that nothing bad would happen to her. I felt so incredibly bad about it when I saw Mom doing that. I tried to comfort her the best way that I could. I resolved that if I ever had to talk with someone again about their care of Mom, I would do it outside of her room, where Mom couldn't see or hear whatever I had to say. I would never, ever intentionally do anything to hurt or to frighten my mom. After the aide left, I told the nursing manager about what had happened, and she said that she would speak to the aide about it.

The next time I saw the aide, she demonstrated an attitude toward me. She also got all of her aide friends on her side, even though they hadn't even been there when it happened. Either way, it was none of their business. I started to get dirty looks from some of the other aides, and they all ignored me in the unit for a while. I would say hi to them, and they would either look at me and turn away or totally ignore me. It was hurtful. I complained to nursing management again. I even had an incident in which one of the aides mouthed off to me in front of the aide with whom I had had the disagreement. I knew that it was an indirect but hostile comment aimed at me. I told nursing management about that too. I also mentioned the incident to one of the aides there who was still friendly with me. She was a personal aide to another resident and not employed by the facility. She knew what was going on and told me that the way the aides were treating me was unfair. I replied, "It's definitely unfair!" She said that whenever one of them has a problem with a caregiver, no matter what had actually happened, the aides would all team up against that person to make him or her feel uncomfortable and unwanted.

Another aide had an attitude about changing my mom when she needed it. I noticed that she was very impatient and tended to be a little rough at times. On several different occasions, I could hear my mom responding in a shrill voice almost every time she was changed by this particular aide. I had to stay outside the room while my mom was changed for privacy reasons, but if I ever felt that an emergency was happening or that I had to check in on her for some reason, I would do it.

I also noticed on various occasions that when I would go into the room after Mom had been changed by this aide, she appeared to be shaken up by the experience. Eventually, it led to an incident between the aide and me, and this was the second time I had had a problem with her within two weeks or so. This particular time, I asked the aide to change my mom. When she came in, she said to me that Mom didn't need to be changed for some reason. I said that I thought Mom needed to be changed. I then went into the bathroom for a second to wash my hands and left the bathroom door open. All of a sudden, I heard the aide move Mom very quickly and abruptly in her wheelchair to a different area of her room, and Mom let out a big yell. I knew right away that the aide was angry about being asked to change my mom.

I talked to the head nurse of the unit about the incident, and the aide was written up because of it. After that, she started giving my sister and me dirty looks. We could also tell that she was either trying to influence or to intimidate other aides to turn against us too. I picked this up because of her strong and dominating personality. I could sense that some intimidation of some of the other aides might be involved because they started to act differently toward us (not friendly, etc.) out of fear or to just go along with it and to not make their work environment any harder for them because of this controlling and dominating coworker's personality. For a while, it became a very hostile environment again, but eventually, some of the other aides started to lighten up in their attitude toward us. However, the other aides would still ignore us or wouldn't act friendly toward us whenever this particular aide was with them. Although the aide continued to harbor resentment and hostility toward us, I would just go on my way and make sure that my mom was being well taken care of. I told my sister to ignore this aide as much as possible. I also spoke to the head nurse about the continuing situation and said that if this aide continued to give me dirty looks, I would confront her about it. I told the nurse that I wasn't looking for anything but that I also wouldn't take any nonsense.

My sister and I have also had some occasional problems with the next aide who was assigned to Mom. This new aide tended to be erratic in her behavior toward us. In the June to July 2011 time frame, I spoke to the nurse manager about her. One of the things that bothered Mary and me was that she refused to call our mom by her first name, choosing instead to call her by her last name. She continued doing this even after we made several requests for her to call our mom by her first name. We also got some attitude from her at times. I asked the nurse to speak to her again and also mentioned that if this was going to continue, I was going to notify the social worker for my mom about the overall attitude problem of some the aides there.

I haven't mentioned all the times that we felt that a nurse or an aide acted inappropriately in a given situation. I believe that the instances I've described here give an idea of the problems that caregivers have to deal with from time to time in nursing homes.

Overall, my sister and I think that our mom is in the best place that she can be in other than at home with us. We still have problems at the nursing home from time to time. Outside of concerns about the behavior of other residents in the unit and its potential impact on our mom, our main concern is dealing with the aides in the unit. Most of the aides are very good and have very good attitudes, while others are good at what they do but can have an attitude at times.

I understand that everyone has a bad day now and then. However, if you choose to work around people with dementia, you must have concern for their well-being at all times. You must really want to do this type of work. Although it may be taxing, the aides in the nursing homes are very valuable employees who have a tremendous impact on the safety and the quality of life of the residents. I know that it's not an easy job, but it is a necessary job to help members of our society who can no longer help themselves.

My sister and I always treat all the staff at the nursing home with kindness, consideration, and respect. The times that we have had to advocate on behalf of our mom have sometimes led to problems between us and the staff. Ultimately, I try to find the best solution possible to any problem or potential problem, but I will always do what I think is best for Mom, no matter what.

The most important goal I have regarding my mom is to make sure that she is always being treated with dignity, kindness, respect, gentleness, sensitivity, compassion, understanding, and caring. She deserves the best care possible. We make sure that she gets it.

6

Alzheimer's Disease Progression

EARLY ON, LITTLE TELLTALE signs caused us to notice that Mom's memory wasn't as good as it used to be. For example, she would forget certain things when she was talking to us, like certain details or where she was in the conversation. Sometimes we would ask her questions, and she would respond with, "I don't remember." It seemed like most of her lapses of memory were related to her short-term memory.

As I mentioned previously, when we first started noticing Mom's memory loss and mentioned it to our dad, he said that it was associated with the normal aging process. A visit to a neurologist resulted in a diagnosis of mild cognitive impairment, which we knew would lead to Alzheimer's disease.

Mom exhibited the normal behavior patterns of someone who is slowly but surely slipping into Alzheimer's disease. Eventually, we could not leave her alone in the house at all. She had to have someone with her at all times.

I showed up after work one day and saw Mom sitting in a chair in the lobby of the nursing home that she was in two weeks after Dad passed away. As soon as I would come in and she would see me, a big smile would come across her face. I would go over to her and give her a kiss on the cheek and a hug. Sometimes I would pull a chair up next to her and just talk to her for a while before we went to her room to have dinner. Other times, I would arrive at the facility and walk down the hall toward Mom's room. Many times, I would see my mom coming from the other end, walking toward me. I knew that Mom spent a lot of time walking up and down the long hallways of this facility because the staff had told me about it. I also knew that Mom loved to walk.

As soon as Mom would recognize me coming down the hall, she would open up her arms with her palms open and facing toward the sky in the most loving and welcoming gesture. It was her way of saying that she was so happy to see me. It was always very dramatic. As we got close enough, I would lean in and hug her. Mom would kiss me and I would kiss her, and we would just embrace. I always told her that I love her and how happy I was to see her.

Sometimes we would walk together back and forth through the hallway of the facility. Other times, we would end up going back to her room to watch some television, and I would go to the dining room later to get her dinner tray and take it back to her room to help her with her meal. My normal stay with Mom was at least two hours every time I visited her. After a while, going to see my mom every day, seven days a week, while working full-time and taking care of everything at home by myself became too much for me. I also helped Mary at my parents' house. I eventually had to work down to visiting Mom six days a week and then five. During this period of time, I had lost a lot of weight. I have always been a slim person. I'm 6 feet tall, and my weight went from 175 pounds down to less than 140 pounds. I lost all of that weight because of all of the incredible stress that I was under during this ordeal. It took me quite a bit of time to get back to my normal weight.

Eventually, the time came to move Mom to another facility because she kept trying to get out of this one. After looking at several different facilities, we found an assisted-living facility with a lockdown unit for dementia patients. As with all Alzheimer's patients, it took Mom and the family some time to adjust to the new facility. Mom still wasn't happy about being in either a nursing home or an assisted-living facility. I completely understood how she felt. The good thing was that this was a lockdown facility. It also had a private room for Mom, like she had had at the previous facility.

Mom was having trouble sleeping at night. She would sometimes get up and walk to the living room area and sleep on the couch. The staff would put her pillow and some blankets down for her so that she could sleep there. Eventually, as part of the progression of her disease, Mom started to have trouble walking. One time, the nurse found Mom sleeping on the floor of the hallway in the middle of the night. She had gotten out of bed and started on her way down the hall, but she had fallen down and had not been able to get back up. On at least one other occasion, the staff found Mom lying on the floor of her room next to her bed. This was because she had tried to get out of bed and couldn't walk, and she must have fallen down. At this point, we already had Poseys (a special undergarment with cushions to help prevent injury in the event of a fall) on Mom. More than likely, it prevented her from injuring herself as the result of these falls.

While Mom was staying at this assisted-living facility, we got her approved for a locator bracelet as part of the Bergen County Sheriff's Department Project Lifesaver initiative. We had to pay a fee and a monthly charge for the service. We wanted it as a backup in the event that Mom ever managed to get away from the facility. If that were to happen, we would have a sophisticated electronic system to help us locate her immediately and bring her back to safety. Luckily, we never had to use the service. Eventually, when we were sure that Mom would not be able to get out because she was confined to a wheelchair and no longer able to walk, we discontinued our participation in the Project Lifesaver program.

When Mom became nonambulatory, the facility referred us to another nursing home that could provide the level of nursing care that she needed. We also knew that this facility was rated as one of the best nursing home facilities in the entire state of New Jersey. After we were able to get our mom admitted there, we were again faced with a period of transition for both Mom and the family. It took a while, possibly six months or more, for Mom to adjust to her new living arrangement. We noticed that she was slowly but surely progressing in the symptoms of her disease. Mom seemed to progress more quickly after Dad passed away and she began living alone in the nursing home.

Although Mom is not able to walk anymore, she has continued to demonstrate that she wants to walk. She occasionally tries to get up out of her wheelchair on her own power. In those instances, my sister and I will explain to her that she can't stand up on her own and that she needs assistance from us. When Mom insists on standing up, Mary and I get on both sides of her and lift her up to a standing position, at which point she usually gets frightened and wants to sit down again. She's not used to standing up on her own, and her legs are probably not strong enough to support her weight. Even if she could walk on her own, she would be unsteady. She would have a problem with her balance while trying to walk because she hasn't walked in a while.

The nursing home attached an alarm to her clothing. If she tries to get up or if she moves too far away from her wheelchair, the alarm will go off and an aide will come over and make sure that she sits down again. Sometimes when I come to visit, they'll have her seated at a table in the dining room with the wheels locked on her wheelchair. Other times, she will be sitting in her wheelchair with a portable table in front of her. The front legs of the table are positioned between the front and back wheels of Mom's wheelchair so that she cannot go anywhere. Anytime I see this, I feel so bad for her. I want to take the table away and take Mom home with me. At these times, one of the aides or I will take the table away so I can take Mom to her room and stay with her there.

Another aspect of the progression of the disease is that Mom isn't able to communicate as clearly or as consistently as she used to. She goes in and out of lucid conversation. Although it's not always the case, my mom seems to function better in the mornings, when her brain is fresh from a night's sleep. In fact, it holds true for most of us. Our brains tend to work better in the morning. So if I want to have the best overall conversation with Mom, it is better for it to happen in the morning or in the early afternoon. There are times when I visit Mom in the evening that she can be fairly lucid. However, it is more likely that I will have trouble understanding what she is saying. In those instances, I will say something like, "Mom, I don't always understand what you're trying to say to me. I'm doing the best that I can. Just know that things are okay, and I'm doing everything that I can for you." I try to be as proactive as possible to help keep the communication open and as clear and understandable as it can be. I also want Mom to know that I'm doing the best that I can to understand her and that I care about what she says to me.

Mom still wants to go home. Sometimes she'll speak to me in a way that is hard for me to understand, but I am able to figure out some of what she's saying and to piece it together. I usually focus on key words when she is communicating to me. Understanding what she is trying to communicate to me at any time is like learning a new language, a language that I will never fully understand. However, I'm trying my best to learn it and to comprehend it as much as possible.

Mom can no longer do the daily things that most people take for granted, like walking and communicating easily. People usually don't realize how lucky they are until they lose something as valuable as this.

I have discovered that dealing with Mom in the throes of Alzheimer's disease is like surfing in the ocean. I have to go with the flow of the waves. If I'm able to do that, then things will usually turn out okay. If I'm not able to go with the flow or to understand what Mom is trying to tell me, I'll get thrown off of the surfboard and tossed under the water. I have to live in Mom's world. She doesn't live in my world. She's not able to. I let Mom be my guide.

7

Caregiver Stress

WHEN I WAS OUT making my way in the world as a teenager, during college, and after college, I used to think from time to time that I had some big problems. I certainly had my share of challenges, but in retrospect, I didn't know what real problems were. Now I do. There are many times when I feel as if I'm stuck in a long, dark tunnel and I can't see any light at the end of it.

The level of stress involved with being a caregiver for a loved one with Alzheimer's disease is enormously high. It takes an incredible toll on a person's overall health and well-being. It drains your energy, and it can take away a lot of the joy and comfort of life.

At one point, I was a caregiver to my dad, mom, and sister all at the same time. I had to help my sister in different ways because she was feeling down about all that was happening. It was even harder for her because Mom and Dad were in the nursing home while she was living alone in the house. I did all this while working full-time and taking care of everything at my own place as well. The stress was compounded by all the paperwork that I was responsible for on behalf of my mom and dad.

Looking back, I'm still not sure how I was able to do it. My stress level skyrocketed. It was hard for me to be as productive at work as I had been, and it also resulted in some substantial weight loss. As I mentioned previously, during this period of stress and uncertainty, I lost over thirty-five pounds.

I really started to experience caregiver stress in August 2007 when I found out that my dad's cancer had come back and spread to his bone marrow. From that day to the present, there's never been a day that I have felt as carefree and free-spirited as I used to. Dad ended up living only another two months. We have been dealing with Mom's Alzheimer's disease since 2000. Mom's disease began before it was even diagnosed in January 2000, as is the case with people who get Alzheimer's disease. As you know, Alzheimer's disease progresses as the patient ages.

When I was arranging for my mom and dad to become residents in their first nursing home, I signed the paperwork for Dad first and then told the estate lawyer that I had done so. He wanted to look at it right away and cautioned me not to sign anything else without his seeing it first. So when it came to signing contracts to get Mom into the nursing home, I made sure that my lawyers looked at them before I signed them. If they had any comments or changes, they would send those to me and I would take them to the facility administrator. If they agreed with the changes, I could then sign the document as amended. If not, I would ask the facility to work out a version of the contract that I could sign off on. However, Mom's current nursing home doesn't allow for any changes to be made to their contract. I found this out only after I had submitted the legal comments on their contract back to them.

In addition, both Mary and I had power of attorney for Mom and Dad. I was the executor of my dad's estate. After Dad passed away, I had a lot of paperwork to do regarding settling his estate. In early 2010, I worked again with the same law office to help me to complete all of the paperwork involved with Mom's Medicaid application.

As I mentioned previously, Mary went into a down period within two months of Dad's passing. She was eventually able to get through it, but it was an extremely difficult time for her. With everything else going on, it was also an extremely difficult time for me. I was always as loving, helpful, and supportive as possible to Mary during her ordeal.

Whenever I hear that someone who I knew from my mom's unit has passed away, I always feel bad for them and for their family. I also feel very bad about it when someone who is well known either is diagnosed with Alzheimer's disease or has just died from it. I can completely relate to it. From firsthand experience, I know how difficult it is not only for the patient but also for the caregiver.

The stress of being a caregiver is omnipresent. I worry about Mom and her overall safety, well-being, and happiness every day. I love her with all of my heart. I am completely and totally devoted to her. Because of the stressful nature of my situation, I must continue to take good care of myself to the best of my ability.

I don't subscribe to the statement "If you don't take care of yourself, you can't take care of anyone else." I believe that you can still take care of someone else even if you're not taking the best care of yourself. However, I also believe that the better I care for myself, the better I can care for my mom and be fully present for her. The difference is the degree to which I can be available to my mom and to her care. I always try to do the best that I can for Mom in all circumstances. When I'm with her, I give her all the love, care, and attention that I can. The key in all this is to strive to maintain balance in my life as much as possible.

There's a whole range of feelings that accompany being a caregiver to a loved one with Alzheimer's disease. As I've said before, I will do anything and everything to help my mom. I try to visit her up to four times per week. I always love seeing her and spending time with her. However, there are times when I don't want to be there. It's not that I don't want to see Mom or that I may have other things to do. It's just that it's difficult for me to see her in this condition. It takes a lot out of me emotionally. So, at times I feel ambivalent about going to see her. That being said, even if I don't feel up to it, I always feel great when I actually arrive and see her in person. My overwhelming love for her comes rushing up inside of me. I also feel Mom's love for me.

8

Paying Medical Bills

PAYING MEDICAL BILLS HAS to be one of the least enjoyable aspects of the caregiver experience. I'm not sure if anyone actually enjoys going through the often unbelievable detail and follow-up that can be required to review and pay medical bills, along with correcting any mistakes that can occur in the billing process.

One of the main keys to success as a caregiver is to stay as organized as possible. In the beginning, Mom was on Medicare with supplemental insurance. Even though I would get statements showing amounts that were covered and not covered by Mom's Medicare and supplemental insurance, I would always call the supplemental insurance company to make sure that the doctor's bill coincided with what we actually owed. There were also times when I had to call Medicare to get information concerning a medical bill.

There were discrepancies many times between what was billed and what we actually owed. It was a painstaking process. My efforts at ensuring that we paid only what we owed and not a penny more definitely saved us money. Later on, after Mom was approved for Medicaid, the billing and payment process was more straightforward.

Sometimes, I get tired of having to be responsible for so many things all the time. There were times when I temporarily put things off, opting instead to deal with them later on. This is just one way of dealing with the stress of being a caregiver and the paperwork that goes along with it.

For example, I had a dispute with a particular facility several months before Mom had to be moved to another one because she needed a higher level of nursing care. I had written a check for the monthly bill and left it with the receptionist at the front desk. I had been told that it was acceptable to do it this way and had done it previously without incident. The receptionist told me that she would make sure that it got to the finance department the next day. This time, however, she forgot to give it to the finance department in time. Consequently, the finance department received it after the grace period had ended and charged us a late fee on the next monthly bill.

When I found out about it, I was furious. I called the finance department and asked them what had happened. They told me that the late fee had been assessed because they received the payment after the grace period. I told them about leaving the payment on time with the receptionist at the front desk. It was either then or a little while later that they realized that the receptionist had forgotten to forward the payment to them in time. It may have been sitting there for a week or more at the front desk, unbeknownst to anyone. Subsequently, I told them that I refused to pay a late fee. They said that they would speak to the director of the facility about it. The director's initial decision was that I had to pay the late fee. My response was, "We'll see about that!" Eventually, they waived the fee. Fair is fair. I make sure that Mom and our family are always treated honestly, fairly, and in a professional manner.

9

Medicaid

THE GREAT MAJORITY OF paperwork that I had to complete on Mom's behalf involved the Medicaid approval process. We hired the estate law firm that we had utilized for my dad's estate to assist me. This made perfect sense on many levels, especially because the legal costs came out of the money that had to be spent down anyway before Mom would be eligible for Medicaid. The law firm kept me on track with all of the paperwork that needed to be completed.

I call the Medicaid approval process the Mount Everest of paperwork. I strongly urge people to either consult with a lawyer or another paid professional who has expertise in the Medicaid approval process to assist them in meeting all of the Medicaid requirements.

In my personal experience, although I provided Medicaid with everything that they asked for, they came back and requested more information to back up things. One of the requirements was that we supply three years' worth of financial information for both Mom and Dad. This included, but was not limited to, all of their bank statements, investment account information, income tax statements, and so on. In fact, even though Medicaid got the list of checks that Mom and Dad had written over the course of the three-year period, they also wanted copies of all of the canceled checks.

At that time, Mary and I couldn't find the previous year's federal and state income tax returns that Dad had submitted for him and Mom. Unfortunately, Dad had already passed away. I had to send requests to both the US government and the State of New Jersey for a copy of the returns, along with a fee. Once I received them in the mail, I forwarded them to the lawyer's office as part of the required documentation.

Many other problems popped up during the Medicaid approval process. One of them didn't have anything to do with dealing with Medicaid at all. We were required to get bank statements for the previous three years. Mom and Dad had accounts at three different banks. One of the banks required us to pay for copies of the bank statements even though they knew that this was part of the Medicaid application requirements. The other banks had provided us with all the statements that we needed free of charge. They do this as a service to people who need this information in order to try to become eligible for Medicaid.

Originally, the charge from this bank was in excess of $200. I spoke to the branch manager and asked if she could waive the fee, mentioning our experience with the other two banks. She said that we could split the cost and that she would charge the account only $100. I agreed to that amount, as there was not much that I could do about it. However, it made me angry. Not only did my parents have accounts there, but my sister and I had accounts as well and had established a good relationship with that branch and everyone who worked there. This particular bank said that it is required to charge for copies of bank statements even though they were being requested as part of the Medicaid application process.

Mom was finally approved for Medicaid in October 2009. However, Medicaid had changed her initial eligibility date to a month later than the originally agreed upon date. When I called and asked the lawyer's office about this discrepancy, they said that sometimes Medicaid does that, but they eventually restore the eligibility date back to its original date.

This did not happen in my mom's case. The nursing home where Mom was living was starting to pressure me to either get Medicaid to correct it back to the initial eligibility date or for me to pay the difference between the Medicaid rate and the rate we had been paying before Medicaid for that particular month. If I didn't get this problem fixed, our family would have owed an additional $8,500 to the nursing home.

I worked really hard and diligently to correct it. I asked both the social worker and the finance department at the nursing home to speak with the Medicaid representative in charge of my mom's account. I also asked the lawyer's office to make calls on our behalf. I called the Medicaid caseworker myself several times. She had talked to me over the phone in some of the other stages of this process. However, she wasn't returning any of my calls regarding changing the eligibility date back to its original date. When my requests to Medicaid, the nursing home, and the lawyer's office to assist me ended up not making any difference in the matter, I took it upon myself to call my congressional representative.

I described the problem in detail to an employee at the US representative's office, and she said that someone would get back to me on the matter. A few days later, she called and told me that Medicaid is taken care of on the state level in New Jersey, so she would forward all my information to my state representative's office to see if they could help me in this matter. She asked that I wait until that afternoon to call the representative. Just as I was getting ready to call, someone who worked in the state representative's office called me. Again, I described the problem in detail. The gentleman I spoke to there said that he would look into it and get back to me soon. He called me back a few days later and told me that he had spoken to the Medicaid representative and her supervisor about the matter, and they said they would review the case again. I told him that I was concerned about what they had said. It sounded to me like they had already made a final decision and that they weren't going to change their minds.

He asked me to wait about one and a half to two weeks before I contacted Medicaid again to see how it was resolved. Within that time frame, I received an e-mail from the nursing home stating that Medicaid had restored the eligibility date to its original date that had been agreed upon. I was so incredibly happy to hear the news after such a long, hard struggle. It was a tremendous relief to me and an important milestone moment in my efforts on behalf of my mom.

Overall, my experience in dealing with Medicaid throughout the extensive application process, along with the effort involved to ensure that the eligibility date remained the same, was cumbersome and, at times, excruciating.

10

Resources for Caregivers

FIRST AND FOREMOST, PLEASE remember that you are not alone. There are many people who serve as caregivers to their loved ones with Alzheimer's disease. Whatever you are going through, many of us are either currently going through it or have already gone through it.

The Alzheimer's Association is a great place to start when looking for resources. You can call them twenty-four hours a day, seven days a week at their toll-free number. You can also check them out on their website at http://www.alz.org/.

The Alzheimer's Association has a tremendous amount of information and resources available, including a list of support groups in your area. There are websites and blogs that are devoted to Alzheimer's caregivers. Consider taking advantage of as many of the available opportunities as you can on the Internet and through social media. You can "like" the Alzheimer's Association on Facebook. You will then get automatic updates on Facebook of Alzheimer's events and related things of interest.

You can also connect with people through Twitter. There are many other ways to get information and to stay connected through social media.

Numerous books have been written on the subject of caring for someone with Alzheimer's disease. Various TV shows that deal with the subject air from time to time. Also, a satellite radio show, currently on Channel 81, called Doctor Radio features a geriatrics doctor. Of course, segments and stories about Alzheimer's disease appear on a regular basis on the national news.

Regarding your loved one, when making the decision about whether or not to have a full-time or live-in aide, or to have your loved one placed into a nursing home environment, it's very important that you do your homework. To find a qualified aide, you can check with various home-care agencies and research their reputations through your local Better Business Bureau. You can also ask them to provide references. In New Jersey, the website titled "State of New Jersey Department of Health, Division of Health Facilities Evaluation and Licensing" has information on home-care agencies, nursing homes, and so on. I recommend trying to talk to people who have their family members in nursing homes or are using home-care agencies that you might be interested in. For example, you may be able to talk with them when you visit a nursing home that you might be interested in. If they're available to answer your questions, please make sure to ask them about their overall experience with the facility.

If you need legal help, it's very important to get in touch with an estate lawyer, who can help you in the event that family estate issues arise. The saying "it's better to know sooner rather than later" is especially true when it comes to legal and financial concerns. Legal help is also important because other family members may be involved. You should be able to get a free consultation with a lawyer to determine whether he or she can be of assistance to you. Likewise, you may have to deal with financial and tax issues and need help in dealing with them. In our case, we hired an estate law firm that my dad had used for his estate, and we also utilized a Certified Public Accountant (CPA) to help us with Mom's and Dad's taxes.

Support groups are very important. In my experience, they have been led by qualified people. It's always good to know that there are other people in the same situation as you. You can obtain and share information, learn new things from someone else's experience and expertise, feel supported and understood, and make new friends. Some support groups bring in guest speakers from time to time who discuss things that may be relevant to you.

I recommend that you journal about your experiences as much as possible. You can write about things that have happened, memorable experiences, happy times, and your thoughts and feelings at any given time. I only wish that I had started journaling from the moment that my mom was placed in a nursing home.

Like any other area of your life, it's very important to stay as organized as possible. Keep up a filing system with all your relevant paperwork. You can also keep a record, either written or on the computer, of incidents that have happened. If you do this, it's important to be as specific as possible. For example, if—God forbid—there is a problem, you can enter the date, time, place, the people involved, what actually happened, and so on. Even if the situation gets resolved in a satisfactory way, it's always good to know that you have this information at your fingertips in the event that it turns into a legal or financial matter. Documenting things as accurately as possible will also help you in the event that it comes down to your word against someone else's.

It's very important to know and to understand on a deep emotional level that you are the best resource for a loved one with Alzheimer's disease. You make all the difference in the world to her. (I'm using the singular pronoun *her* because I'm speaking in reference to my mom in this case.) You are her best doctor, nurse, and aide because you love her. You always want the very best care and treatment for her. Also, you know and understand your loved one better than anyone else. The amount of time that you spend with her, the love and care that you give her, the time it takes to do her paperwork and any other follow-up activities, and the time and effort spent advocating on her behalf whenever necessary make a tremendous difference in her overall quality of life. It can dramatically increase her health, happiness, safety, and longevity. It also benefits you because you get to spend quality time with her while you're still fortunate enough to have her in your life. It's all comes from love. Besides, you definitely don't want to feel like you have any regrets after your loved one passes away.

Whenever you feel stuck or uncertain of what to do next, please don't ever be afraid, anxious, or hesitant to ask for help. It's always there if you need it. Look at seeking help as a sign of strength, courage, and wisdom. Also, there are people out there (professionals, caregivers, etc.) who may know things that you don't know. It's better to ask if you don't know or aren't sure about something. In some situations, you may want to ask to make sure that what you're doing is actually the best thing for your loved one.

Your loved one is counting on you to be as organized, informed, and devoted to her care as you can possibly be. You have to take appropriate action whenever the situation calls for it. It makes all the difference in the world to her. It will make a difference to you, also.

11

What My Mom Means to Me

I MADE UP A saying that goes like this: "I've met a lot of people in the course of my life, but I've never met anyone as wonderful as my mom."

I know that I'm being partial because she is my mom. However, I'm glad that I have her and that she is the person that she is. She is the most wonderful and amazing person in the world to me. She has so many gifts. She is also extremely loving, kind, compassionate, and special, and she is a lot of fun to be with.

I've learned a tremendous amount from her, like to always do the right thing in any situation and to use common sense in life. Mom also taught me to treat everyone with respect. She is also the most sensible, spiritual, sensitive, and intuitive person that I know.

Whenever I am with Mom, even these days in the midst of her battle with Alzheimer's disease, I know that I am with the most precious person in the world. Every moment that I share with her is sacred. We have an incredible bond. I'm grateful for this and for many other things that have happened as a result of the closeness that I have with her. My humanity is elevated whenever I'm in her presence. That's how good of a person she is and the wonderful effect that she has on me.

I'm sure that I speak for millions of people when I say that I'm hurt and angry about what people with Alzheimer's disease have to go through. It's a terrible burden for Mom as well as for her family. I cannot have the normal conversations with Mom that I used to have. I always cherished our conversations about life, living, doing what is right, being good to myself and to others, and many other topics of interest. I'm also deprived, to some extent, of her heartfelt expressions of love, wisdom, and guidance.

Since Mom did so much for me growing up, I feel that I owe her a lot. No matter how much I do on her behalf, I can never do enough. I'll always feel that way.

Mom helped make me the person that I am today. I like to say that even on my best day, when I'm doing great work, being a really good person, and helping people out, I'm still not half as good as my mom. I really and truly believe that. In fact, whenever I'm with Mom, my spirit and all of who I am is lifted to a higher level. As I stated before, I always feel like a much better person whenever I'm in her presence. I sincerely feel that I love my mom more than I love myself. I'm not saying that I don't love or care about myself. I'm just saying that the love that I have for her is infinite and boundless. It is an unselfish love that says, "I love you, Mom, more than anything else in the world. And I'll show you how much I love you by all of my daily thoughts, feelings, and actions on your behalf."

Another aspect of Mom's wonderful personality is that she has a great sense of humor, a wonderful smile, and a love of laughter. The light and beauty that are inside of her comes out whenever she smiles. It is apparent to anyone who's ever met her. Like I said before, Mom could light a room with her personality and her presence. She could also light up a person's heart with her smile.

My mom is filled with such goodness. Being with her is the closest thing to being with God that I can experience here on earth. I really see her as someone who is the closest a human being can be to being as pure, beautiful, and wonderful as God. She could be the queen of the world. She would be the kindest and most benevolent, compassionate, understanding, and just leader the world has ever known.

Mom means everything in the world to me. I think about her every day, and I pray for her every night. I pray really hard for her. I pray for a cure to Alzheimer's disease. Although a cure may not happen in her lifetime, I still pray fervently for it. I pray for all of Mom's medical issues to go away. I also do whatever I can for Mom and advocate, whenever it's necessary, on her behalf.

I visit Mom as often as possible, partly because it hurts me to think about her being alone at the nursing home. She is there without a family member for the majority of the day. I don't want Mom to ever think that we have forgotten about her, that we don't know that she's there in the nursing home, or that we don't care.

One day while I was attending a course titled Computer Concepts and Applications in 2010, we were working on Microsoft PowerPoint. The test for that portion of the class was to create a PowerPoint presentation on either a company that we created or a cause that we cared about. I knew right away that it had to be about Alzheimer's disease. We had to give our presentations on Thursday and Friday of that particular week. As it turned out, I ended up being the last person to go up on Friday. I started out by asking the class not to leave during my presentation, saying that if they tried, I was going to call them out like President Obama. They laughed.

I started the presentation by talking about Alzheimer's disease, what it is, how many people it affects, famous people who have had the disease, and so on. As I neared the end of the presentation, I talked about how much my mom means to me. I started by saying, "Maybe I'm being partial . . . ," and I started to choke up and almost started to cry. My voice was breaking. I was trying to control myself. I wanted to finish the presentation, but I couldn't speak for about thirty seconds or so. Then, unexpectedly, a woman friend in my class reached her hand out for me to hold for support. I grabbed her hand and held it for about ten seconds. It meant the world to me. It helped me to compose myself and to continue.

I went on to say, "But my mom is the best person that I've ever met in my whole life." I explained why I feel that way, describing some of the wonderful things that she's done in her life and why she's such a good person. When I finished the presentation and the lights were turned back on, I could see that many people in the class were either crying or had tears in their eyes. When the class ended about ten or fifteen minutes later, several people came up to me and told me how moved they were by my presentation. Some of them shared stories of their own as they related to family members who suffered from the disease. I also received a voice message later that day from another friend in my class. Her message basically said, "It was heavy stuff and really beautiful in the way that you shared it." She said how touched she was by it. It was so meaningful to me to get that feedback from people. I know that they meant it and that they really cared about what I was going through. I knew that I had touched their hearts.

In today's world of celebrities, Mom is the greatest celebrity of all. If anyone should be celebrated for whom he or she is, it's my mom. Knowing her like I do, I believe in my heart that she could have been the most famous and well-loved person in the world because of all the incredible goodness and love within her. I feel that there should be a big parade in her honor down the Canyon of Heroes in New York City. I've never met anyone who comes close to her with all her wonderful qualities and gifts. I feel so lucky that she is my mom. I'll always be grateful for that.

12

Selected Events and Conversations with Mom

ALTHOUGH I HAVE ONE entry in this book dated from March 2009, I actually started taking notes on conversations I had with Mom on October 29, 2009. I regret not taking notes for the first two years that she was in the nursing home environment. I do remember certain events that happened during that time span, and I have included some of them below.

On one occasion when I was visiting Mom in the nursing home, we were walking down the hallway together and talking. All of a sudden, I saw a woman sitting in a wheelchair in the hallway that we had just turned into. I pointed to the woman and said to Mom, "Mom, see that woman over there? She's almost one hundred years old. Can you believe it?" Mom said, without hesitating, "She looks it!" I started laughing. It was just another example of her wonderful sense of humor.

One day at this same nursing home we had moved Mom to after Dad passed away, they were having a special event, complete with food and a band. During the performance, they played "Day-O (The Banana Boat Song)," made famous by Harry Belafonte. Mom got excited, jumped up, and started dancing to it. I wished that I had been able to videotape it. It was so much fun to see Mom being spontaneous and really enjoying herself. At another point during the band's performance, Mom got up, went over to the band, and touched the singer's arm. The singer seemed to be upset by it, so I pulled Mom away and explained to the singer that she couldn't help it.

Another time, I had taken Mom home for part of the day to get something to eat and to let her see her house again. We stayed there for a couple of hours or so. When we were getting ready to leave, Mom didn't want to go. I understood why. She was home again and wanted to stay there. I didn't blame her at all for feeling that way. It was very hard for me to convince her that she had to leave the house with me. I called the nursing home, spoke to the unit nurse, and asked for advice. She just told me to keep trying. She suggested that I tell Mom that I was taking her out for a ride at that time.

So I told Mom that I wanted to leave and take her for a ride, but Mom is so smart. She asked where I intended to go. I was deliberately vague with her. I really hated having to lie to her to get her to go back to the nursing home. It broke my heart. Mom continued to resist, but eventually, she said that she would go with me. I think then that she knew that I was taking her back to the nursing home. I would have given everything in the world then to be able to give her a great big hug and a kiss and say, "Mom, I love you with all my heart. I never, ever wanted for you to be in a nursing home in the first place. You won't ever have to go back there. You can stay here at home with me. I'll find someone to help us take care of you." This is yet another example of the heartbreak, suffering, and trauma that is associated with people who suffer from Alzheimer's disease along with their loving caregivers.

On another occasion, Mom had to be taken to a local hospital because she had fallen down and gotten some bruising. After I got the call, I went right over to the hospital to meet her there. As we were waiting for a room to open up so that she could be examined, we walked past a woman and her husband who were sitting down and waiting for something. We talked briefly, and I ended up telling the woman why we were there and what my mom has.

While Mom was in the examining room, she started to yell when the nurse came in to examine her. I asked if I could help, but the nurse said that everything was okay. Mom kept yelling because they were trying to keep her on the examining table, and she was scared. When the doctor was going into the room to examine her, I told him, "She has Alzheimer's" to explain why she was acting like that. The doctor turned to me as he was walking in and replied harshly, "I know that!" He spoke to me as if I annoyed him by saying it. I only said it because I was anxious and wanted to make sure that he knew about it. I was upset that he had responded to me like that. It hurt my feelings. I considered talking to him about it when he was done tending to my mom, but I eventually decided against it. I regret not saying something to him about it or calling back later to complain to the hospital administration about the way he spoke to me. I understand that he may have been in a rush. However, he should understand and have compassion for what caregivers go through on a daily basis. Maybe he should care about how his reactions or attitude can adversely affect someone else.

Also, just before Mom and I left the hospital, the woman I had been speaking with in the hallway earlier made a comment to me about Mom making a lot of noise. I was really annoyed by her comment. I had to explain to her again that Mom has Alzheimer's disease and that was why she had been yelling. Some people either don't get it or don't want to get it.

A while after Mom was placed in her current nursing home, she had to be taken to the hospital because she was having a problem with her heart and lungs. Her oxygen was low. I was visiting with her when it was discovered. It turned out that she had congestive heart failure. I accompanied Mom to the hospital in the ambulance, and I held Mom's hand as she lay on the stretcher. She had an intravenous line in her. She was looking at me the whole time. She wouldn't take her eyes off of me. En route to the hospital, I was talking to the paramedics about the economy, and I said that being a paramedic is a good job in this economy. Mom said out loud, "No, it isn't!" Everyone in the ambulance laughed. Even under these kinds of circumstances, Mom listens closely to everything that is being said, and sometimes she'll comment on it.

Regarding the journal entries that I've included in this chapter, there are some entries that may sound similar in nature to others. I have done this to emphasize that Mom's responses are both interesting and different. I also have included entries if they provide deeper insight into Mom and her disease or if they describe an event that happened in the nursing home. For example, I say, "I love you, Mom" to her a lot whenever I visit. I want her to know that and to remember it the best that she can. Many times she makes me laugh. Other times, it amazes me how profound she can be with just a few short words.

The following entries in this chapter help to provide an inside look and a detailed account at some of the things that can happen on a daily, weekly or monthly basis to a loved one with Alzheimer's disease and to their caregiver(s). I have made this chapter a significant part of this book to provide the reader with stories, insights and to help them to benefit from my overall experience as a caregiver.

March 16, 2009

I'm Not Comfortable With Mom Being Asked Questions

I was visiting with Mom, and I said, referring to the nursing home dining hall, "I know why they don't have any juice. The trucks couldn't get through because of the storm." Mom said, "I just thought of it." I laughed. I thought that her comment was very cute.

At one point, I pointed to the wedding anniversary portrait of Mom and Dad that is in her room. I said, "Remember Dad? I pray to him every night for you." Mom replied, "That's great!"

Sometime later, an aide saw me with Mom and asked Mom if she knew me, being playful. Mom said yes, and the aide said, "Do you know his name?" Mom said, "I like him." I said to Mom, "Mom, my name is Bill." In hindsight, the aide's questions made me uncomfortable. I talked to the social worker about it the next time that I visited. She helped me come up with a response to use if it were to happen again. I could say, "I know that you're being playful and trying to help my mom. However, I'm not comfortable with her being asked questions that she's not able to answer."

As I was leaving, I said, "Happy St. Patrick's Day, Mom! Keep those Irish eyes smiling." Mom laughed and smiled that wonderful smile of hers.

October 29, 2009

What Do I Do Now?

I showed up around 12:10 p.m. to see Mom. As I walked into the dining room, Mom said, "Billy!" It made me feel like I had just won the lottery.

When I first got there, Laura (a resident in my mom's unit) said that Mom was too smart for this place. She meant that Mom was more advanced and sophisticated than the other people in the unit.

During the visit, as I was helping Mom with her lunch in her room, she said that she loved me. I said, "I love you too, Mom." At different points, Mom asked, "How's your mother?" and I replied, "*You're* my mother." Mom just said, "Okay."

Mom also mentioned her own mother to me. I told her that her mom was in heaven and was watching over her. I told Mom that Mary would be visiting with her that night, and she said, "Good." She asked if others were coming to see her, and I said that her other two sons would see her over the next week.

During that same visit, she said, "What do I do now?" I said, "You don't have to do anything, Mom. We're taking care of everything." Mom says that because she wants to feel useful. She hates not having much to do. I completely understand. Before she got Alzheimer's, she was used to doing things during the day instead of having to rely on people to help her.

At one point, Mom called me "Daddy." This is common among people who have this disease. Since I am one of Mom's main caregivers and I'm a man, she refers to me as Daddy. I help to take care of her, and I look after her.

When I was leaving and saying good-bye, Mom said, "Be careful." I said, "Thanks," and then added, "Be happy, healthy, and safe."

January 17, 2010
Where Is My Husband?
When Mary and I were with Mom for a while, Mom said, "Where is my husband? I love him." Whenever Mom asks about Dad, I always tell her what happened to Dad and that she sometimes forgets that he passed away. I also console her and tell her that we'll take care of her. A short time later, she said, "You have to go home. This isn't right. I can't take it." When she said, "You have to go home," she meant, "I have to go home."

She sometimes mixes up her personal pronouns because of her disease. Since I already know this from personal experience, it's easier for me to understand what she is saying and to respond to her.

Later on, while Mary was in the bathroom, I said out of the blue, "You're my mom, for gosh sakes!" Mom started laughing. She said, "Thank you" several times to us when we were leaving, showing us her big, beautiful smile.

March 3, 2010

Why Are You Here?

Mom turned to me at one point and asked me why I was there. When I asked her if she recognized me, she said that she didn't know who I was. It always hurts when she says something like that to me. I know that she can't help it; it's a result of her disease. I explained who I was and why I was visiting her.

When I was leaving about an hour later, I said good-bye to her one more time, and she started saying, "Bill, Billy, Bill, Billy." I rushed back over to her and started hugging and kissing her. I was so happy that she remembered my name in that moment. I also felt bad because I was leaving her. The fact that Mom said my name just as I was leaving made it even more of a dramatic and difficult departure for me.

March 7, 2010

Have Some Sensitivity!

Mary and I were taking Mom for a ride in her wheelchair on the main floor and down the hallways of the facility. They have artwork and photographs on the walls, along with a nice aquarium. When we were coming back around and headed toward the main lobby, Mom started to yell out. Sometimes we don't know why she is yelling, and Mom can't explain it to us. We may or may not be able to figure it out in the moment. After

Mom yelled out, I immediately tried to comfort her and to calm her down. A woman was in the area with her husband and an elderly patient in a wheelchair, probably a parent. They were getting ready to get on the elevator. They were standing about a hundred feet away from us at that time. The woman yelled out, "What an act!" I was stunned. I couldn't believe that someone would say something as ignorant and hostile as that. They know that the nursing home houses people with dementia along with people who need assisted living and physical rehabilitation.

I walked over toward them to discuss it with them, but they had already gotten on the elevator and the door had closed. As the elevator started to go up, I said loudly through the door, "Have some sensitivity!" I know that they heard me through the elevator door. I called the nursing home the next day and complained to the social worker. She asked me if I knew who the people were so that she could speak to them. I said no but that if anything like that happened again, I would find out who they were and let her know. I was absolutely furious that someone would say something so incredibly insensitive and inhumane. I guess that they feel it is okay to say that to someone else even when they may not understand or care to understand what's really going on—unless of course it happens to them or one of their loved ones. The woman who said it is a rude and ignorant fool.

When we took Mom back into her unit after the tour of the facility, she said, "Chand." I said, "Do you want Mary to hold your hand?" and she said yes. I said, "Mom, I'm getting to understand your language." She replied, "Good."

April 21, 2010
A Large Bruise on Mom's Left Forearm
I spoke to the head nurse, June, about a large bruise on Mom's left forearm. I also mentioned that Mom had tried to eat a sugar packet in the

dining room and that no one had prevented her from doing it. I said that I had first noticed the bruise when visiting Mom on April 20, 2010. At that time, I had brought the nurse Ray over. He looked at Mom's chart and said that he had checked the bruise after the CNA noticed it on April 19. He said that Celia, another nurse, had told him that it was in Mom's chart. However, the last date that a bruise on her left forearm had been recorded in the chart was March 11, 2010. I told Ray that I didn't think that the current bruise was the same one from forty days earlier and that I would call June about it, which I did the next day. Also, I asked why the CNA would have only just noticed it if it wasn't a fresh bruise.

May 9, 2010
I Can't Do Anything!
While Mary and I were visiting Mom, Mom said, "I can't do anything!" She paused momentarily and then said, "I can't help it!" Mary went over and comforted her. I felt so bad for Mom. Outside of everything that we do for her, I wish that I could cure her of this awful disease.

This is another example that people with Alzheimer's disease do suffer. Imagine what it feels like knowing that you're a prisoner in your own body and that you can't do much to help yourself or others or to feel that you're accomplishing things every day.

May 12, 2010
Do You Want to Walk, Mom?
Mary was visiting Mom by herself on this particular day. Mary told me that Mom started shaking her wheelchair at one point with a fierce look on her face, and then she screamed. Mary asked her, "Do you want to walk, Mom?" and she said yes. Mary said, "I'll take you for a ride." Mary took Mom to Ray before taking her for a ride in the wheelchair and told him about what had just happened. Ray gave Mom her medicine a little

earlier than normal to calm her down, and within five minutes, Mom was back to her normal self.

It must be so frustrating for Mom to be unable to walk, to know that she can't walk, and to not be able to communicate her thoughts and feelings like she used to.

May 30, 2010

Bye, Now

I was with Mom in her room, busily preparing her dinner by setting up the tray the best way for her to eat, cutting the food into smaller pieces, and so on. Mom looked over at me and said, "You're so cute." I said, "Thanks, Mom. I get my looks from you and Dad."

As I was getting ready to leave, I started getting the room ready for the aides to come in and change Mom. Mom said, "Bye, now." I said, "Mom, I'll be leaving in a few minutes. I'll let you know when I'm leaving, and I'll say good-bye." I felt so badly that Mom had said it. She was anticipating that I would be leaving and thinking that I would just walk out of her room without saying good-bye. Of course, I would never do that.

June 5, 2010

Of Course, Of Course, Of Course!

At one point, Mom looked at me and said, "What's the matter?" because she could see the look on my face. I said, "Nothing, Mom. I just have a few things on my mind, and I worry about you." I then said, "Do you worry about me, Mom?" Sometimes it's nice for me to be reassured about how she feels and to know that she can still communicate it. Mom said, "Of course, of course, of course!" She said it three times in a row! I thanked her. What a doll!

June 8, 2010

Mine? Mine?

When I was first arriving to see Mom, she saw me and said, "Mine? Mine?" This is Mom's way of saying, "You're my child, right?" I said, "Yes." Mom said, "I love you," and I said, "I love you too, Mom." We gave each other a hug and a kiss. I'm so glad that she's my mom.

July 1, 2010

That's What She Said

When I walked into the dining room, I was looking at Mom and she was looking back at me. When I approached her, she said, "Why?" I said, "Because I'm your son and you're my mom, and I love you." Mom then seemed to recognize me. I told her that I was taking her to her room so that we could hang out together and she could have her dinner there.

Later on, we were watching *Oprah*, and the cast of the movie *Twilight* was on. The actor Robert Pattinson was stopping by unannounced at the houses of *Twilight* fans, and the girls and women all went crazy when they saw him. Mom seemed to be getting a kick out of it. I said, "It's funny, isn't it?" and Mom replied, "That's what she said," without any emphasis on the word *she*. I started cracking up because it was so unexpected, because of the expression itself, and because I say that exact same thing sometimes when responding to something that someone says. I'm not sure if I had ever used that expression in front of Mom. Some aides had just come into the room, so I explained to them and to Mom what she had just said and why it was so funny to me. The aides laughed too.

Subsequently, I was explaining to Mom that if I had a lot of money and didn't have to work for a living, I would have her live with me and take care of her. I said that the reason she was there at the nursing home was so that she could be in a place where the people would take good care of her. Shortly after that, I went to the bathroom. When I came back,

Mom's right eye was tearing up, and a tear had run down the side of her left cheek from her moistened left eye. I asked her if she was crying, and she said yes. I asked her if she was sad, and she again said yes. I then asked her if she was sad because of what she has. She said yes. I told her that I was sorry if I had said anything that hurt her feelings. I also told her that I would never hurt her feelings. I never want my mom to cry or to feel bad. It hurts me tremendously.

July 17, 2010

What about Bill?

As I was taking Mom into her room, I mentioned that I needed to straighten up the room. I added that my work is never done, and Mom said, "What about Bill?" I was glad to hear her say that and to see that she was still able to express herself that way. I said, "You're right, Mom. I need to worry more about myself, too." It demonstrated that Mom cares about me and knows what's best for me.

A little while later, Mom said, "I like her." I said, "Who, Mom?" and she replied, "Mary." This was Mom's way of saying that she missed Mary. Mary comes with me to visit Mom on the weekends, but during the workweek we usually visit Mom on different days.

July 18, 2010

I Want to Go Home!

A little while after Mom finished eating her dinner, she started yelling something. She started out by saying, "I want to go home!" I felt terrible about it, as I always do whenever she says anything like that. I explained to her in the moment, as is my practice in these situations, why she was there. I told her that the people there take good care of her and that I see her as often as I can. As I've stated before, I would love to have Mom at home with me with a round-the-clock aide to help me take care of her. For me, it comes down to not having the money and resources to make it happen.

July 26, 2010

Go Away. Go Home. Go. Go Home.

After my meeting with Jill, I went upstairs to visit Mom for a while. Jill is a social worker at the nursing home. We discussed Mom's Medicaid application and her prescription drug coverage.

I had my writing pad and my pen in hand, including some important paperwork. I wanted to drop them off in Mom's room before I got her from the dining room so I could wheel Mom into her room without things in my hands. As I was walking past the window and looked in at Mom, she started waving to me. She seemed to be calling out my name repeatedly. I made a motion with my index finger to indicate that I would be back in one minute.

After I dropped my materials off in Mom's room, I went right back to her area in the dining room. I first stopped in front of the window that Mom was facing and started waving to her to let her know that I was back. She seemed to be looking right past me. She had a dejected look on her face, and her head was leaning on her right hand. She didn't acknowledge that I was there when I was waving to her through the window, so I went into the dining room to get her. When I went up to her, she looked annoyed.

She said, "Go away. Go home. Go. Go home." My first response was, "No, I'm not leaving." Then I said, "Are you mad at me?" and Mom said yes in a tone of voice that conveyed that she was feeling hurt. I explained why I had walked by the dining room on my way to drop off my stuff and then came back for her. I told her that I was sorry and that I didn't mean anything by it. I explained why I did it. I told her that I love her and that I wouldn't do anything to hurt her. It really hurt me to see how Mom felt. If I had known at that time that Mom wouldn't understand why I didn't come in to the dining room right away, I would never have done it. Although I completely regret what happened, it was another valuable insight for me.

After I had expressed myself to Mom, I noticed that her expression started to slowly change from one of hurt and anger to a look of relief. I noticed the beginning of a smile crease across her face. Just to make sure, I asked her if I could give her a kiss, and she said yes. After I leaned over and kissed her, I stood up and prepared to take her to her room. About thirty seconds after I kissed Mom, she grabbed my left hand and started giving it her "bunny rabbit kisses." I called out to Dana, the nurse on staff, to look, and she said to Mom, "You love him." I replied, "I love her more," and Dana said, "I'm sure you do."

Although I felt sad at the time that it happened, I was also glad to see that Mom's short-term memory was working okay. I would never let it happen again. Next time, I would just go right in and get Mom, no matter how many things I had to carry. Otherwise, I could go in on the other side of the dining room where Mom probably wouldn't see me come into the unit, drop my stuff off in her room, and then go back and get her. This way Mom wouldn't know that I had gone to her room prior to getting her. A potential problem, that was unintentional on my part, would be avoided.

Later on, Tammy, the head nurse, came into Mom's room to explain the change in Mom's medication to me. I mentioned what had happened when I first arrived. Tammy said that sometimes the residents surprise them with what they can do.

While I was with Mom in her room, I said, "I love my mommy so much!" Mom said, "That's good." I repeated it and laughed because I enjoyed her comment. Mom replied, "You bet!" Then I said, "Mom, tomorrow, I'll have lived in my apartment for twenty years!" Mom said, "Wow!" A little later on, I asked Mom if she had had enough to eat for lunch, and she replied, "Just about!"

August 1, 2010
He's a Nice Boy
When I took Mom outside after dinner, I told her that Mary was going to join us in a few moments. I asked her if she liked being outside, and she said, "I love it." A little while later, I asked her if she wanted to go back in. She replied, "No, thanks." I then said, "Mom, you're so wonderful," to which she responded, "So are you." When Mary came, she asked Mom if she liked being a mother. Mom said, "Sure." Mary then asked her, "Do you like being a grandmother?" Mom said, "No." Mary and I laughed. Mom tends to say no a lot, even if she doesn't mean it. I then asked Mom, "What does it say on Mary's shirt?" Mom can sometimes still read words. She replied, "Simply." The word was actually *simplify*. I said, "Very good, Mom. Close. The word is *simplify*."

Later on, Mom counted to six, and we helped her count into the teens. She later said, "Twenty," "twenty-one," and "thirty." She continues to surprise and amaze us. God bless her and her beautiful soul!

Later on, when we were bringing Mom back inside the nursing home, she started yelling. She had said that it was okay to go back in, but she was protesting. I calmed her down the best that I could. We took her down the hallway in the wheelchair and showed her some of the pictures on the wall. A few minutes after she calmed down, Mom said that she was sorry. It seemed that she understood what had happened. However, she can't control it because of her disease and how it affects her in so many ways. I said, "It's okay, Mom." She then said to Mary, "He's a nice boy." I asked, "Me, Mom?" and she said, "Yes." It made me feel like a million dollars.

August 8, 2010

I Want to Get Better

Mary and I went to visit Mom and took her to her room. A little while later, Mom said, "I want to get better." I said, "Oh, Mom, I want you to get better, too!" I got up and gave her a loving hug. I feel terrible about what Mom has to go through on a daily basis. However, I'm grateful that she still has the awareness to speak about her condition and the ability to express herself this way.

Before Mom's dinner arrived, she started to try to lift herself out of her wheelchair. She said, "Take me." I said, "I wish that I could take you with me. I wish that I could have you with me every day." I bent down and gave her a big hug. I explained to her that she couldn't walk unless two people were holding her up.

August 15, 2010

Pray That We Can Go

When I first arrived and went in to see Mom, she looked up at me and said, "Me?" This is her way of asking, "Are you here for me?" and checking to make sure that I'm someone whom she knows and who knows her.

I was in Mom's room. All of a sudden, Mom said, "Pray that we can go." I said, "Mom, I pray for you every day, and if I had the money, I would buy a big house and take you home and give you the best of everything. This is the best place for you right now. But if my situation changes, I will be happy to take you home." I was happy to hear Mom use the word *pray* in a sentence. It showed me that she is still able to retrieve from her long-term memory. It also showed Mom's awareness of prayer and the important role that it plays in her life.

August 17, 2010

I Hope

I came up from behind Mom to greet her. When she saw me, she said, "What?" I repeated the question to try to stir her memory. We went back and forth a couple of times. When I realized that Mom wasn't going to recognize me in that moment, I said, "Mom, I'm Bill. I'm your son, Bill." She started to smile, and I gave her a kiss.

When we were back in her room, the nurse came to talk to me. I ended up telling her how wonderful Mom is and why I feel that way. Mom said to me, "So are you." I was both surprised and happy to hear Mom say that.

Mom later said, "I hope . . ." Somehow I understood what she was trying to say to me because of the context of the moment. I asked, "Mom, are you saying that you hope I know that you appreciate me?" She said yes, and I replied, "I know that, Mom. Thank you. I appreciate you, also. That's one of the many reasons why I see you a lot."

I know in the bottom of my heart that my mom wants to go home and that she wants to be with her family all the time. I also want her to come home and to be with her all the time.

August 19, 2010

Is That My Business?

After meeting at the nursing home for the quarterly interdisciplinary care meeting regarding my mom, I went to visit with her. I found out that she was outside with the other residents in the back of the facility. When I went up to her, she asked, "Is that my business?" I said, "Yes, Mom. I'm here for you." I thought that it was so cute that Mom expressed herself that way to me. It was her way of asking if I was one of her children.

I took Mom back inside with me. We got on the elevator to go back to her unit. She was saying something to me that I couldn't understand. I could tell that she was anxious by the tone of her voice. I said, "Don't worry, Mom. I'm looking after you," and she replied, "No, I don't think so." My guess is that Mom was saying that she didn't think that I was looking after her because she was still in the nursing home.

I took Mom to her room and then went out to check on her lunch. When I went back to her room, I smiled at her. I asked how she was doing. Mom pointed at me and said, "Happy." I said, "Me, Mom?" and she said, "Yeah." Mom was trying to tell me that she was happy that I was there. I replied, "I'm always happy when I see you."

August 24, 2010
Stay with Me
When I walked in, Mom was looking down at the table. All of a sudden, she picked her head up and looked directly at me through the window. It seemed that she had sensed my presence before I even entered the room.

A little while after Mom finished her dinner, she said, "I'm scared." She said it in a way that was a little garbled, but I could pick it up. I said, "I'm scared for you too, Mom." I then proceeded to explain that I was on her side, that I would always be with her, and that I would fight on her behalf.

Two aides went in to change her. Just as they were leaving, Mom said to them, "Stay with me." She had probably forgotten that I was out in the hallway waiting for her. She was very happy to see me when I came back into the room.

Later on, when I was taking Mom back out, I told her that her birthday was in one week. She said, "I hope so." I took her into the dining room and said good-bye. As I was leaving, I poked my head back into the room and said, "Good-bye, Mom" again. I looked back at her and saw her turn in the direction of my voice. I started smiling and waving good-bye to her through the window. Mom started laughing, and I heard her say, "Bye."

September 4, 2010

That's Up to Yourself

When I walked in to see Mom in the dining room area, Mary was already with her, getting her ready to bring her out of her room. Mom looked up at me and said, "There he is." It was good to hear Mom refer to me that way. She recognizes me not only as her son but also as someone who's a very important part of her life.

We were with Mom for a while, and at one point when Mary was in the bathroom, Mom said, "He's a nice guy." I said, "Me, Mom?" and she said, "No." She likes to say no a lot. It's easier for Mom to say "no" than to say than "yes." I was still curious. So I said, "Am I a good guy or a bad guy?" and she replied, "That's up to yourself." What a truly wise and profound thing to say. Mom's right, as always. Mom really does know best. If I live my life the way that Mom wants and expects me to, the way that I should be living my life, I'll truly be who I'm meant to be in this world. I'll also be happier and have less to worry about.

September 9, 2010

Get Out of My House!

It was around six thirty or seven p.m., after Mom's dinner. Mary and I had already been with her for some time. Mom suddenly turned to me and said, "Who are you?" I asked Mom if she knew my name in order to test her on a different level. She said no, so I told her who I was. A little while later, Mom asked me if I liked her. I said, "Mom, I like you and I love you." It's heartbreaking to me whenever Mom asks me this question. Just to be reassured because Mom can't express herself like she used to and because people with Alzheimer's disease lose the ability to think abstractly, I asked her if she liked me and loved me. She replied, "Yes," and I said, "Thank you, Mom."

Mary and I were taking Mom back to the dining room because we were getting ready to leave. I leaned over to Mom and gave her a kiss on the cheek and a hug. I didn't realize it, but she may not have been expecting it. She started to yell at me and ended by saying, "Get out of my house!" She also may not have recognized me in that moment, which would explain why she reacted that way. It really hurt, although I know that she can't help it because of what she has. It was a reminder to me to either make sure that Mom is open to being touched by her expression and body language or to ask her ahead of time in case I'm not sure.

September 17, 2010
You Look Just Like Me!
While I was visiting with Mom, she turned to me and said, "You look just like me!" I said, "That's because I'm your son, Mom." She said, "That's right!" I was so happy about her comment. The fact that Mom recognized her features in my face showed both her awareness of herself and of me as her offspring. It was truly an amazing, memorable, and wonderful comment to me.

September 19, 2010
I Don't Want to Be Like This. I Want to Be Free.
Mom wanted to go outside. I told her that maybe we would next time because it was getting late. It was already past six-thirty. Then, Mom said, "I don't want to be like this. I want to be free." The way that she

said it—so clearly and powerfully—startled me. I felt very bad for her. However, I'm always glad when she can express herself and what she is thinking and feeling. It demonstrated to me again that people with Alzheimer's disease do suffer on an emotional level. I've experienced it firsthand with my mom. I've also seen other residents in her unit who are suffering. I said, "Okay, Mom. I understand. We'll take you outside for a while." It was the end of the summer, so it was still light outside.

I then told her, "I love you so much, Mom." Mom replied, "I know you do." It's good to know that Mom understands how much I truly love and care about her.

October 12, 2010

Have You Seen Him?

When I first arrived to see Mom, she was agitated and yelling. She even yelled at me and told me, "Get out of here." I took her to her room anyway. I asked her a few minutes later if she had been yelling because she was frustrated, and she said yes. She then made a reference to "him," and I asked if she was mad at Dad because he wasn't there. "Yes," she answered. I explained again that he had passed away, and Mom said, "Oh, I didn't know." I replied, "That's because you forget sometimes, Mom. It's okay."

Later on, as I was sitting next to her, I said, "I love you, Mom." She grabbed my hand and started kissing it. A little while later, she asked me if I saw him. I initially said yes, not realizing at the time that she was talking about Dad. I then said, "Do you mean Dad, Mom?" and she replied, "Yes." I explained the situation again and gave her my standard reassurances.

One of the many unfortunate aspects of this disease is that Mom can ask about Dad, I will tell her what happened to him, and then she may ask me again later on because she doesn't remember. Because of her memory loss, she sometimes thinks that he abandoned her and reacts accordingly.

It's very hurtful to know that Mom has these thoughts sometimes and that she feels abandoned, betrayed, hurt, and angry.

October 19, 2010

ABC World News Segment on Alzheimer's Disease

I was talking to Mom and said, "Mom, like I told you before, there are a lot of good moms out there, but you're the best mom." She said, "Great!" and flashed her wonderful smile. Mary and I started laughing.

At one point, Mary said, "I only had one slice of pizza this afternoon." I replied, "The world won't be a safe place for the next hour." Mom and Mary both started laughing.

We started watching ABC's *World News with Diane Sawyer.* Diane Sawyer was interviewing Maria Shriver about Alzheimer's disease and being a caregiver for someone who has it. I was sitting next to Mom and rubbing part of her back periodically throughout the segment. I felt so terrible about it. Watching something on Alzheimer's, especially when I'm with my mom, brings up the sadness and frustration that lies deep inside me. Mom was watching it intently, but I'm not sure how much of it she understood. Tears started running down my cheeks. I went to get tissues and dry my eyes, and Mom looked at me with a surprised look on her face. She could tell that I was sad and that I had tears in my eyes. I told her, "Don't worry, Mom. I'm okay."

Sometime after the broadcast was over, I was sitting off to the side writing notes. Mom looked over at me and said to Mary, "Who is he?" Mary said, "That's your son, Bill."

A little while later, when we were leaving Mom for the evening, Mom said, "Can we go now?" It always breaks my heart when she says things like this. I know that she wants to come home and live with her family. It is my fervent wish and hope that that will happen someday.

October 24, 2010

No, I Just Know It

While Mary, Mom, and I were together for a while, I said, "Mom, there's a lot of love in this room. There's a lot of love between us. Can you feel it?" Mom said, "No, I just know it."

Afterward, she had to be changed. When we went back into her room, I helped her with setting up the rest of her wheelchair, putting the pedals back on, and so forth. Mom said, "Thank you very much." I said, "You're welcome!" and Mom said, "You bet!"

Mary then said to Mom, "Mom, do you feel better now that you've been changed?" Mom replied, "Yeah. Do you?" Mary and I laughed.

A little while later, Mom noticed that I was writing notes. I explained, saying, "This is for my book, Mom." She said, "Your what?" and I replied, "My book." She said, "Oh, drat!"

Mary went to lie down on Mom's bed and fell asleep. Mom and I were watching the movie *Braveheart* on TV. I said, "You hear the Scottish accents in the movie? You're a Scot, Mom." She does have some Scottish blood in her ancestry. Mom said, "I'm a Scot," and I replied, "Yes, you are!"

October 26, 2010

Grandma!

I wasn't able to make it this particular evening, but Mary visited Mom. Mary said that she had been in the room with Mom and had fallen asleep and started snoring. She was tired from going on a class trip earlier that day with her students. The nurse told Mary later on that when she came into the room to give Mom her medicine, Mom said, "Shh" so that the nurse wouldn't wake Mary up. Mary was so happy to hear that. She knew that Mom still looks after her children.

Later on, Kathleen, Mom's aide, came into the room. She told Mary that it was getting late and that she had to get Mom ready for bed. When Mom saw Kathleen, she said, "Grandma!" Mom said that because Kathleen is her aide and she takes care of Mom. Mary said, "Mom, that's not Grandma. That's Kathleen." Mom said, "Kathleen?" and then started cracking up. (Kathleen is not her real name; I changed her first name for the purposes of this book.) Mom probably laughed because Kathleen's real name is a little uncommon. Mary worried that Kathleen might be offended but said that she didn't appear to be.

November 2, 2010
I Don't Want to Be Like This
Mom said, "I don't want to be like this." She was again demonstrating an awareness of her medical condition. I felt so bad for her. However, I was also surprised and happy that she could recognize and articulate that things had changed for her. I went over to her to give her a warm hug and a kiss. I said, "I don't want you to be like this either, Mom. It's not fair. It hurts me, too."

November 3, 2010
How Much?
I went in early on this day so that I could be with my mom during her dental cleaning. As we got on the elevator to go down to the dental office at the facility, I said, "I love you, Mom." She asked, "How much?" I thought that was so cute. I responded with, "With all my heart and then some."

Mom had some difficulty with the dental cleaning, more so with the lower portion of her mouth. After leaving the dentist's office, I was taking Mom back to her unit and said, "The hard part is over, Mom." She said, "Do you think so?" She is so funny.

Later on, I was talking to Tammy, the head nurse, about Mom and how she had done at the dentist. Tammy said that Mom was at peace because she could see me and hear my voice, saying that my presence was comforting to her. I was so happy to hear that. It was also good to have a medical professional tell me that she noticed a real difference in Mom when I'm with her. It gave me an extra level of awareness and appreciation that what I do for Mom really does make a difference to her and to her life.

I mentioned to Mom that she was more alert that day than usual. She responded, "What's that mean?" so I explained it to her. I forget that sometimes Mom doesn't understand the meaning or context of words that I may take for granted. It's because of her disease. When she notifies me that she needs clarification, I make sure that I explain it to her. Otherwise, if I just sense that what I'm telling her isn't clear, I take the time to explain it to her or repeat it to make sure that she understands.

When I was getting ready to leave, Mom asked, "Where are you going?" I told her about all the things that I had to do, which included paying her monthly bill, going food shopping, doing my paperwork, making phone calls, and so on. I also told her that I wished that I could be with her all the time. I really do.

November 6, 2010
Mom Makes the Sign of the Cross
While I was visiting Mom, a New York Giants commercial came on with music in the background. I started dancing in front of Mom. I do that sometimes to entertain her and to make her laugh. I said, "You would

dance with me if you could, Mom," and she replied, "You bet!" I wish Mom could do all of the things that she used to do. I really miss Mom the way that she was.

A while later, Mom made the sign of the cross to herself. I was surprised but happy to see her do it. I'm glad that she remembers these things from time to time. It comes from her long-term memory. She was probably saying a prayer for herself or asking for help from God. I would do anything to take my mom's disease away from her and make her better again.

November 7, 2010
Mom Dances with Her Hands
When I went in to see Mom, I took her downstairs to the art and craft fair that the facility was hosting. I wanted her to enjoy the music and being around other people. Carl, the musician, was playing and singing, and Mom and I started moving our hands together to the rhythm of the music. I said, "This is just like we're dancing together." She gave me her wonderful smile and said, "It sure is." I was really enjoying this special moment with Mom. I was so happy to see her smiling and thoroughly enjoying it, also. It made me realize that even though she is confined to a wheelchair, she still has the ability to enjoy the music and express herself. She can't dance on her feet anymore, but she can dance with her hand movements and with her wonderful facial expressions. It was a great insight for me. It opened up another opportunity for me to really connect with her. God bless Mom!

November 11, 2010
Can I Go, Too?
After being with Mom for a while, I was taking her out of her room. I told her that I had to go home for dinner, and she asked, "Can I go, too?" There's nothing I want more in the world that to have my mom

live with me. I told her, "I wish that I could take you home." I explained to her why she was living there and why I can't take her home with me. I always say it in the most loving and compassionate way possible. It's so heartbreaking to have to say these things to her. I hate what this disease does to her and to us.

November 16, 2010

My Son, My Son

When I went in to see Mom and she saw me, she started smiling and said, "Mine. Mine." I said, "Yes, I'm yours, Mom." I gave her a big hug and a kiss. When I took her to her room, I told her that I was sorry about what she was going through.

A little while later, I helped set up Mom's dinner. When she started to eat, she said, "My son, my son." I said, "That's right. And you're my mom." I went over to her, and we gave each other a kiss.

During her dinner, Mom said, "Home. I want to go home." I told her that I know she wants to go home, gave her a hug and a kiss, and then consoled her. I told her, "Mom, I would take you home with me if I could, but I can't right now." I went on to tell her that this was the best place for her to be at this time. I also told her that she wasn't being punished and that she hadn't done anything wrong. She said, "I know." I said, "Good, because I don't want you to feel that way."

November 21, 2010

Astoria

Mom had finished eating her dinner, and I was trying to get her to eat some yogurt. I said, "C'mon, Mom. Eat your yogurt. It's good for you." Mom said, "You eat it." I started laughing and then Mom started laughing. I said, "You're a riot, Mom."

We were watching *America's Funniest Home Videos* on ABC. Something came on that made Mom say, "Oh, my goodness." It's one of her sayings.

I took Mom back out to the dining room because I was preparing to leave. She didn't want to go back out there, but I have to take her there when I leave. I can only leave her alone in her room when she's already been put to bed for the evening. I asked Jose, the nurse, if it would be okay to put Mom across the hall, facing him at the front desk. He said that it would.

As I was talking to Mom before I left, she said, "Astoria." I looked in the direction that Mom was looking and noticed that she was reading the nameplate on the wheelchair of the woman nearby, which said, "Astoria Surgical" on it. I told Jose about it. He was happy to hear it. I was overjoyed that Mom could still read some words. She really surprises me with the things that she can do.

November 30, 2010
Why Are You Here?
I was visiting Mom. Around 6:50 p.m., Mom turned to me and asked, "Why are you here?" In moments of memory lapse, she doesn't remember who I am or why I'm with her. I replied, "Because you're my mom; I'm your son; and I'm here to love, support, and take care of you."

A few minutes later, I asked Mom, "Do you recognize me?" She said, "No." I asked her again, and she still said, "No." I explained to her that this happens sometimes because of she suffers from memory loss but that I'm her son and will always be there for her. A few minutes later, Mom looked over at me and asked if I was staying with her. I said, "Yes, Mom, for at least another half an hour." Mom said, "Good." A little while later, Mom said, "I'm good." I said, "Yes you are, Mom. You're the best!"

When I took Mom back out to the dining room area and put her next to Rose, an aide, Mom said, "I don't want to sit." I felt so bad for her. It hurts even more to know that I can't fix these things for her. I explained to Rose that Mom wanted to walk now and that she loves walking. Turning to Mom, I explained to her that she can't walk right now but that I understood that she wanted to. As I was saying good-bye to Mom, I saw that Rose was rubbing her hand and talking to her. I appreciated it.

December 7, 2010

Take It Easy!

I got Mom from the dining room to take her to her room for dinner. As we were passing the nurse's station, Mom said loudly, "Here I am!" I laughed and kissed her on the head. She's so funny!

Later that day, I relayed to Tammy that one of the aides wasn't being gentle enough with my mom when checking to see if she needed to be changed. Once, she bent Mom forward abruptly without notifying Mom first. Then she talked to me in a loud voice after checking the back of my mom's underpants. Just after that, she grabbed Mom twice in a hard, fast way to check to see if her private area was wet. I was startled the first time she did it. After the second time, Mom started to yell at her. I said to the aide, "Take it easy!" I told Tammy that the aides always need to be gentle with my mom and explain things to her first, always treating her with dignity and in a humane way. I said, "Don't they realize what my mom and the others are dealing with?" I could tell that Mom was listening intently to everything that I was saying to Tammy. In the end, I said, "How would the aide like it if I did that to her mom?"

Tammy said that they have to constantly remind the aides—she called them the backbone of the unit—to be gentle and to put themselves in the other person's shoes. I also told Tammy that Mary and I like that particular aide, and we can tell that Mom likes her, too. I said that we're happy with her overall. I don't think that her intent was bad, but she needs to always be gentle with Mom and sensitive to what she is dealing with. I think that part of the problem is that they become desensitized to the patients' needs because they deal with them at work all day. However, if they're going to be that way, then they should find a different industry to work in. It's a very important position. The residents and their families are counting on them. You always have to be sensitive and compassionate whenever you're dealing with people with Alzheimer's disease and dementia. People with this disease can't help it. Their brains are damaged by this disease. They need our help.

December 8, 2010

Human Resources Representative Has Mom with Dementia
I interviewed for a concierge position at a high-rise building in my town. I was anxious to start working full-time again. I completed the application and then got my forms together so I could be drug tested in New York City.

I went to the company's human resource department in New York. After I told the woman in human resources a little bit about my mom, she told me about her own mom's experience with dementia, probably a result of minor strokes. She said that her mom forgets people's names and that she once turned the house upside down when she saw a story on TV about bedbugs in New York City. I recommended that she take her mom to a psychiatrist specializing in dementia and elder care. She replied that her mom didn't want to go to the doctor and didn't want to go into a nursing home. I told her that I understood but recommended that she be proactive about it. I said that she could call the psychiatrist or maybe get her mom evaluated by a psychiatric nurse who could visit her at her home. I told her several times that I understood how heartbreaking it is because I've already gone down that road. I said that her mom wasn't capable of making good judgments about herself. They were letting her mom be the train conductor even though she wasn't qualified to run the train.

I gave her examples of when we put Mom back into the nursing home after Dad passed away and how I cried my eyes out when I left. I suggested that she could make the best decision by having the most information available to her. I also told her that it would be better to get her mom on medication as soon as possible, if it were determined to be what she needs, because of the progressive nature of the disease. She told me that she would consider it.

As our conversation was winding down, I got a phone call from Mom's nursing home. I asked the HR lady if she minded my taking it. It was the psychiatric nurse there, asking to increase the dosage on one of my mom's medications because she was having more outbursts. It is probably due to Mom's disease, her being afraid of what she has and where she is, and her not knowing if we know or care about her being in a nursing home. It must be so frightening and overwhelming for her.

I said okay to the psychiatric nurse. I knew that it was the right thing to do. I don't want Mom to suffer, and I don't want the other residents to be upset by her. I got choked up during the call and had tears in my eyes when I got off the phone. It's so incredibly difficult to bear. I want Mom to always be as happy, peaceful, and content as she can possibly be.

December 9, 2010
I Better Be
When I was walking down the hallway toward Mom, I could hear her voice in the dining room. She was yelling at Diane, another resident in her unit. I'm not sure why she was yelling at her. Something may have transpired between them before I arrived.

When I walked into the room and Mom noticed me, she said, "Oh," and suddenly stopped yelling. Mom said to me, "I love him," and then, "My father." Mom may sometimes call me Dad because she knows that I'm a family member who takes care of her. As a way to remind her and be helpful to her, I said, "Mom, I'm your son." I then asked her not to yell at anyone and said, "Sorry," to Diane, who was crying. I explained that Mom hadn't meant anything by it and that she yells at me sometimes, but she doesn't mean to do it. As I was taking Mom out of the dining room to go to her room, I went over to Diane and gently rubbed her shoulder. Mom also reached over and started rubbing Diane's back. I thought that it was so sweet of Mom to do that. It was probably her way of saying that she was sorry for yelling at her.

Later on, Mom started yelling again. She wasn't eating her dinner and may have been yelling because she didn't like it. I went to the front desk and ordered her an egg salad sandwich. I went back to the room and said, "Don't worry. You'll be okay, Mom," and she said, "I better be." I feel so bad for my mom. I wish that there was a way that I could at least stop it from progressing. I wish that I could kiss her on her forehead and make it go away.

December 12, 2010
I'm Hurt
Mary and I were visiting Mom, and early during our visit, Mom said, "Are you going to get me out?" It always hurts when she says those things. I told her that I'd do my best.

At one point, Mom started yelling at Mary and me. I went over to her and said, "Mom, are you scared? Are you frustrated?" She replied, "I'm hurt." I couldn't understand all of what she said right after that, but I was able to understand enough that I knew what she was trying to say. She was saying that she felt hurt inside because she was living in a nursing home and wasn't at home with her family. Even though comments like that are hurtful, I'm so grateful that she's still able to communicate her feelings and that we're still able to understand her. I said, "Mom, don't be hurt. I know that it's hard for you. I'm trying to help you, and I'm doing the best that I can." She said, "I know you are."

When Mom was lying in her bed, she started running her hand through her hair. I had turned off the overhead light so that it wouldn't shine in her eyes. She asked me, "What's the matter?" She can always tell when something is bothering me. I said, "I'm just worried about you, Mom. I'm worried about you." I never stop worrying about her.

December 16, 2010
Be Careful
Corina, a food service employee, updated me on an issue that I had spoken to her about earlier that week. Mom's dinner had included a chicken bone, and I brought it to Corina's attention. Obviously, it's dangerous to have something like that on her plate. Mom could have put it in her mouth and choked. I thanked Corina and gave her a hug. As Mom and I were leaving the area, I said good-bye to Corina and the nurses, and Mom said, "Bye, girls."

A little while later, Mom grabbed my hand while I was sitting next to her. She folded my thumb and then started running her hand over my fingers. She then started rubbing my hand with the palm of her hand. This is something that she likes to do to people. It shows how warm and loving she truly is. Mom said, "This is nice." I replied, "Yes, it is."

When I was leaving and saying good-bye to Mom, she said, "Be careful," as I was walking away. I said, "Thanks, Mom. I will."

December 19, 2010
Quiet, Quiet, and Then Go to Bed
Mom was eating her meal while Mary and I were visiting, and I said something to her. Mom replied, "All right. Quiet, quiet, and then go to bed." She then looked at Mary and winked. I thought that it was so cute that Mom was talking to me like I was her kid back at home when we all lived together. It brought back memories of the good old days.

Later, Mary said something to Mom about me while I was in the room, and Mom replied, "He's beautiful."

December 22, 2010
Home Is a Concept
I turned to Mom at one point and said, "I love you, Mom." She replied, "I'm glad."

During my visit, Mom said, "I want to go home." The Alzheimer's Association says that "home" is just a concept to people with Alzheimer's disease. In some cases, they may not remember where they lived, but they do remember the feeling of being in a loving home surrounded by their families. They don't like to be in a nursing home surrounded by people they don't really know and who aren't family. As I always do under these circumstances, I went over to Mom, hugged her, and said, "Oh, Mom, so do I!" and then explained that I would do the best that I can do for her.

January 1, 2011
Me, Too!
Mom and I were watching TV together, and I said, "Look, Mom, the baby!" Mom loves babies, and the commercial that was on had one in it. She loves seeing them in commercials, shows, and movies on TV. Mom

pointed to herself with her thumb and then said, "Me, too!" I laughed. I think she meant that she was like a baby because she knows that she needs assistance and a lot of love and affection to help keep her going.

January 4, 2011
It Shouldn't Be Like This!
Out of the blue, Mom said, "Where's Mary?" I think that Mom expects Mary to be with me every time that I visit because Mary and I usually visit Mom together on the weekends. I explained that Mary wasn't able to see her today but that she'd be back the next day.

A little while later, Mom turned to me and said, "How are you feeling?" It makes me happy when she says that. It's wonderful that she's still capable of asking how I'm doing and demonstrating that she truly cares about me.

Later on, Mom started banging her hands on the table in front of her. She yelled out, "It shouldn't be like this!" I comforted her. I totally agree with her—it shouldn't be like this. I resent that Mom has this disease. I don't understand it at all.

When I was leaving, Mom said, "Where is she?" I explained that Mary would be there the next day and that I'd try to be back in a few days. After I took Mom back out to the dining room, I said good-bye to her and started walking away. I turned back to look at her, but she was facing away from me. I almost started crying at the thought of leaving her for the day, knowing what she has.

January 18, 2011
Mom Takes a Swing at Me
Mary went in to see Mom first while I was parking my car. When I got to Mom's room, Mom smiled when she saw me. She asked, "What's

your name?" I said, "Do you recognize me, Mom?" and she said, "Yeah." I said, "I'm Bill. I'm Billy. I'm your son." I leaned over, kissed her, and gave her a hug.

At one point, I was talking with Mary in the room when Mom started banging on the table. I went over to ask her what was wrong. When I leaned over to see what was going on, Mom grimaced and swung at me with her open right hand, aiming to smack me in the face. I pulled my head back just in time to avoid being hit. I said, "Mom, you almost hit me. Please don't hit me." She said, "I had to do it." I repeated myself and Mom did the same. I think she said that because she sensed that she can't help it. She doesn't have much control over her emotions and isn't able to use good judgment because of her disease. I understand it and feel the utmost compassion and love for her. In fact, even if Mom had been successful in smacking me in the face, I would never hit her back or yell at her for it. I would just say something like, "Mom, you just hit me. Please don't hit me. It's not nice." Mary suggested that Mom was mad because we weren't talking to her at that time. That may have been true. She may have felt that we weren't paying attention to her. Of course, I didn't realize it at the time. I would never ignore my mom or make her feel that she wasn't part of the conversation.

After Mom's dinner, she was eating some yogurt for dessert. She got a little bit of yogurt underneath her lower lip, and I wiped it off with a napkin. I told Mom what I was doing and said, "I can't take you back out there later with yogurt on your face." Mom said, "So what?" I laughed, and Mom started laughing.

January 20, 2011
I Know Who You Are
After I had been with Mom in her room for a while, she turned to me and said, "Who are you?" I replied, "You don't remember me?" and she said,

"No, I don't." I said, "Are you sure you don't remember me, Mom?" and she replied that she didn't. I started to feel upset. Mom asked, "What's the matter?" I said, "It bothers me, Mom, that you don't remember me. It happens sometimes. It's what you have. It's not your fault. I know that you're doing the best that you can."

About one and a half hours later, as I was coming out of the bathroom, Mom smiled and said, "I know who you are." I said, "That's great, Mom. You forgot before, but you remember now. I'm so happy now." Mom said, "Yeah." I leaned over and gave her a kiss. In hindsight, Mom may have remembered that she didn't know who I was earlier in this visit and saw that I was upset by it. That's why she said, "I know who you are" later on. If that was the case, I'm so happy and proud of her for being able to do that. Of course, I'm always proud and in awe of her.

When I took her back out to the dining room area, I told her that I had to go but would see her in two days. Mom said, "Where to?" I said, "I'm going home to eat dinner. But I'll see you in two days." I also told her, "Be careful. Be safe. Be strong." I kissed her good-bye a few times and then left.

January 23, 2011
Please Forgive Me
I took Mom to her room while Mary was parking the car. When Mary came in, she greeted Mom and said, "Mom, can I give you a hug?" Mom said, "Maybe." Mary and I laughed.

After we had been with Mom for a while, Mary said something to Mom while standing in front of her, and Mom started yelling at her. Mary moved to the window and sat in the chair. I stood in front of Mom and asked her to please not yell. Mom said, "Please forgive me. Please forgive me." I said, "It's okay, Mom. I know that you didn't mean it. It's what you have. You get frustrated." I was grateful that Mom still had the realization that she sometimes can't control herself. I understand that her occasional outbursts come from a combination of her disease, her knowledge and fear of Alzheimer's and what it does to her, and the fact that she doesn't have the same quality of life because she's in a nursing home.

After Mom finished her dinner and had her drink of Ensure, I went into the bathroom for a few minutes. When I came out and looked at Mom, she said, "I'll be back." I laughed. Mom said that to me because I say that to her. For example, I'll say, "I'll be right back, Mom," when I'm getting her more juice to drink or when I'm checking on something for her.

When we were leaving Mom by the nurse's station and saying good-bye, I told Mom that I'd see her in two days, on Tuesday. Mom said, "Good. Don't forget." A few minutes later, I told Mom that the nurse would put her to bed soon, and Mom replied, "That's nice."

January 25, 2011
I Want to Go to the House
When I was walking into the dining room to get Mom, Frances, an aide, said to Mom, "Look who's coming in." Because Mom was looking down at her plate at the time, she started yelling at her. Frances may have startled Mom a little. I went over to Mom and gave her a second to recognize me. I then said, "Hey, what did I tell you about yelling at people?" Mom looked surprised but was apparently happy to see me because she stopped yelling right away. When I took her into her room to help her with her lunch, she said, "I want to go to the house." I hugged her and said, "Aw, Mom. I know that you want to go home. I'm working on it for you." Later on, I mentioned to Mom again that if I could get money and get her home soon, I would. Mom said, "Good."

January 28, 2011

You're Writing about Me

When we got to Mom's room, she seemed a little bit confused. I told her who I was and that she had just greeted me with open arms a few minutes earlier. That was a beautiful sight and a great feeling, especially when Mom started giving me her bunny rabbit kisses. I then took a picture of myself as a ten-year-old red-headed kid out of my wallet and showed it to Mom to help spur her memory. I said, "Do you like it?" and she said, "I like it!" I told her that I'd be right with her because I was writing some notes for my book. Mom said, "You're writing about me." I said, "Yes, I am, Mom. I'm writing a book about us. Hopefully it will make enough money so I can spend most of my time helping you and being with you."

When Rose came in with Mom's food tray, Mom was happy to see her. Mom called her over and started giving her bunny rabbit kisses, also. Rose said, "Thank you," when she was leaving, and Mom said, "Thank you," back to her. I told Rose that Mom liked her. Mom later asked me what I thought of her, and I said, "Mom, I love you. I think you're fantastic. You're the best!" Because of Mom's disease, she will sometimes ask what I think about her. In those moments, I always reassure her by saying things like "I like you," "I love you," "I'm crazy about you," and so forth.

January 29, 2011

Mom Gets Really Happy When She Sees Me

Mom smiled when I arrived. When I got close enough, she put out her hand with her palm facing her, moved my head close to her, and started giving me her bunny rabbit kisses. I started to laugh gently. It touches my heart every time.

When I took Mom back into the dining room, I placed her across the table from Stan, and Mom started yelling at him almost immediately. I had heard that they argue with each other from time to time. It made me angry that anyone would argue with my mom. However, when I reflected on it later, it also made me feel grateful that Mom's short-term memory was still working. I moved her next to Margie, an aide, who told me to put Mom there. I told Margie that I guessed Mom didn't like Stan, and Margie said, "No, they're always arguing with each other."

Margie also told me before I left that Mom gets really happy when she sees me. I was so happy to hear that.

February 1, 2011

She's an Angel on Earth Who was Brought Down Here from Heaven

I had been with Mom for a while and left the room for a few minutes to check on something for her. I usually walk in and say, "Mom, I'm here," but I don't think I did that when I returned this time. Mom started yelling at me, "Get out of here! This is my house! Get out of here!" I was surprised. I realized the next day that I may have startled her by walking back into her room unannounced. Also, she may have forgotten who I was in that moment.

Later on, when an aide was getting Mom ready for bed, she had to weigh her. She had Mom on a special device that lifts patients in order to weigh them. Mom looked so cute and adorable as she was being lifted off of the bed. I held her hand and told her several times not to worry because they were just weighing her. I was happy because Mom seemed to be enjoying it.

I said good night to her when I was leaving. She looked so beautiful, calm, and peaceful lying in bed, like she always does. She's an angel on earth who was brought down here from heaven to be my mom. I said my final good-bye and was preparing to leave her room. I turned off the overhead light but left the bathroom light on. Mom said, "Bye, dear." I said, "Bye, Mom." She is such a doll!

February 4, 2011

Car

When I showed up, Mom was looking at a magazine, and her back was to me. When I walked up to her, she said something like, "He said . . ." and I interjected, "He did?" Mom smiled and started laughing, and then she grabbed and pulled my head closer to her and started giving me kisses.

I took her to her room and set her up with the magazine. After a while, she started laughing. I asked why she was laughing, and she said, "I can't read it." I said, "Oh, well, you're doing the best that you can, Mom." Mom said, "I guess so." A little while later, I asked her if I could turn on the TV so she could watch it. I said, "Don't worry. I'll put on something that you will like." She said, "I hope so."

Later on, Mom turned to me and said, "Car." I asked, "Do you want to go for a ride in my car?" and she said, "Yeah." I said, "Do you want me to take you home?" knowing that she makes this request from time to time. She said yes. I replied that maybe we could take her out in the spring. Taking her in and out of a car several times each trip involves a certain level of risk. I also said that if I could make enough money to take her home, I would do that.

After Kathleen finished changing Mom—the door was closed for privacy—she said to Mom, "I'm going to a party. Do you want to go?" Mom said, "Yes, I do. I'm going." Kathleen laughed. When she told me about it, I thought that it was cute, also. I'm glad that Mom still has the fighting spirit to want to go out and do fun things and to really live her life.

March 2, 2011

Don't Be So Sure about That

Tim, the nurse practitioner, came in to check on Mom. I spoke with him for some time about Mom, and during our conversation, he had to take a phone call. He told me that he'd be right back. I was using the bathroom when he returned. When I came out of the bathroom, Tim told me that Mom had said to him what her first name was. I was glad that she remembered her name and was able to express it to Tim.

I stayed with Mom for a while longer before getting ready to leave. I said good-bye to her, and she said, "Bye" and "thank you." Before I left, Mom saw a private duty aide and started pointing at her. The aide came to talk to us and told me that earlier that day she had asked Mom, "I'm your friend, right?" Mom replied, "Don't be so sure about that." It's another one of Mom's famous expressions. I laughed. I knew that Mom was joking with her, and the aide knew it also. I could tell that she liked and appreciated my mom. Of course, I really appreciate it when I know that the staff likes my mom. She's so lovable!

March 8, 2011
Are You Angry with Me?
When I was visiting Mom, she said, "Are you angry with me?" I told her I wasn't. Maybe she wanted to know if I was angry with her because of all that I have to do for her. She may realize that it takes a toll on me. I told her that I'd do anything for her, and she said, "Thank you. Thank you very much."

A little while later, I had to leave the room for a minute. I told her that I'd be right back. She asked, "How long?" I said, "I'll be back in a minute, Mom." I was glad that she asked me that.

After some time had passed, Mom said, "Do you like me for me?" I'm amazed that Mom can still express herself so clearly while saying something to me that is deep, profound, and to the heart of the matter. She isn't sure of where she stands sometimes because of her disease. I said, "Of course I do, Mom. I like you and I love you."

March 22, 2011
I Don't Care
I went in to see Mom after being away for a week at a seminar in California. When I arrived to see Mom, I explained why I had been away, and she said, "I don't care" on two separate occasions. She meant that she didn't care why I had been away because she was so happy to see me again. I also knew this because she hugged me and gave me lots of kisses on my face when she first saw me. She had really missed me, and I had really missed her too. It hurts me when I'm away from her for more than a couple of days. Of course, I try to be with her as often as possible.

I noticed that Mom didn't eat much of her dinner, so I went out to the small kitchen area and got a half-sandwich for her. I also got her an Ensure to drink. When I took them to her, she started shaking her hands and said, "If you don't stop, I'm going to start crying." I said, "Mom, don't do that." I kissed her on her head, and she smiled. I realized then that she was kidding with me. I'm grateful that she can still play a little joke on me every now and then. I said, "Oh, Mom, you really know how to get me." Then I said, "I love you, Mom." She replied, "Thank you, sweetheart." I then said, "I'm crazy about you, Mom," and she said, "Are you?" I said, "Of course I am." Mom replied, "That's wonderful."

March 25, 2011
That's What I Said!
When I first showed up and saw Mom, she said, "I know you." I said, "Of course you do, Mom. I'm your son, Bill." A look of recognition came across her face. I gave her a hug and a kiss.

I took her into her room and said that I'd be right back. I went to check with the nurse regarding a red mark next to Mom's eye. When I went back into her room, I said, "I'm back, Mom." She said, "That's what I said!" I think Mom was trying to say, "That's what I say." She's so cute!

Later on, I had my back to Mom as I was preparing to help her eat some soup. I heard her say, "Who are you?" I turned around and explained who I was. I also explained to Mom that she has memory loss and that's why sometimes she doesn't remember me. I never say the word *Alzheimer's* in front of her. I said that I'll always be by her side, no matter what. When I asked her later, "How are you doing?" she said, "Okay." I said, "I worry about you, Mom," and she replied, "Yeah, I know."

April 2, 2011
Mom Picks Up on My Feelings
While I was visiting with Mom, she turned to me and said, "What's the matter?" Earlier that day, I had had an argument with one of my siblings, and I must have been thinking about it in that moment. Mom picked up on it right away. I told her that I was okay and thanked her for asking. I certainly don't want to tell her anything upsetting that might add to all that she has to deal with on a daily basis.

April 8, 2011
Where Are You Going?
When I went to see Mom and stay with her at lunch, the nursing home employees had karaoke music on and "When Irish Eyes Are Smiling" was playing. I walked up to Mom, greeted her with a kiss, and started singing the song to her. Mom said, "I like it." I said, "I like it, and I like you, Mom."

After she had lunch and had been changed, I started preparing to leave, getting the room in order. I started to take Mom back out to the dining room area, but she said, "Where are you going?" I felt bad because I don't like leaving her. I told her that I had to get a new phone, go pick up my prescription, and then go home to get some things done.

When I took Mom back out, Faith, one of the employees there, came up and started telling me how funny Mom is and what a good mood she'd been in recently. I told Faith the story about something Mom had said at another facility (about the woman who was a hundred years old and Mom's response was, "She looks it!"). We both started laughing. Mom said, "What?" with a smile on her face. I told her the story, but Mom didn't know what I was referring to.

April 17, 2011
I Want to Go to Church
I went to see Mom in the morning because I had to meet a friend for some social media work in the afternoon. I took Mom downstairs to the café and bought her a cup of tea and got a cup of coffee for myself. I situated Mom so that she was facing the backyard of the facility, giving her a good view of the pond, the trees, and the beautiful blue sky and clouds.

I told Mom about her family origins, her relatives, and how she and Dad originally met. A little while later, out of the blue, she said, "I want to go to church." I had told her a little earlier that it was Sunday, April 17, 2011; maybe it was a coincidence that she said that on a Sunday. Regardless, it was amazing that she said it. I told Mom that she wasn't expected to go to church anymore because the church came to her on Saturdays to give her communion. It really felt like there was a communion then, a communion of souls—mine and Mom's—connecting on a very deep, personal, and spiritual level. Mom has always been and will always be the most important person in the world to me.

April 19, 2011
Promise Me
Mom was saying something to me, and I heard the word *home*. I said, "You want to go home, Mom? You want to be home with your family?"

She said yes. I said, "It's going to take a lot of money. If I can make the money, I'll take you home." I said that I would try to do it. Mom said, "Promise me," and I said, "I'll try." She again said, "Promise me," so I said, "Okay, Mom. I'll do everything that I can to get you home again. I promise."

Mom was looking at me while I was writing notes and said, "Here." I put my hand and forearm on the table in front of her. She said, "Billy," and I said, "That's right, Mom. I'm Billy!" She touched my hand and said, "Okay." A few minutes later, Mom asked if I had "told him." I said that I had and that I'd get her back home as soon as I could.

I kept writing notes in my notebook, and everything was quiet for a while. When I turned to look at Mom, she was looking at me with a look like she was wondering what I was doing. It caught me by surprise. I laughed. I thought that it was so cute.

April 23, 2011
He's So Sweet and Nice
I pointed to Mom as I approached her. When she saw me coming closer, she started saying, "Dad! Dad!" I approached and greeted her with a hug and a kiss. I said, "I love you, Mom. Do you love me?" She replied, "You bet."

She looked over at me and started tracing my nose from a few inches away with her index finger. She said, "He's so sweet and nice." I was delighted that she was able to say that to me. I replied, "Thank you, Mom. So are you." She said, "I know."

Later on, I turned to Mom, kissed her on her upper arm, and said, "I love you, Mom." She replied, "Me, too!" meaning that she loves me, too.

April 27, 2011
It Hurts Me That I Can't Get Up
I told Mom that I was going to get her dinner and that I'd be back in two minutes. She said, "And then," and motioned with her hand palm down toward the floor, indicating that she wanted me to stay with her while she ate her dinner. I smiled. I was happy to see Mom gesture in communication with me. I told her that I'd stay with her for a couple of hours.

Mom said later, "It hurts me that I can't get up." I was surprised to hear her say it so clearly. I repeated it back to her to make sure that she had said it, and she confirmed that she had. I said, "Oh, Mom. It hurts me, too. You can't walk because of what you have. I know that you want to walk."

As I was saying good-bye to Mom, I could tell that she didn't want me to leave. She kept talking to me and holding onto me. She asked me if I loved her, and I said, "Yes, Mom. I love you." She replied, "Oh, that's lovely."

May 3, 2011
It Was the Sugar in My Mom That Did It to Me
When I first showed up, Mom looked at me and said, "What did you do?" or something like that. I smiled and said, "Hi, sweetheart." Mom smiled back and said, "My sweetheart." I leaned in and gave her a kiss on the cheek, and she started kissing me back.

I helped Mom with her dinner, and afterward, she said, "I can't stand this!" She means that she can't stand having this disease, that she's in a nursing home and can't be at home with her family, and that she can't function as well as she used to. I understand. I'm constantly amazed at how she's still able to demonstrate such grace, strength, and courage while under the circumstances that she's in. I said, "Do you want to go downstairs, Mom?" She emphatically replied, "Yes."

As I was taking Mom through the hallways on the first floor of the nursing home, we stopped in the lobby and started talking. I said that I was sorry about what she was going through, and she asked, "What?" I explained that she had some memory loss, which affected her in different ways, including making her unable to walk. Mom said, "It was the sugar in my mom that did it to me." I was shocked that she was able to even say this and to make a connection to sugar. There is a growing body of evidence that points to a link between diabetes and an increased risk of getting Alzheimer's disease. If what Mom said to me ends up being a medically correct statement of fact, it demonstrates a deep and abiding spiritual presence inside her. It also has a metaphysical, magical, and mystical quality to it. It's just one of her many amazing gifts and talents. Just to make sure, I repeated what she had just said to me and asked if that's what she meant, and she confirmed it. Mom had also asked for "the girl." She said, "I love her." I said, "You mean your daughter, Mary?" and she said, "Yes." I said, "She loves you too, Mom. She'll be here to see you tomorrow." A little while later, I asked Mom a question—I don't remember what the question was because I didn't write it down—but she replied, "Yes, really and truly." "Really and truly" is one of her famous sayings. I hadn't heard it in a while.

At another point, Mom was saying something I didn't understand. I got up, stood in front of her, and said, "Don't worry. I'm here for you. I love you." She said, "I know you do." She started rolling up the left pant leg of her sweatpants, and I said, "Mom, you're showing off your sexy legs." She replied, "Yeah, so you say." I leaned over to her, kissed her on her arm, and rested my head on her upper arm. I said, "You're so wonderful, Mommy." She said, "I don't believe it." She probably responded this way because of her disease and all of its ramifications. I said, "Mom, believe it. You are wonderful."

May 8, 2011 (Mother's Day)

You Know What to Do

Before Mary and I took Mom down to the café for her Mother's Day lunch, I wheeled her through the hallway of her unit. One of the aides said, "Happy Mother's Day!" to her, and Mom said, "Boo!" The aide started laughing. She told Mom how funny she was. I agree. Mom can be so funny. It's another bonus of being with her. I get to witness her wonderful sense of humor firsthand.

We continued down to the café, and Mom was really enjoying getting out of her normal routine and taking in the view of the grounds that she could see from the café. After she finished her dessert, a Dove ice cream bar, she said, "It's delicious!"

Later on, we took Mom back to her room, where my brother John showed up and joined us. Mary fixed the back of Mom's shirt because it was sticking up, but Mom wasn't expecting it and let out a scream because it frightened her. Mary said that she was sorry. Mom looked at me and said, "You know what to do." Mom said this to me because I spend so much time with her, I'm very sensitive to her and her special needs, and I know how to communicate with her in a meaningful way. I went over to her and consoled her with a hug and a kiss. I told her that it was okay.

A little while later, John was telling Mary and me about all the problems he was having with his girlfriend, and Mom started banging on her table. I went over and said, "What's the matter, Mom?" and she answered, "Me!" as she pointed her thumb back to herself. She wanted the attention back on her because John was going on and on. We didn't realize at the time that Mom felt left out in that moment. I said, "You're right, Mom. You! It's always about you." I was being sincere. It is always about Mom, anyway.

May 22, 2011

I Want to Go to the Store

After being with Mom for a while, I took her out of her room to the dining room area because I was getting ready to leave. She said, "I want to go to the store." She wanted to get out and do something that she liked. Mom just wants to live a normal life. She wants to have the life that she used to have back again. Anyone in her shoes would feel the same way. I feel so badly for her. It breaks my heart to see her going through this ordeal and having to deal with all of the limitations that it places on her mind, body, and spirit. I said, "Don't worry, Mom. We're going to get you out soon."

May 28, 2011

How Much?

While I was visiting Mom, she yelled out, "I can't stand this place!" I told her that I understood and that I was doing everything I could for her. I wish that I could take this terrible disease away from her.

I later got a call from my credit card company about some fraudulent charges, and I told Mom about what had happened after the call. She asked me, "How much?" It was wonderful that Mom was able to ask me an appropriate follow-up question. Thank God that she can still understand me and respond to what I'm saying to her.

June 5, 2011

Are You Laughing at Me?

I took Mom down to the spring concert that the facility was hosting. I was holding her hand, and we started swaying our hands together side to side to the rhythm of the music. After the concert, I got some fruit salad from the table and took it into the café with us.

While we were there, I went over to get a plastic knife to cut the fruit into smaller pieces. On the way back to our table, I talked to another resident from Mom's unit along with her son. I said something funny to them, and they started laughing. A few seconds later, I rejoined Mom at the table, and she asked me, "Are you laughing at me?" I said, "No, Mom. I would never laugh at you. I only laugh *with* you." I felt terrible that she would say that, but I was glad that she could verbalize it and tell me how she felt. I'm also grateful because Mom seems to speak up more now on her own behalf when something bothers her. It's ironic, but I think that her disease helps to block any inhibitions that she may have had in the past to speak up when she feels the need to do so. Although Mom is restricted in many ways by her disease, she also is more consistently related to what's going on inside herself in the moment. She is then better able to communicate her thoughts and feelings back to us.

June 13, 2011
Mom Loses a Tooth
I called Tammy, the head nurse, and asked her how Mom was doing. The past Saturday, a tooth in her lower left jaw had come out. I wasn't visiting her at the time because I was just getting over an illness.

When it happened, Mom had somehow gotten a paper napkin in her mouth and was chewing on it like it was a stick of gum. This has happened several times in the past. A nurse was trying to it out of her mouth and started to put a spoon in Mom's mouth to help open it up. Mary said that the tooth must have already been loose because it popped out very easily, without much pressure from the spoon. I realized after that happened that Mary and I had to be better at getting Mom to brush her teeth each time we visited her. I know that Mom, along with the other residents with Alzheimer's disease, doesn't like it when we try to brush her teeth. She doesn't understand that we're trying to help her. It probably seems intrusive. I also conveyed again to Tammy that I'd like the staff to try to help Mom brush her teeth at least once per day.

Tammy told me their plan for following up on the missing tooth, and I requested that she call me if she needed me to be there when Mom was seeing the dentist.

Tammy went on to tell me that they had given Mom a magazine to look at that morning. She said that she and another nurse were watching Mom look through the magazine for a little while and that Mom was so cute to watch because she seemed really happy as she was going through it. She said that Mom was looking really closely at the pictures. That's my mom! She's so adorable!

July 5, 2011

I'm Allowed to Express My Opinion

I went in to visit Mom and help her with her dinner. As I was preparing to take her to her room and help her, I noticed that CNN was on. They were announcing that Casey Anthony had been found not guilty on all the major counts against her. I said something like, "I can't believe it—not guilty. What's this country coming to?" I was just expressing my opinion. I was shocked and disappointed in the verdict, like most Americans. An older man who was across the table from my mom—he was there taking care of a resident, who may have been his wife—stood up and said to me in an annoyed way, "All right! All right! They're having their meal now." I turned to him, looking directly at him, and said, "I'm allowed to express my opinion." He looked away and sat down. I was angry that he had spoken to me as if I had done something wrong and as if I was upsetting the residents in the dining room, neither of which was true.

A little while later, after I had taken Mom to her room with her dinner tray, I called Mary to relay the news about the Casey Anthony verdict to her, and I told her about the exchange I had had with the man in the dining room. I finished the story by saying, "If he's allowed to have his emotional response, then I'm allowed to have my emotional response," and I added that I wished I had said that to him at the time. Mom said, "Yep!" as if she agreed with me and understood my position. It made me feel good that Mom understood and agreed with me.

July 16, 2011

Oh-h-h!

As I was entering the dining room to get Mom, she started to get agitated when an employee took her dinner tray over and put it right in front of her. It may have startled her. She started to raise her voice and smack her hand on the table several times. I came up from behind her, grabbed onto her left arm, and said, "Hey, take it easy!" She turned toward me and started to raise her voice to me for a few seconds. Then, when she realized that it was me, she said, "Oh-h-h!" She gave me her great big smile, and we gave each other a kiss.

The nurse and the aide who were there started laughing. It was so cute and funny to see Mom change her demeanor so quickly once she realized that her son was the person who grabbed her arm. She had gone from being highly agitated one moment to loving, kind, gentle, and happy the next. I wish that I had captured that moment on video.

July 20, 2011

When I Go Home

We had an updated family portrait taken on this day. We would now have a picture to help Mom remember her children as we look today and to also serve as a family heirloom.

Later, while Mom was being changed for bed (Mary and I were waiting outside of her room), we heard Mom say the phrase "when I go home" to the aide. We both felt really bad when we heard that. The next day, July 21, I was so inspired by that phrase. I just knew that I had to use her comment as the title for this book. Her comment emphasizes in just four words all of the pain, frustration, agony, sense of powerlessness and so on that both Mom and we feel about her daily struggle against this terrible disease. However, it also shows a side of Mom that still has hope burning inside of her. It burns like an eternal flame with the hope that someday soon she will be back home, safe and sound, surrounded by her loved ones in a warm, cozy, comfortable, and intimately familiar environment. By utilizing what Mom said in that particular moment, I wanted to clearly emphasize what Mom and we are going through, what she really wants, and what we really want in our hearts and souls for her. Mom's comment summed it up for me. That's my mom. She really knows how to get to the heart of the matter with a few simple yet powerful and profound words. God bless her always!

July 23, 2011

You Can See Me as Much as You Want

I dropped Mary off to get Mom ready. When I went into the unit and was walking down the hall toward Mom, Mary said, "Look, Mom. It's Bill! It's Bill!" When Mom recognized me, she gave me a big smile and started waving her hands back and forth excitedly. I walked up to Mom and leaned in toward her. She started kissing me on the cheek. I kissed her back and said, "I love you too, Mom." Mary said, "Mom wasn't kissing me like that." I said, "That's because this is the fourth time that I'm seeing her this week."

When I stood up, Mom said, "You can, you can, you can . . ." as if she was trying to tell me something. I said, "You can see me as much as you want." Mom said, "You bet." It's good for me to be tuned into Mom, her personality, and the context of what she's saying to me. This helps me to piece things together so I can better understand what she's communicating.

July 29, 2011

How's Your Father?

When I looked at Mom through the window into the dining room, she recognized me and started waving. I motioned for Celia to watch before I did it so that she could see Mom's reaction. Celia got a kick out of it. I took Mom out of the dining room and back to her room, and Celia asked Mom if she knew who I was. I stood in front of her, bent toward her, and said, "Mom, I'm your son, Bill." She said, "You have to stay here." She wants me to always be by her side. I said, "I wish that I could stay here, Mom. I always want to be with you."

A little while later, Mary called and wanted to talk to Mom, but Mom didn't say much during their conversation. It's harder for her to communicate with someone over the phone than it is in person. At one point, I said, "I think that Mom's not saying anything because she doesn't know what to say." Mom laughed. I said, "It's okay, Mom. I know that you're doing the best that you can." A few minutes later, while I was still talking to Mary, Mom said, "How's your father?" I felt terrible about it. I explained to her again that Dad passed away in October 2007. She said, "That's too bad." It hurts me to think that Mom doesn't remember that Dad died. She may think from time to time that he abandoned her, especially because she needs him now more than ever. It's another terrible aspect of her disease. I never want Mom to think or feel that she's been abandoned or left to live alone in a nursing home.

August 9, 2011

Why People Make Jokes about Alzheimer's Disease

For my volunteer organization meeting, I had arranged for Annie, a representative from the Alzheimer's Association, to be our guest speaker. Annie was great and very informative. At the end of her presentation, she answered questions. A member of our club, trying to be funny, said, "I would give you my business card, but I forgot to bring it." This was the second time that this particular person had made a joke about Alzheimer's and memory loss. I turned to him and said, "Bad joke." I was so happy that Annie turned to him and said right away, "Then I'll give you mine!"

One of the reasons that some people might joke about Alzheimer's disease is that they're afraid of it. It's not something you can see. It sneaks up on its victims. It can settle into a patient's brain years before it's even diagnosed. Society frowns upon people making fun of other people who have physical handicaps. The same standard must be applied for people with Alzheimer's disease. They are handicapped mentally, physically, and emotionally. People may also joke about Alzheimer's disease because they're not directly affected by it. They don't have it and probably don't have a loved one who has it. If they did, they probably wouldn't try to joke about it.

Afterward, Mary and I went to visit Mom at the nursing home. We took her to her room, and I saw that Mom was admiring what I was wearing—navy blue dress slacks and a cranberry-colored striped dress shirt. I said, "Do you like it, Mom?" and she said, "Great. It's great!"

Mom said something to me, and I asked, "You want to go for a ride, Mom?" She said, "No." I said, "Do you want to get out of here?" and she replied, "Yeah." I said, "I'll get you out of here soon, Mom." "Okay, good," she said. Mary said, "It's heartbreaking."

As we were getting ready to take Mom back to the dining room area, I gave her a hug and a kiss and said, "I love you so much." Mom said, "How much?" and started laughing. Mary and I also laughed. I told Mom how cute she is. Needless to say, my love for my mom is infinite. There is no beginning, and there is no end.

August 31, 2011

I Don't Like You

It was Mom's birthday. I arrived early to get her to the hair salon to get her hair done for the occasion. When we were back in her room, she said to me, "I don't like you," twice in a row. I don't remember why she said that now. She may have said it because she was feeling disappointed or annoyed about something. It may have been because I took her from the salon back to her room for a little while. Later on, I took her back downstairs to the social room, where we were had a nice birthday celebration for her.

After the birthday party, Mary and John came up to join me in Mom's room. John said something to Mom, and she replied, "Oh, for goodness sakes"—just another one of her famous expressions.

Later on, I said to Mom, "Mom, do you like being here with your family?" She said no and started laughing. We laughed, also.

I could tell that Mom was happy that we were with her and that we were spending so much time with her on her special day. She seemed more energized and enlivened by the experience. It helps to prove what the Alzheimer's Association representative told me: "Home is a feeling."

September 24, 2011
Reading Mom's Body Language

I had been visiting with Mom for over three hours, and the aides came in to get her ready for bed. After the aides had completed getting Mom into bed and left her room, I went back in to check on her. I wanted to stay with her for a little while longer before I left for the evening. She seemed to cringe when I first walked in like she was frightened. She was probably thinking, *Who is this man coming into my room?* I said, "Mom, it's okay. I'm your son, Bill. I'm Billy!" I repeated similar comments to her over the next minute or so, and finally, a bright smile creased across her beautiful face like the sun breaking through the horizon. She said, "I know." I said, "Oh, Mom, you're such a kidder!" I realized a little while later that Mom may not have initially recognized me when I walked into the room. I based this observation on her body language. She then may have said, "I know" to cover up her inability to recognize me right away. She may have been embarrassed by it. I totally understand why she would feel that way. It must be so hard on her. I still thought that it was very cute and clever of her to finally say to me in that situation, "I know."

Before I walked out of Mom's room, I turned back, like I always do, and said, "Good night, Mom. I love you. Sleep with the angels. I'll see you tomorrow." Sometimes she'll say "Okay" or "Good night, sweetheart," but this time she didn't say anything. I walked out of the room and proceeded to leave the nursing home into the cool, yet muggy, September night.

September 25, 2011
She's Dead
When I first arrived to see Mom, she said a few things that I didn't understand. Then she said, "She's dead." She was probably referring to Mary because she hadn't seen her in ten days. Mary had been busy the previous week and then got sick with a cold and a respiratory infection,

so she wasn't able to see Mom for a while. I said, "Do you mean Mary?" She didn't answer, so I told her what was going on with Mary and why she couldn't be there. I know that Mom missed Mary. She didn't understand why she hadn't seen her in a while.

After the aides got Mom ready for bed, I went back into her room to say good-bye for the evening. I talked to her for a few minutes, telling her that I had to leave but would be back in two days. Mom said, "Good." Mom seems to communicate better at night when she's lying in bed. I believe it's because she gets more blood flow to her brain when she's lying down, which enables her to communicate more clearly.

October 7, 2011
It's a Sacred Relationship
I went in, greeted Mom, and took her back to her room. After settling Mom in her room, I went back to talk to Tammy about some of my concerns with the aides. Tammy said that they tell the aides during in-service trainings to give warnings when they're about to do something with the residents. For example, when they're changing the residents and getting them ready for bed, they should always address the residents by name and let them know what they're going to do before they actually do it. If you were in their shoes, could you imagine an aide coming in, taking your clothes off quickly, changing and cleaning you, and then putting you to bed without saying much of anything or without interacting with you on a personal and humane basis? When Tammy told me about the continuing in-service training, I was happy to hear it. I was glad that I had brought it up and followed through on it.

I went back to Mom and told her, "I'll be here, Mom." She said, "Good." A little while later, I had another conversation with Tammy. I told her that I don't want to seem to be complaining a lot. I appreciate everything that the staff there does for my mom. I also explained that there is such a powerful connection between Mom and me. It's a sacred relationship. She gave birth to me; I feel that she is part of who I am and I am part of who she is. We are inseparable. I told Tammy that this is the reason I'm so concerned about my mom and that I periodically check on things for her to make sure that she is okay. Tammy understood. I think she appreciated my saying those things, particularly because she is a mom, also.

I took Mom back out to the area where the residents were congregated. As I was leaving, a female resident yelled out to me and asked me to help her get into a chair. She was sitting in her wheelchair at the time. I told her that I was sorry but that one of the aides, who were standing off to the side at the time, had to help her. When I started walking down the hallway to leave, I turned once more to Mom and said, "I love you." The woman who had asked me for help couldn't see me anymore. I was already around the corner from her. However, Mom could still see me from where I was standing. The woman yelled back to me, "You love me, but you won't help me sit down!" Some people laughed. I replied, "No, I love my mother. I was talking to her." I wanted the woman to understand that I wasn't talking to her. I then walked down the hallway and left the unit.

October 11, 2011

I'm Tough!

It was very early in the morning. I went to my first meeting with a men's group. I had been invited by someone I knew. The group basically discusses what it means to be a man in today's world and whether or not we're keeping our word and staying in integrity, performing acts of service for the community, and so on. If I was a good fit and wanted to join the group, I could do so. I already knew some of the men from past circumstances, but the rest of them I had just met that morning.

During the meeting, one of the men said that he had been out of work and had spent his dad's inheritance. He was depressed and was having a hard time getting a job to make things work out. Many of the men gave him advice. He was also looking for support and encouragement.

I told him that I understood because I had been out of work for a while too. One of the men suggested that we exchange information so that we could support each other. The man who was out of work said, "No, I want someone who is tougher." I was offended. It was a really inappropriate thing to say to someone, especially since he had just met me. He didn't really know me. Besides, I knew that it wasn't true at all.

As one of the men in the group started to give him some more advice, I spoke up. I said, "Let me tell you something." Another man interrupted me, but I was determined to speak my mind. I said, "Let me finish." I said something along these lines: "My mom has struggled with Alzheimer's disease for over eleven and a half years now. I love and adore my mom with all my heart, mind, and spirit. Helping my Mom fight this disease makes me feel as if I'm stuck in a big, ongoing battle and that the battle will never end. I feel this way every day of my life, seven days a week. I don't get any days off. Unless any of you men have either gone through it or are going through it, you don't really know what it's like. It's tough. *I'm* tough!" I think that I made my point. Some of the men in the group looked over at me with a mixture of surprise and respect for what I'd just expressed written on their faces. They had just seen mild-mannered Clark Kent transform into Superman before their very eyes. I didn't even use my telephone booth. One of the men used the word *compassion* in response. He's right. I'm battle tested and a real warrior when it comes down to taking care of my mom.

October 18, 2011

She Can't Help It

After visiting with Mom, I was taking her back out to the dining room because I had to leave, and I saw Kathleen in the hallway. She said to leave Mom in front of the nurse's station and that she would come back and get her in a little while. I mentioned to Celia what Kathleen had said. After I positioned Mom, I joked to Mom, "You can make faces at Celia." Celia and Jose, the nurses, started laughing. Then Celia said playfully to Mom, "And no yelling." I knew that Celia was joking, but I thought that it was in inappropriate and insensitive to Mom. Celia should know better. I defended Mom, saying, "She can't help it. She gets scared. I understand her language." I'm glad that I spoke up when I did. I then said good night to Mom and to the nurses.

October 24, 2011

Wotz

I had been away Friday, Saturday, and all day and into the late evening on Sunday at a seminar in New York City with Mary. I really missed seeing Mom. I try to see her four times a week. I could tell that she had missed me by her initial reaction when she saw me.

When Mom saw me through the window of the dining room, she smiled her beautiful smile, started rubbing her hands together excitedly, and then clapped her hands together a few times. As I was coming around to get her, she looked at me through the window again and started blowing kisses at me. She is absolutely adorable!

I gave her a nice, warm hug and kissed her several times on the side of her face while saying that I love her. I explained that I had been away for the weekend at a seminar. When I took Mom back to her room, Mary had just arrived after parking the car. She started hugging and kissing Mom too.

After I finished writing these notes, I turned around and saw Mom looking right at me. She was eating her lunch earlier than normal because she had a scheduled doctor's appointment off site. Mom said, "You can." I think that she meant that I can continue to do whatever I was doing when I was writing my notes. I replied, "Yes, Mom. Thank you. I can, and I will." I could also take it to mean that I can accomplish things in my life.

We rode together in the ambulette to Mom's doctor's appointment. We were stopped at a red light. All of a sudden, Mom said, "Wotz." I looked up and realized that she was reading a word on the back of the truck in front of us. I told Mary about it. I said, "Very good, Mom. *Wotz.* That's what it says." The word on the truck was actually *Wotiz*, but it was close enough. I am constantly surprised at what Mom is still capable of doing, like reading certain words. It's good to know that she's still trying to read and keep her mind active. I'm so proud of her!

October 28, 2011
Hi, Billy. How Are You?
Mom started smiling as soon as she saw me. I gave her a big hug and a kiss. I was so happy to see her, as always. I took her to her room, and then I went to get her lunch and took it back to her.

While Mom was eating her lunch, I went to the bathroom. When I came back out, I walked over to the desk area and waved to her as I walked past her. She smiled and said, "Hi, Billy. How are you?" Mom doesn't say my name that much anymore. When she does, it means so much to me. I was so happy to hear Mom say my name, and I told her so.

A little while later, I was helping Mom with her lunch. I said, "I'm here for you." Mom said, "I know. Um-hmm!" *Um-hmm* is one of my favorite things that Mom says to us.

After she finished her dinner, I took her tray back to the dining room. Mary was in the bathroom. When I went back into the room, I stood close to Mom, and she motioned for me to come closer. She then started rubbing my face with her hands. She said, "That's my baby." When Mary came out of the bathroom, I told her what Mom had just said, and Mom said, "Yep!" Mom's just so adorable!

November 6, 2011
Woman at Arts and Crafts Fair Shows Understanding and Compassion
The nursing home was holding an arts and craft fair on the ground floor that day. I took Mom downstairs so that she could enjoy looking at all the different displays and seeing all the people. Mom knew some of the people there because they work in the nursing home and were either helping out or doing some browsing of their own.

As I was taking Mom down one of the hallways where items were displayed, we bumped into Mary. She had decided to buy something there before she went upstairs to see Mom, and she greeted Mom with a kiss.

A little while later, after going all the way down the hall that had the most exhibits, we turned Mom back around. There was a little too much noise and commotion going on for Mom, and she started to get agitated and then started yelling. I leaned over in front of her, calmed her down, gave her a kiss on the forehead, and told her that we were going to take her back upstairs. Mom said, "Good." A woman who was working at the fair was standing behind one of the displays near us and saw the whole thing. I explained to her what had happened, that Mom couldn't help it and had gotten overwhelmed by what was happening around her. The woman smiled warmly at me and told me that she understood. It means the world to me when people truly understand and have compassion for what my mom has and how truly difficult it is for her, along with how difficult it is for us.

We were watching *Pandora Unforgettable Holiday Moments on Ice* on TV. All of a sudden, Mom said, "Grandma. She's here!" Mom brings up her grandma, who raised her from age four to fourteen, from time to time. Mom also used to go back during the summer breaks from high school to live with her grandma and grandpa in Massachusetts. Her grandma was really like a mom to her. God bless her grandma! I explained to Mom that her grandma was in heaven but was looking after her. I also told her that we are also looking after her.

A few minutes later, Mom and Mary were holding hands as Mary stood in front of Mom. They then started rocking their hands back and forth between them. This is something that I had discovered a few months earlier as another way of connecting with Mom. People with Alzheimer's disease are more sensitive to and in tune with the power of the human touch than the general population, who tend to take it for granted. They are gradually losing the ability to do other things. The importance that they place on the things they *can* still do becomes heightened because of their greater reliance on it as a way of communicating and relating. They connect better to their environment in this way and in other ways that are not so apparent to the casual observer.

While Mom and Mary were rocking their hands back and forth in unison, Mom was smiling away and Mary was laughing. It was good to see the two of them really enjoying the moment. Mom then said to Mary, "And your grandfather." Mom was referring to Mary's grandfather, Mom's grandfather, or Dad, our father. Sometimes Mom uses family words interchangeably.

A little while later, Mary and I were preparing to leave. Mary said to Mom, "It was so nice spending so much time with you today, Mom." Mom replied, "Yes, that's what I'm saying." I laughed.

As we were leaving, I popped my head into the dining room to say good-bye to the residents and the aides. I said, "Good night, girls! Good night ladies!" After I walked out of the entryway, Mary walked into the dining room and said, "Good-bye." A female resident who is usually loud and outspoken yelled out to Mary, "Good-bye? Where are you going?" Mary replied, "We're going home." The woman then said, "You've got some nerve! You're going home and leaving us here!" Everyone started laughing, with the exception of the woman who said it. She was serious. It just demonstrates that they're lonely, they're bored, and they miss the known comforts of home and family. That's really where most, if not all, of them want to be. And who can blame them? I would feel the exact same way if I were in their shoes.

November 8, 2011

No, I'm Not Interested

Before I went to see Mom, I met with some friends for lunch. I was sitting next to a woman whom I'd known for over seven months at that point. After the luncheon ended, she asked me how my mom was doing, and I said, "Okay. Thank you." I told her that I was going to a doctor's appointment later and would then be going to see my mom.

This woman has asked me many times about my mom and how she's doing. Because she is retired and may have a more flexible schedule, I asked if I could ask her a question. I prefaced it by saying something like, "I don't know if you would be comfortable with this, but I was wondering if you'd like to come with me sometime when I visit my mom." She responded right away by saying, "No, I'm not interested." I was shocked by her response and immediately taken aback by it. It was very abrupt and insensitive. Considering the polite way that I made my request and the context of the situation, it was a horrible way to respond. I stated that I was sorry and didn't want her to feel uncomfortable, but I had asked because she always asks about my mom. She said, "Well, you know that I worked in that business." I told her that I wasn't thinking about that when I initially asked her. She ended up saying something about not being comfortable going to visit Mom. I recognize her right to say no; I just didn't like the way that she first responded to me.

I would have much preferred that she say something like, "No, thank you, Bill. I'm sorry. I don't want to hurt your feelings. It's just that I worked for a long time in that industry. I wouldn't be comfortable doing it. I know that your mom is very special to you, and I know that you wouldn't just ask anyone to join you in visiting her. It must have been difficult for you to even ask me to join you. Thank you for thinking enough of me and for having the courage to ask me in the first place."

After I reflected on it, I realized that she had responded to me in a way that was dismissive of my feelings. It came across as self-centered. She didn't care how it sounded to me when she said it. It seemed as if she also didn't care about my feelings for my mom. That made matters even worse because it concerned my mom. Needless to say, I'm very protective of my mom. My feelings are heightened whenever it concerns her. She is my mom, and she's vulnerable and defenseless because of her disease. It makes me that much more protective and sensitive about things that are said in reference to her.

November 10, 2011
Thank You
When I first arrived to see Mom, I went in from behind where she was sitting at the table. I went to her side, smiled, and asked how she was doing. I could tell that she didn't recognize me right away. I told her that I was her son and repeated it several times. After about one minute, I could tell that she recognized me by her facial expression. A lot of our communication is accomplished through body language. I have to wait until she recognizes me. If I don't, she might get scared or start yelling

at me. When I noticed her recognition of me, I gave her a kiss on the cheek. I told her that I was taking her to her room to hang out and have lunch there.

After she had finished her lunch, I told her that I was going to trim her fingernails with a nail clipper. She was generally cooperative while I did so. After I was done, I asked Mom to look at her fingers to see how nice they looked. She looked at her hands and said, "Thank you." Even though she resists a little while I'm doing it or may not understand what I'm trying to do, after it's done she really does notice the effort. Thankfully, Mom can sometimes express her appreciation to me for something that I've just done on her behalf. It means a lot to me to help her in every way possible. It's not only the right thing to do, it feels great knowing that I'm helping her and making a positive difference in her life.

Mom in early childhood.

Mom's mother.

Mom's father.

*Mom as a young girl in Massachusetts. Mom's paternal great grandmother
is on the left side. Her paternal great aunt is on the right side.*

Mom in her teens in Miami Beach, FL.

Dad's high school graduation from St. Cecilia's in Englewood, NJ.

Dad in an action photo in his U.S. Army uniform.

Dad in his U.S. Army uniform.

Mom at around 19 years old.

Mom in her early 20's.

Mom in her early 20's.

Mom in her early 20's taken in her Mom's house.

Mom as a young lady before she met Dad.

Mom and Dad in front of Dad's childhood home in Englewood, NJ when they were dating. Dad's mother is on the front left. Mom's mother is on the front right.

Mom and Dad in front of Mom's home in Englewood, NJ.

Mom in front of Dad's childhood home in Englewood, NJ.

Mom and Dad's wedding day on January 26, 1952.

Mom and Dad leaving St. Cecilia's Church in Englewood, NJ on their wedding day.

Mom and Dad dancing at their wedding reception.

Mom and Dad's wedding reception. Mom's stepfather and mother are on the far left.
Her paternal grandparents are 3rd and 4th from the far left. Dad's parents are on the far right.

*Mom's wedding day with her paternal grandparents who raised her from the
age of 4 to 14. She also spent her high school year summers with them.*

*Mom's wedding day. Her Dad on the left side of Mom in the
picture. Her paternal grandparents are on each end.*

Mom as a bridesmaid at her sister-in-law's wedding.

Mom in her mid 20's when she and Dad were first married.

The author as a young boy. I had just turned three years old in this photo.

Photo of the author from my high school graduation yearbook. I was 17 at the time. I wish that my hair was still red.

Mom and Dad in Houston, TX in August 1983.

Mom and Dad's 50th Wedding Anniversary portrait in January 2002.

November 16, 2011

Dentist Visit

I went up to see Mom because she had an appointment with the dentist at the nursing home. She had lost a big part of her tooth the week before. During the appointment, I had to hold Mom's hands down. She doesn't understand what is happening to her when the dentist opens up her mouth, so her natural instinct is to lift up her hands to protect herself. I had talked to Mom numerous times right before the dentist saw her regarding what was going to happen during this checkup, saying that the dentist was going to look in her mouth and look at her tooth. I tried to prepare her for what was about to transpire. I think that it helps a little bit to get her to understand the process ahead of time. Regardless, I always feel better whenever I do it.

When the dentist looked at Mom's mouth, he pressed on the area of the gum where she had lost a tooth, and then he pressed on the gum area above the tooth that had just been partially lost. Mom reacted by raising her eyebrows at the pain. The dentist knew that he had to pull that tooth. As I was trying to get my hands back from Mom, she held onto them and started squeezing my wrists, holding my arms down. Then she started yelling at me. She didn't understand that all of this was necessary in order to check out her teeth. I told her that I was sorry several times and that it was all over. I hugged her and kissed her to help comfort her.

Before I left, the dentist told me that when I brought Mom back to see him the next week, he would clean her teeth and remove the two teeth that were damaged. I asked him if he would put some gel on her gums before injecting her with the Novocain. The dentist responded, "Yes, if you want me to." I told him that I did.

Before I took Mom back up to her unit, I took her with me to the café, where I bought myself a large coffee and got a piece of cake for Mom. I took off the plastic covering on the cake and placed it in front of her. She picked up the whole piece and started eating it. I could tell that she was thoroughly enjoying it. I'm glad. She deserved it, especially after having just been checked out by the dentist. I was happily sipping on my cup of coffee and watching Mom enjoy her cake. When she was done eating, she looked at me and said, "How much?" I said, "How much? Mom, it's my pleasure. It's on me. I paid for it already." I was surprised and touched that she said that. Mom is so incredibly sweet. I say this because of the fact that she would even consider paying for her own cake. The fact of the matter is that I owe her so much anyway. It's a debt that I can never fully repay. I absolutely adore her. I would do anything for her.

Later on, we were back in her room. Mom ate her lunch, and then we watched *Who Wants to Be a Millionaire?* As the contestant was answering a question, I made a clicking sound with my tongue, indicating disappointment. I knew the right answer and would have answered it correctly had I been on the show. Mom picked up on it right away. She turned to me and said with concern in her voice, "What's the matter?" I told her that I had successfully auditioned to be on *Who Wants to Be a Millionaire?* on two separate occasions but the show hadn't called me, which was true. I said that if I had been on that show, I would have been able to answer that question. It's amazing how Mom can still pick up on the slightest deviation in my mood or voice and express her concern for me. She's such a blessing to our family. I'm so glad that we still have her in our lives.

A little while later, I had to leave. I took Mom out to the area where the other residents were congregated. I said good-bye and told her that I'd be back in a few days to visit her. Mom said, "Be careful" three times between the time we left her room and when I was walking away. The love of a mom is the most awesome and incredible love in the world. I love her with all of my heart.

November 19, 2011

When They Find Out about This

Mom smiled and greeted me warmly when I arrived. I gave her a big, loving hug and a kiss on the cheek. I hugged her for thirty seconds or more. When I stood back up, I could see that the nurse's aides were all smiling. They said, "Enjoy her." I said, "Thanks. She's the best!" They're right. Part of my journey with Mom is to enjoy every moment that I'm there with her. Whenever I'm visiting with Mom, I feel as if time is standing still. I'm with Mom in a special place that isn't affected by it.

After I took Mom to her room, she said something to me that I didn't fully understand. I said, "You're so cute, Mom." She asked, "Me?" I replied, "Yes, you, Mom." She said, "That's cute."

A little while after dinner, Mom started to bang her hands lightly on her table. I sensed that she was frustrated and asked, "Do you want to go home, Mom?" She said, "Yes, I do." I said, "I want you to come home too, Mom." I looked right at her when I said it, and she smiled back at me. Magical!

I got ready to leave, and as I was taking Mom out, she put out her arm and tried to grab the door to stop me from leaving. Then she started to yell. She didn't want me to leave. I leaned over and said some comforting words to her. I told her that I understood, that I didn't want to leave but that I had to, that I live close by, and that I would be back the next day.

I decided to stay with her for an extra five minutes or so. A woman in Mom's unit who was also in a wheelchair started to complain loudly. She must have been new to the unit. I'd never seen her before. She was speaking to an aide in a loud voice. She said something to the effect of, "I know some people, and when they find out about this, they're going to do something about it." My heart really went out to her. I'm sure that my mom and most of the other residents feel the same way. Even though they get medical care, food, lodging, and social activities there, it's still not the same as being at home with their loved ones.

I interpreted this woman's comment to mean that it's criminal that they have to live in a nursing home and can't be at home being taken care of by their loved ones. I agree. I'm not sure if there currently is a program, but I wish that there was a program in New Jersey (or the entire United States, if possible) that would help family members to stay at home and take care of their loved ones with Alzheimer's disease with the help of a live-in or a twelve-hour-a-day aide. It might be a feasible alternative to having to place loved ones in a nursing home.

November 21, 2011
Mom Visits My Dentist
I had reservations about using the dentist in the nursing home. I was lying in bed the evening of Mom's most recent visit to the dentist, and it really bothered me that I had to ask him to put a numbing gel on her gums before giving her a shot of Novocain in the event that he performed dental surgery on my mom. It was painfully obvious to me that it would be important to use numbing gel in this situation, especially when you're dealing with someone with Alzheimer's disease. It's bad enough when I get it done for myself. I can't imagine what it would be like to not have numbing gel applied to my gum area before a shot of Novocain was administered there. So, on the morning of November 17, 2011, I called my dentist and asked him about it. He said that he would see if he could help her. I trust my dentist because he does such an excellent job with my teeth.

Mom and I went to his office on November 21. I had told the staff ahead of time that she wouldn't cooperate because of her Alzheimer's disease. Mom seemed really excited to be in a new environment with me and to meet the nice and friendly staff there. It definitely helped that I was with her. She knew that she was in the care of someone who is family and who truly loves and cares about her. Of course, I will always be there whenever it's necessary to help her. Before the dentist entered the room (we had already placed Mom in a dental chair), she was holding the hand of one of the dental aides. She was smiling. She gave a big, wonderful smile to every staff member that I introduced her to. My dentist came in and said hi to Mom. When he started to work, Mom was resisting all attempts to open up her mouth. My dentist then said that he couldn't help her. He didn't want to fight with her to get her to open her mouth. It's natural that she resists it. She doesn't understand what is happening to her and that it's being done to help her.

My dentist recommended that Mom be sedated so that some of her teeth could be removed. He recommended for me to either take her to an oral surgeon or to a hospital where they would perform that service.

Luckily, I was able to get an appointment set up for the next day at a local hospital that had an oral surgeon who could apply sedation, if necessary. At the time, they said that they were just going to look at Mom's mouth to do an evaluation.

November 22, 2011
Mom Gets Dental Surgery
I went with Mom to the hospital to get her teeth looked at. Once there, I had to fill out all of the necessary forms for her. They already had a copy of Mom's medical record.

I went into the examination room with her and explained Mom's medical situation to the dentist and the dental assistants. The assistants were there to help out because it was the dental surgery center at the hospital. They were trying to get Mom to open her mouth so that they could look inside. I told them that even though they were trying to do the right thing, Mom wouldn't understand that they were asking her to open her mouth. I said that they would have to have something to keep her mouth open while they were taking X-rays.

They put an X-ray bib on Mom and one on me to protect me while I was holding the slide in place. At one point, my bib fell off, but the dentist told me not to worry about it because it was a low dose of radiation. I told him that I wasn't worried about a little radiation and that I'd face a hungry tiger for my mom.

Mom resisted during the whole process. We were able to get X-rays of her upper jaw and the lower part of her mouth where she was having the problems. The dentist showed me that a post that was located under a crown that had fallen off had to be removed. He also said that the tooth next to the post had to be pulled. On Mom's bottom jaw, a tooth had popped out months before, and only the root of the tooth was left. It would need to be removed, also.

At this point, the dentist informed me that he was going to have to take out all three teeth, and he was going to do it then and there. I asked about sedating Mom, but he said that if he did, she may not wake up because of her age and medical condition. I knew right away that this wasn't an option. I agreed that he should go ahead and do what needed to be done. The sooner this work was done, the better that it would be for her. I didn't want her to have any more mouth pain or to let an infected tooth or other areas in her mouth get any worse.

To keep Mom's mouth open during the oral surgery, they inserted the same device they had used while they were taking the X-rays. When they started working on the upper part of her mouth, I felt so incredibly bad for her. Although the injections into her upper mouth went well because of the gel that they applied on her gums, I still felt helpless in the moment. At some point during the surgery, I started to cry. Of course, Mom was resisting. One of the dental assistants and I were holding Mom's hands down so that she couldn't interfere with the work that was being done. I hoped that Mom understood on some level what they were doing for her. I know that I had explained things to her ahead of time. However, I'm not sure if she remembered or fully understood what I was saying at the time.

Things got really bad when the dentist moved to the lower part of Mom's mouth to get the root of that tooth out. After he put the gel in her mouth, he injected her with Novocain. She started to yell, probably because she felt the needle this time. A minute later, the dentist started trying to extract the root, but Mom started yelling again. I know my mom really well. I could tell by the way she was yelling and the pitch of her voice that she was still in pain. I asked the dentist to please inject her again with Novocain, and he did. He also showed the other dentist who was present there why he had injected my mom again. He said that there was another area that could be injected to prevent pain when working there. I'm not sure why he didn't give Mom the two injections in that area in the first place. Regardless, the dentist said that after the second injection, she wouldn't feel any more pain in that area. When he got back to extracting the root, Mom started to yell again. The dentist said that she couldn't feel any pain but was feeling the pressure of him working on that area.

I started to cry again. Again, I felt helpless in that situation. I never want to see my mom suffer at all. However, I knew that the dentist was doing what needed to be done. To not do anything at all would have made matters worse. Throughout the oral surgery, the dental assistant, the dentist, and I kept encouraging Mom. On a few different occasions, the dentist looked at me. He said that he was more worried about me than he was about Mom. I told him that I was fine and would be okay.

When the surgery was completed, I leaned over and kissed Mom gently on the cheek. I told her that it was all over. I was so relieved for her.

I had my arms wrapped around her from where I was standing behind her to comfort her and make her feel protected and loved. Within a minute or two after I told Mom that it was all over, she started to gently pat my hand with hers. It was as if she was trying to comfort me, also. I'm sure that she had heard me crying in the background during the surgery. I also believe that she was relieved that it was over, as anyone would have been. This is especially true of an eighty-four-year-old woman who was diagnosed with Alzheimer's disease almost twelve years earlier at that point. I am so proud of my mom for going through it. It was so wonderful that in the midst of all the pain, suffering, chaos, and confusion, Mom still wanted to comfort me in her time of distress. I couldn't ask for a better mom. She's the best!

On the way out of the surgery room, the dental assistant offered to get me a cup of water. She said that I looked pale. I accepted the water and thanked her for it. I also thanked the dentist and the rest of the staff.

November 27, 2011
Mom Says She's Still Here
I went in to see Mom and sensed that she recognized me to some extent but couldn't place how she knew me. I told her who I was and why I was there, and her expression changed to one of recognition. I leaned over and gave her a hug and a kiss. I snuggled up to the side of her face. I know that Mom really enjoys the closeness, as do I.

A little while later, Mom grabbed my hand. At first, she placed it up on the tray in front of her. Then, she brought my hand up to her mouth and started kissing it. She was telling me that she loves and appreciates me. I said, "Thank you, Mom."

Later on, she reached over and started to gently pat the back of my head. I said, "Mom, are you worried about me?" She said, "Yes, I am." I said, "Thanks, Mom. Don't worry. I'll be okay. I'm worried about you, too." It's amazing to me that Mom still is concerned about her children in the midst of her disease. I appreciate that she can still express herself this way. I wish that all of the worrying and praying that I do for her would help improve her condition.

After dinner and some TV with Mom, I took her back out to the dining room area because I had to leave for the evening. When we got there, two residents in the unit were arguing with each other, so I decided to stay with Mom for a while to make sure that she was okay. We sat at a table a good distance from where the residents were arguing. I turned to Mom and said, "Don't let them bother you, Mom." She said, "I know, I know, I know."

A little while later, I turned to Mom and said, "I'm still here." She looked at me, gave me her great smile, and said, "So am I." I thought that this was her way of telling me that she wanted to go home. I am grateful that my mom still has her wonderful sense of humor. I ended up staying with her for an extra half hour.

November 30, 2011
Mom Says, "I'm Sorry"
After Mom finished eating her lunch, I helped her brush her teeth. She thanked me after we finished brushing. I said, "You're welcome. It's my pleasure." She knows that it's good for her. I'm sure that she feels better after brushing with her teeth clean and her mouth fresh.

A little while later, Mom said, "I'm sorry. I'm sorry." I think that Mom says this to me every once in a while because she sees all that I do for her and she knows that it can take a toll on me. She also realizes that I'm spending my time with her and taking care of her needs while possibly neglecting doing things for myself and my life. However, I always enjoy being with her and I love being able to give back. Sometimes it does get to be a little too much for me. In those instances, I try to take stock, make sure to take better care of Bill, and try to maintain a more balanced approach. So, I told her that she didn't have to say she was sorry, and I added, "I like you, and I love you." She said, "So do I." I said, "You like me and you love me, Mom?" She smiled and said, "Yes!" I said, "Thank you, Mom."

Mom then began saying something to me that I couldn't understand. She said, "He . . . ," and I replied, "He did, Mommy?" She said, "Yes, yes, yes" and started laughing. In those situations when I'm not sure what Mom is saying, I either try to go along with her or tell her that I don't understand what she is saying to me. If I tell her that I don't understand, I also tell her that I'm doing the best that I can to communicate with her, that I understand that it's difficult for her sometimes, and that I'm taking care of everything so there's nothing for her to worry about.

Later on, Mom saw something on TV and said, "He's a redhead." I said, "Redhead—that's me!" I actually grew up as a redhead. Mom then said, "That's me!" and pointed to herself. I laughed. It's true, in a way. My red hair comes from Mom's side of the family. And, of course, she brought me into this world.

December 3, 2011

Mom Gets Agitated

Mary and I went together to see Mom. While Mary was parking the car, I went up to get Mom and take her to her room. As I walked into Mom's unit, I could hear her voice from down the hall. She was yelling, agitated about something. I ran down the hallway to get to her. If I ever hear Mom being agitated when I first come into her unit, I rush over to her as soon as possible. I don't ever want Mom to feel agitated or to suffer in any way.

When I got over to her, she was turned away from me and facing the nurse's aide. I went up to her and said, "Mom, Mom, what's the matter? Don't yell, Mom. It's okay." She looked over at me. She didn't seem to recognize me for about five to ten seconds. When she did recognize me, she smiled. I gave her a kiss and a hug.

When I was back in the room with Mom, I asked her, "Who's the most beautiful woman in the world?" Then I answered my question by saying, "You are!" She replied, "I am!"

A little while later, I said, "Are you happy, Mom?" She said, "Yeah, sure!" I then said, "You're so adorable," and she replied, "I know."

I had to leave Mom's room for a minute. When I came back, I said, "Hey, gorgeous!" and she said, "Yes!" She's so cute!

After that, I gave Mom a magazine that she had in her room. There were two cute babies on the cover, and Mom put the magazine up to her face and started kissing the baby pictures. Mary and I started laughing. Mom said, "What's so funny?" We replied, "You are!" Mom loves seeing babies on TV and in print. I wish that I had a real baby to bring in to her when I visit her.

December 7, 2011

Mom and Big Band Music

I first dropped off my stuff in Mom's room and then went back and looked through the window into the dining room at Mom. She looked at me for a few seconds and then recognized me. She pointed to herself and said, "Me?" a few times in a row. She has said this to me before. I could read her lips.

I pointed back to her through the window. I went to the room to get her. I was saying, "You. You, Mom." I waved to her, and she waved back to me. When I got into the dining room and went up to see Mom, I said hi. Music from the big band era was playing in the background. I told one of the aides that this was my mom's music. I held her hands, and we started moving our hands back and forth to the rhythm of the music. I said, "We're dancing, Mom. This is how we dance with each other." After a few minutes of this, I took Mom back to her room to help her with her lunch.

At one point, I was coming out of Mom's bathroom and back into her room. Mom started saying, "Mary, Mary, Mary." I said, "Are you saying *Mary*, Mom?" to make sure that I had heard her correctly. Mom said yes. I said, "Mary will be visiting with you this evening. She's working now. I'm with you now, and Mary will see you later." Mom says "Mary" sometimes because she misses her. She doesn't understand when I'm visiting her and Mary isn't there with me. This is because Mary and I have gone together many times to visit her. Also, aside from Dad (rest in peace), Mary is the most prominent person in Mom's long-term memory. Mary lived with Mom and Dad for some time. Therefore, Mary figures large in Mom's long-term memory because of the amount of time they lived with each other and the time that they spent together.

December 10, 2011
Don't Worry about Me
I went in to see Mom, we got into her room, and I got her set up. Mom said, "The funny thing is . . ." I said, "Mom, that's one of your sayings." I asked her, "Do you want me to sit there?" after she looked at the chair next to her and then looked at me. She said, "I think so." We both laughed.

Mom clapped her hands while watching some of the TV shows and commercials. I love because it means that she's enjoying herself and she's happy.

A little while later, I told Mom that I love her. She replied by saying, "Oh, I don't think so." I explained to her that I really do love her. A few minutes later, I decided to wash Mom's hands with soap and water. As I was doing it, she called me Dad.

While I was talking to Mom, I told her that I worry about her. She replied, "Don't worry about me." She said that to me because she's strong and she wants me to live my life and not worry about her too much. I replied, "I have to, Mom. I love you, and I'm concerned about you." I'll always be connected to her in so many ways. Loving and caring for Mom is in my DNA. It's a big part of who I am as a person. I wouldn't have it any other way.

I tried to straighten Mom's leg in the wheelchair because she was sitting a little bit off center, and she let out a little noise because it hurt her. I said, "I'm sorry, Mom. I was trying to straighten your leg out. I would never hurt you." Mom smiled and said, "I know that."

I was getting ready to leave and kissing Mom good-bye. I said, "Okay, sweetheart." She said, "No, I'm not." I think she said it to make me laugh, and it worked. The nurse and I laughed. Mom looked up at me and smiled.

December 11, 2011
Mom Says Her Name
Mary and I went to see Mom. After a few minutes of conversation, I wanted to see how her memory was doing. I said, "What's your name, Mom?" She said her first name, and I said, "Mom, you said it! You said

your name!" I was so excited that she was able to respond so quickly. Because we're so involved with Mom's care, we usually know what she's capable of doing. It's a real joy when she surprises us with something like that in the moment.

We were all in Mom's room. We gave her the abominable snowman, one of the stuffed toys that we have against the wall in her room. She was acting excited when she had it in her hands to make us laugh. A little while later, she started rubbing noses with it, and Mary and I laughed again. It's such a treat being with Mom. She started laughing later and said, "I'm telling you!" At another point, she said, "Isn't that the funniest thing?" These are two of Mom's many sayings.

December 17, 2011
The *Wizard of Oz* Hug
Mary and I visited Mom, and I had brought the family portrait with us that we had taken as a birthday present for her. We had finally received the finished portrait in a frame. Everyone remarked about how beautiful it looked. We set it up in her room hanging on the wall in a place where she could easily see it.

We took Mom to her room and watched Christmas movies on the Hallmark Channel. At one point, I turned to Mom and said, "You're so beautiful, Mom." She smiled, winked at me, and said, "I know." I laughed. She's so cute!

A little while later, we were watching *The Wizard of Oz*. Mary had gone in to use the bathroom, and there was a sad scene in the movie. It made me feel sentimental about Mom. I went over to her, kissed her on the forehead, and gave her a nice long hug. I held her close to me. I told her that she shouldn't have to go through this. While I was hugging her, she started to rub the back part of my upper arm. She appreciates the closeness and the comfort of knowing that someone really loves her and cares for her. I appreciated it, also. It was a very special, loving, and spontaneous moment between Mom and me. I'll remember it as our "*Wizard of Oz* hug."

December 20, 2011
Friend Shows Lack of Sensitivity and Compassion Regarding My Mom
While I was visiting Mom, I received a phone call from a friend of mine who was returning my call from earlier that day. We were on the phone for about five to ten minutes. I noticed that Mom was starting to get agitated. I told my friend that I would have to call her back later because my mom needed me.

After I got off of the phone, Mom started to raise her voice to me. She was annoyed because I had been on the phone longer than she wanted. In Mom's condition, she needs attention. Even when I'm with Mom and we're watching TV together, she still feels like she has my attention because I'm not being distracted by anything else. Sometimes when Mom feels as if she's not being noticed, she gets agitated. I understand. Mom is limited in her capacity to understand what is going on. Although I visit her as often as possible every week, I'm not there all of the time.

I got some bottled water for Mom and gave it to her with ice in a plastic cup. She prefers to drink fruit juice. While Mom was sipping on the water, I said, "'Cause I'll do . . ." and then jumped in the air toward Mom and landed in front of her. Then, I finished it by pointing my index fingers at her and saying, "anything for you." Mom said, "I know," raised her eyebrows, smiled, and chuckled. I love to make her laugh. She's so cute!

After I left Mom to go home, I returned the phone call to my friend. I explained why I had to get off of the phone earlier. My friend didn't seem to understand. I explained to her as clearly as possible that my mom doesn't understand what is going on when I'm on the phone for a while in front of her. My friend responded a few different times in a way that indicated that she was still offended. I kept repeating that my mom doesn't understand why I'm on the phone and not being present with her or giving her my attention.

After I got off of the phone, I felt really hurt and angry about my friend's response and her apparent lack of sensitivity and compassion. I thought that she would understand. She knows that my mom has Alzheimer's disease. I explained to her several different times in that conversation that my mom didn't understand. It's amazing to me when people really don't seem to understand why people with Alzheimer's disease act the way that they do, even after it's been explained to them.

If I had known that this woman would feel this way in response to my explanation, I would never have told her the reason that I had to get off of the phone in the first place. I would have said something like, "I need to get off of the phone to help my mom with something." It's unfortunate, but in the future I'll make sure never to explain things about my mom to anyone unless I absolutely feel the need to do so.

December 23, 2011
I Would Have Died
I went to the nursing home to be with Mom when she got her hair done. I got there twenty minutes before the scheduled appointment time and discovered that she had already gotten her hair done earlier. They had an early opening, and she took it. She looked great. I went downstairs to the salon to thank the women for taking such good care of her.

When I got there, the woman who cut my mom's hair said that Mom had told her when she was done, "I want to come back next week." I was so happy to hear that. Mom knew that they had done a really good job.

Another woman working in the salon told me that Mom had given her a hug and a kiss after she had taken Mom back. Mom really appreciated having her hair done. She recognizes the opportunity to be treated in a salon to a haircut and style and given kindness and compassion. Just like any other person, it's good for her to be taken care of in this way. I can't think of anyone more deserving of this special care and attention than her.

When I was back in Mom's room, she was saying something to me. I couldn't understand what she said at first, but then she said, "I would have died." I was shocked to hear Mom say that to me. I told her that I wouldn't let anything bad happen to her. I realized later on that she may have been talking about her stay in the nursing home. She may have meant that if she wasn't in the nursing home, she would have died. If Mom meant that, she doesn't realize that we would either have been taking care of her in a nursing facility or at home. I would never, ever let anything bad happen to my mom. I would do anything for her and I'd willingly devote my life to her.

January 3, 2012
I Emphasize Mom's Emotional Needs to the Staff
Mom had been kept in her room since December 28 while she was being treated for a skin rash. This was Mom's first day back out on the floor of her unit. I came to visit her after she was initially treated for it. I didn't know then that she was being kept in her room until they decided that it was okay for her to go back out into the unit. They had kept Mom in her room in case her skin rash was contagious. I told the nurse that I wished she had told me right away that they were keeping Mom in her room. I would have gone right up to see her. The nurse apologized and acknowledged that she had told me only that Mom was being treated with antibiotics.

I went on to say that Mom wasn't going to understand why she was being left in the room alone; it was a significant change from her normal routine. I also said that Mom might think that she had done something wrong and was being punished. She might even think that she would always have to stay in the room and would never be able to come out again. I asked the nurse to tell Mom every time that she or an aide went in to see her the reason they were keeping her in the room for now. I made sure to mention it to Mom every time that I visited with her during this period. I also told the nurse that I would appreciate it if, in the future, someone would call me and let me know whenever Mom would have to stay in her room for any reason.

It's amazing to me that the nursing staff didn't tell me about it upfront. Even though they have more contact with Mom and see her every day, they aren't as tuned into her emotional needs as I am. Maybe they'd be more sensitive to Mom's and her family's emotional needs about her being quarantined if she was their mom. Either they're not doing what they're supposed to be doing regarding contacting a family member, or they just don't care. Because they are nurses working in an Alzheimer's unit, I would expect more sensitivity to a patient who is stuck in her room and to the importance of notifying a family member about it. It must have really frightened Mom when she was going through it without knowing why. All of a sudden, her daily routine was turned upside down. In this particular situation, she had to stay in her room for seven days straight.

I took Mom from the unit back to her room with me to hang out and to help her with her dinner. Afterward, as I was leaving, I placed Mom across from the nurse's station. The nurse waved to Mom, and Mom waved back at her with her hand sideways under her nose and her fingers going up and down in a humorous way. We started laughing. There was Mom displaying her wonderful playfulness and sense of humor again. Before I could leave, Mom held my hand. I knew that she didn't want me to leave her for the evening, so I stayed for a while longer. I promised her that I would be back to see her in a few days and that Mary was coming to see her the next day. I gave her a hug and a kiss and told her that I'd see her in a few days. Leaving Mom for the day or the evening is the hardest part of any visit.

January 7, 2012

Aide Tells Me That Mom Can Tell Her if She's Hungry (Really?)

While Mom was eating her dinner, she started to rub her nose with her hand. As I was getting her a tissue, she put her hand under her nose and pushed up on it to make a funny face. She said something to me, and I knew that she was doing it to be playful and make me laugh. I laughed. I was glad to see Mom displaying her sense of humor again. I gave her a tissue for her nose.

A little while later, Mom started to pour some of her juice onto her dinner tray. Mom sometimes does this because she is being playful. I said, "No, Mom. Don't do that!" She looked up and stuck her tongue out at me. I laughed again.

When Mary came out of the bathroom, I told her what had happened. She was happy to hear about Mom being playful with me. Then, Mary told me that she had been visiting with Mom that past Wednesday, January 4. She said that Mom was eating a tuna fish sandwich as part of her dinner. I don't know whether or not Mom was enjoying it or felt that she couldn't eat it all, but Mary said that when Mom thought that she wasn't looking, Mom took a piece of the sandwich off and tossed it underneath her wheelchair. Mary laughed when she told me the story. Mom had done it thinking that Mary wouldn't notice. She is so cute!

During her dinner, Mom stopped eating and drifted off to sleep. I tried a few more times over the next half hour or so to get her to eat more, but she kept sleeping. We decided that it was time to have Mom changed and put into bed for the evening.

When Kathleen came in to change Mom and get her ready for bed, I told her about Mom's not eating much of her dinner. I said that Mom might get agitated later because she would be hungry and not be able to communicate it. Kathleen told me that Mom can tell her if she's hungry. I was shocked by her response. I couldn't believe that she said that. I guess Kathleen thinks that she can communicate better with my mom than anyone else, including me, can.

I pointed out that Mom sometimes can tell people when she's hungry, but other times she cannot. Mom usually can't verbalize "I'm hungry" or "I want some food." I told Kathleen that I was just telling her this to keep the lines of communication as open as possible.

My purpose at that time was to advocate for her and to make it as clear as possible what might happen after I left. I work hard at keeping the guesswork out of the equation as much as possible. Mom can't speak up on her own behalf as well as she used to. I'm more than happy to do it for her. It's vitally important to be as proactive as possible, especially when it concerns issues that need to be communicated to the staff. It's important to anticipate things and to advise the staff accordingly.

January 17, 2012
I'm Not Here! I'm Not Here!
Mary and I were visiting Mom. A little while later, Mom started talking and sounded like she was going to start crying. I said, "What's the matter, Mom?" She said, "I'm not here! I'm not here! I'm not here! I'm not here!" I started asking her questions to try to figure out what she was trying to say. Mary said, "I know what she's saying." I said, "What is it?" Mary said, "Mom is saying that she's not herself." That sounded good

to me. I asked Mom if her saying "I'm not here" meant that she wasn't herself anymore, but Mom didn't answer me. About ten minutes later, I reminded Mom about what she had been saying and then asked her if she meant that she wasn't the way she used to be. Mom said, "Yes." I felt so bad for her. However, I was content knowing that she could still express herself in a way that we could understand. I was grateful that Mom still has the awareness that she has a problem that prevents her from functioning as well as she used to.

It also proves that the belief that people with Alzheimer's disease don't suffer is a fallacy. They suffer great emotional pain as a result of this disease, especially when they still have the awareness of what it's doing to them. They also suffer physically, for example, when they lose the ability to walk and their muscles start to atrophy from a lack of movement and exercise. I know that they're given physical therapy when they're not walking anymore, which is helpful. Also, their spirits suffer because their overall quality of life has diminished. This is one reason why frequent visits and taking them outside, when possible, can make a big difference to them.

January 19, 2012
I'm Fifty-six Years Old
I went up to Mom's room to drop off my jacket and to charge my cell phone before attending the quarterly interdisciplinary care meeting for Mom. I was going to visit with her after the meeting.

Before I went downstairs for the care meeting, I went into the dining room to talk to Maria, the recreational aide, about how Mom was doing. Then I went over to say hi to Mom. She looked up at me and smiled. Then, about five or ten seconds later, she realized that it was me and a big smile came across her face. Mom said, "My sweetheart! My sweetheart!" I went up to her and gave her a hug and a kiss. I told her that I had to go downstairs for a meeting and that I'd be back in twenty minutes to a half hour.

After the meeting, I also met with the recreation department regarding my offer to volunteer to help Mom and the people in her unit with painting and arts and crafts. Subsequently, I went back to the unit to get Mom. I took her back to her room, set her up for lunch, and turned on the TV. While she watching TV, she said, "How old . . . ?" I couldn't understand the rest of what she was saying, so I asked, "Do you want to know how old I am, Mom?" She said, "Yes." I said, "I'm fifty-six years old." She replied, "Fifty-six! So am I!" I laughed out loud and said, "No, Mom, you're not fifty-six. You're eighty-four." She is so adorable!

Shortly before leaving, I told Mom that I had to leave in about fifteen to twenty minutes. She said, "Why?" in the ingenuous way of an innocent child. I explained why I had to leave and what I had to do after I left. I told her that I want to be with her all the time, but I have some things that I have to take care of. I took her back out to the area where the other residents were and said, "I'll be back in two days, Mom. I'll be back on Saturday." She said, "Oh, good." She is so sweet.

February 4, 2012
Aide Becomes Defensive When I Ask Her Some Questions
I helped Mom with her dinner as we watched *Pandora Unforgettable Moments on Ice* with Kenny G. performing. He was playing his hit "G-Bop." I danced to it in front of Mom for a few seconds. After I sat down, I told her, "I wish that you could dance with me like you used to, Mom." She said, "That's all right." I felt bad for her but was glad to hear her express herself so clearly.

When it was time for Mom to get ready for bed, Kathleen came in to change her while I waited outside in the hallway. At one point, another aide, Martha, went into the room to help Kathleen with Mom. While they were in there, I heard Mom let out a scream. When Martha left the room, I asked her why Mom had screamed, and Martha replied that she always screams when they change her. I knew that this wasn't the case. I have been outside in the hallway many times while Mom was being changed and hadn't heard her scream at all.

A little while later, Mom screamed again, but this time the scream was long and very loud. The door to Mom's room was open a little bit, so I pushed it open a little more and looked in. It seemed that Kathleen had done something while changing Mom without letting her know about it. I'm sure that it frightened Mom a great deal. We had had some problems with Kathleen in the past, the main one being that she was too rough at times. I believe that part of this might stem from cultural differences. I also believe that some of the aides become desensitized to the needs of the residents and the residents' families because they perform these tasks day after day. However, there is never any excuse for treating anyone with insensitivity or indignity, especially people who have Alzheimer's disease.

A few minutes later, I heard Kathleen saying something to Mom, but I couldn't hear exactly what she was saying. Mom yelled out, "Go home!" in an angry way.

As Kathleen was leaving the room a few minutes later, I thanked her for changing Mom. I also asked her why Mom had screamed so loudly. Kathleen told me that Mom always screams. I asked her if she had told Mom what she was going to do beforehand. She said that she had, but I didn't believe her.

I could tell that Kathleen was being defensive with me by the way she responded to my questions. She seemed irritated that I was asking them. Regardless, I have every right to ask her questions concerning my mom.

I didn't trust her or her answers based on some of my past experiences with her.

I called Mary and told her about what had happened. I had already resolved to talk to the nurse manager about it. Mary said that she would join me in discussing it with management when she was up there with me during the week.

I went back into Mom's room, said good night to her in my loving and comforting way, and put the safety mat down on the floor for her. I told her that I would be back to see her the next day.

February 14, 2012
I Want to Go with You
It was Valentine's Day, so I just had to see Mom. She's my number one sweetheart! She will always be number one with me. Mary and I got her a really beautiful card. I also bought her a bunch of helium-filled balloons that said, "I love you," and had different Valentine's Day designs on them.

We had a nice visit with Mom. Just before we were getting ready to leave for the evening, Mom grabbed Mary's hand and said, "I want to go with you." We both felt so bad for Mom. I explained that we were doing all that we could for her and that if we had the money, she could stay with us. I also told her that it would cost a lot of money and was something that we could not afford right now. I added that she was in the next-best place to being home and that we would see her as often as we could. I told her that if I could change things, I would do it. It's so heartbreaking to have Mom in a nursing home and not at home with us. I never want Mom to think or feel that we would ever want her to be in a nursing home and not be home with us.

February 25, 2012

Big! Big! Big!

When Mary and I were finishing our visit with Mom, we took her out and placed her by the nurse's station. Mom wouldn't let go of our hands. She didn't want us to leave. Mom does this from time to time. She wants us to stay with her as long as possible. I don't think that Mom ever wants us to leave her side. I don't blame her at all. It's understandable. I would feel the same way if I were in her shoes.

All of a sudden, Mom started yelling out, "Big! Big! Big!" She said it seven or eight times in a row, sounding like she was distressed and calling out for help. I didn't realize until the next day that Mom was calling out to Dad. Our Dad's name was Ben, but Mom wasn't able to say "Ben" at that time. So, she said a word that was very similar to his name. It broke my heart even more when I realized what Mom was trying to say and who she was reaching out to. I told Mary about it the next day, and she agreed with my conclusion. Mom knew that I was leaving, and she wanted her husband to be with her.

It is good for me to know whenever Mom is trying to say something but the exact words aren't coming out. If I can get some clues, I can try to piece together what she might be trying to say. There are many instances when I'll be proactive. I tell her that although I can't understand everything that she is saying, I am trying. I also tell her that everything is being taken care of and that I'm doing all that I can for her.

March 1, 2012

Aide Takes Mom Away Before I Get to Say Good Night

I went to see Mom and was greeted warmly by her. As I was on the way out of the dining room with her and heading back to her room, she reached out her arm and touched a woman I privately refer to as the Mayor. The Mayor talks very loudly and acts as if she runs the show there. She tries to be in everyone's business, whether they want her to be or not. I was happy that Mom reached out and touched her shoulder. I know that the Mayor likes my mom and tries to look after her. The Mayor was drifting off at the time, and she woke up when Mom touched her. I told her that it was my mom, and she smiled. I told her that Mom touched her because she likes her.

I took Mom back to her room. I said, "I love you, Mom," and she replied, "Good. Let's go." I felt terrible. I always do whenever Mom expresses a desire to go home because I know that it's not possible right now.

I responded by saying, "I would love to take you home, Mom," and went on to explain why it wasn't possible at this time. However, I told her that if I could do it, I'd be happy to have her home with us.

Later on, Mom said something to me that I didn't understand. She then called me over and started kissing me on the face. It was Mom's way of saying that she appreciates me and all that I do for her.

Before I left, I took Mom back out to the area where the residents were congregated. On the way out, I was intercepted by Alice, a nurse's aide. She came up to me and said, "I'll take her. I'm going to change her." It happened so suddenly that I was caught off guard and said okay. After Alice took Mom away, I felt bad. I realized that I hadn't said good-bye to Mom before I left. I always kiss her on the cheek and tell her when I'll be coming back to see her.

I called the nursing home later and spoke to Tammy, the head nurse, about it. I told her that I knew that there wasn't any bad intention involved. However, I asked her if she would talk to the aides about giving me a moment in those situations to say good-bye to Mom before they take her away. Tammy understood and said that she would speak to Alice about it. I emphasized that I wasn't angry with Alice. Tammy said

191

that she would simply ask her to be more sensitive to caregivers' family members. I thanked her for doing this for me. I have been encouraged in the past to speak directly with the nurse manager or one of the nurses in the event of any problem or concern that I may have with one of the aides rather than discuss it directly with the aide involved.

March 3, 2012

Coconut Oil to Improve Memory

When I first saw Mom and greeted her, I told her that I had read that adding coconut oil to a person's diet could help improve her memory and reduce her symptoms. I went on to say that we may be able to do that for her. I asked her if she liked that. Mom emphatically said, "Yes," grabbed my hand, and held onto it with both of her hands. It seemed like she was hanging on to me for dear life. She understood what an opportunity this discovery could hold for her. It made me realize on a more profound level how much she has to deal with every day knowing that her memory and other functions aren't working as well and are slowly getting worse.

Mary showed up, and we took Mom out of the dining room to her room. On the way over, we stopped at the nurse's station to tell them about coconut oil. Mom was still holding tightly to my hand with both of her hands. I felt so bad for her. I realized how frightened she is of her condition and how desperate she is to get better. I would feel the exact same way if I had Alzheimer's disease.

March 4, 2012

I'm Slipping!

After Mom had her dinner, she started to fall asleep for a while. I asked the nurse if she could get Mom's aide to put her to bed early, and she said that she would.

I took Mom out to the hallway across from the nurse's station. I was saying good-bye to her. At one point, the nurse manager walked up. All of a sudden, Mom said, "I'm slipping!" I turned to the nurse manager and said, "Did you hear what my mom said?" The nurse manager said that she had. I knew what Mom meant. She realized that she was mentally slipping and was not as good as she used to be. I told Mom that I was working on getting something into her diet soon that might help her. I'll do anything possible to help her.

March 11, 2012

Mom Meets My Friend Stacy

I was with Mom in the café on the main floor, and my friend Stacy happened to be there. I originally met Stacy at the nursing home sometime in the fall of 2011, when she was there with her mom, who needed physical rehabilitation. It turned out that we had grown up in the same town and knew a lot of the same people from our high school years. It was fun talking about the old times and the people we knew and generally catching up on things.

This was the first time that Mom had met Stacy. Stacy joined us at our table for a while, and Mom started reaching for Stacy's handbag. I guess that she liked the color of it. I said, "No, Mom, that's her handbag." Stacy was okay with it. It was nice that she understood what Mom was doing and why she was doing it. She let Mom hold her handbag and look it over. Stacy asked if I had a handbag at home for Mom, and I said that I did. Stacy recommended that I bring one that had some color to it, in the event that I had one like that. I said that I would.

While Stacy was still there, I blew a kiss to Mom, and she responded in kind. I thought that it was so adorable. After Stacy said good-bye and left, Mom took my hand and started kissing it. It was Mom's way of saying that she was glad that I had taken her to the café and that she enjoyed meeting someone new. Mom has always appreciated the simple joys of life. She appreciates them even more now.

March 20, 2012

Confronting the Mayor

I visited Mom with Mary, and we had a nice visit. When we were taking Mom back out, we asked Ray, a nurse, if we could leave Mom out across from the nurse's station, and he said we could. We were getting ready to leave Mom for the evening, so Mary and I were saying good-bye. At this time, the Mayor was coming down the hallway in her wheelchair, asking if someone could take her to the bathroom. As she got closer, she even asked me if I could do it. I told her that I couldn't, that an aide would have to take her to the bathroom. At that same time, an aide walked right past us, and the Mayor asked me if she was an aide. I didn't answer. I didn't want to get the aide mad at me. I didn't know whether or not she was on her way to do something else. Also, unfortunately for the Mayor, it's not my responsibility to ask the aide to help her. Both the unit nurse and the aide were right there at the time she made her request. Ray, the nurse, told the Mayor that he would get someone for her. In the event that a resident ever needs some type of assistance and the staff isn't aware of it for some reason, I have always notified them of it. Besides being a loving and devoted caregiver to my mom, I'm also a good neighbor and champion for all of the other residents in her unit.

My instincts told me to stay in the area until the Mayor's problem was taken care of. I know that Mom doesn't like a lot of noise, and I had a feeling that she might react if the Mayor kept talking loudly and complaining, although I did understand where the Mayor was coming from. I would have felt the same way if I were in her shoes. I expressed my concern to Ray that something might happen between Mom and the Mayor if we left then, but he said not to worry, that he would take care of everything.

Mary and I said good-bye to Mom. We were walking down the hallway and starting to make the turn down the next hallway to leave the unit. I asked Mary to wait another minute to make sure that everything was going to be okay. Sure enough, the Mayor started talking very loudly and complaining again. Mom made a comment to shush her in order to get her to talk lower. The Mayor turned to Mom and said, "Shut up," adding something about it not involving her. As soon as I heard that, I made a beeline over to the Mayor, with Mary following close behind. I said to the Mayor in a firm manner, "You don't tell my mom to shut up. Don't you speak to her that way!" Mary reiterated what I'd said, and the Mayor seemed surprised when we showed up and defended our mom. She said something to me, although I don't remember exactly what it was. I then said, "I don't want you to ever speak to my mom that way. She can't help it. She doesn't like a lot of noise." Ray was listening in and took our side.

I told Ray, "You see? I know my mom. I had a sense that something was going to happen." I leaned over to Mom to say good-bye again. As I was trying to give her a kiss on the cheek, Mom turned her face toward me and kissed me on the lips. I knew right away that this was Mom's way of saying thank you. She really appreciated what we had just done for her.

I'm happy to do anything that I can for my mom. Like I say sometimes, I would get into a cage alone with a hungry tiger if I had to do it in order to protect my mom. I will do anything, absolutely anything, to help my mom at any time.

March 21, 2012
Lesson in Empathy
I called the nursing home to speak with the nurse about the possibility of reducing some of my mom's prescription medicine. I was mainly concerned about the amount that they were giving her on a daily basis

to help keep her calm. When I called, I got to speak with Ava, the nurse on duty at the time. She said that she would relay my concern to Tammy. I also mentioned what had happened the day before between my mom and the Mayor, and Ava said something like, "Well, you know that these people don't know what they're saying." I felt like saying, "I appreciate your empathic response." I ended up telling her that I didn't think that was the case in this situation. I said that the Mayor is a much higher-functioning person than Mom is and knew what she was saying when she said it. I continued by saying that I had handled the situation in an appropriate manner. I told Ava that I was firm with the woman and spoke to her in a calm and direct way. I also told her that I have the right to defend and protect my mom at all times, no matter where an attack or danger comes from. I could feel the tension between us. I got the impression that Ava didn't like what I had to say. If that was the case, then it's just too bad. I'm sure that she'd feel differently about it if her mother or someone else that she really loved was in the situation that my mom had been in.

March 22, 2012

Request to Reply to Message within Twenty-Four Hours

I called the nursing home to follow up on some things with Tammy, and Ava answered the phone. I asked her if Tammy was available, but she said that Tammy was in some meetings that day. I said that I would call back later. As I was thanking her and saying good-bye, Ava hung up on me without saying good-bye. I felt as if she was retaliating against me because of our tense phone conversation the day before.

I called back and spoke to Tammy around four o'clock. I told her that I was concerned because there had been a delay of over twenty-four hours on my request to speak with her about my mom's medications, and she said that she hadn't gotten the message. Tammy asked if I wanted to make a suggestion, and I said that whoever answers the phone and takes a message should write it down right away and put it in her message box. I didn't know whether Tammy was offended by my pointing out that I hadn't heard back from anyone in over twenty-four hours. I said that I apologized to her if I had ever hurt her or anyone else's feelings. I like to be direct when I feel the need to do so, but I always try to be as diplomatic as possible.

I also told Tammy about the incident between my mom and the Mayor and made a direct request that Tammy help ensure that no one ever speaks to my mom that way again. I told her that my mom is the sweetest person in the world and doesn't mean anything personal when she speaks up like that. I went on to say that I appreciate the efforts of the staff and that I try to strike the appropriate balance between advocating for my mom and allowing the staff to do their jobs.

April 1, 2012

Mom Asks for Her Grandma

Mary and I went in to see Mom. When we took her to her room, Mom said something that I didn't understand. I wasn't sure, but I thought that she might be talking about one of her relatives. I said, "Are you talking about your grandma, Mom?" Mom replied, "What did she say?" It hurts me to know that Mom thinks that her grandma (the woman who raised her) is still alive. It also hurts that Mom would think that her beloved grandma is alive and isn't trying to see her or to get in touch with her. I explained to Mom that her grandma had passed away and that she was watching over her from heaven. As I stated before, my mom's grandma raised her for ten years of her childhood. Mom then went to live with her mom and stepfather through high school. However, she always returned to Massachusetts to stay with her grandparents during her summers off from school. Mom's grandma was really her mom. I know that my mom loved her like she was her mom. I also know that Mom's grandma loved her like she was her own daughter.

Later on, I was telling Mom how wonderful she is and how I would rather be with her than with anyone else in the world. Mom listened and said, "Good." I laughed and told Mary what Mom had said, and Mom said, "Sure," with her New England accent. I laughed again.

A little while later, I was sitting next to Mom and telling her how wonderful she is again. I sometimes repeat things to her during a visit to enable her to remember them better. I also do it to make sure that she knows how much I love her and care about her. I told her that I wished that I could sit next to her and hug her all day. Mom said, "No, thank you." I laughed. She's so funny!

April 15, 2012
Stars and Stripes Forever
After I helped Mom with her dinner and dessert, I cleared the area and cleaned off her glasses. A short time later, Mom reached over to me and ran her hand down the side of my face and the back of my head. This was Mom's way of saying that she loves and appreciates me.

During my visit, Mom and I watched the *60 Minutes* tribute to Mike Wallace. During a portion of the program, Mike Wallace was interviewing pianist Vladimir Horowitz, and Wallace got Horowitz to play "Stars and Stripes Forever." When Mom heard the song, she said, "I like that." I said, "Yes, Mom. It's the 'Stars and Stripes Forever.'" I was happy to hear Mom indicate that she recognized the song. I'm sure that it brought back memories for her. Mom and Dad were always very patriotic.

When I was getting ready to leave and taking Mom out of her room, I said, "I had a lot of fun with you today, Mom." She asked, "Did you really?" as if she didn't believe it or wasn't sure. I said, "Of course I did, Mom." I told her that I would be back on Tuesday, in two days. Mom said, "Okay."

I left Mom across from the nurse's station and said my final good-bye. As I was walking away, I said, "Good-bye, Mom. I'll see you in two days." Mom smiled her world-famous smile, said, "Okay, thank you," and winked at me right after she said it. Priceless!

April 24, 2012

Zone of Protection

I saw Mom and greeted her in a very warm and loving way, like I always do. I said, "Hi, Mom" and started calling her a sweetheart. Mom said, "Sweetheart," back to me. Mom really is a sweetheart. She's the sweetest person in the world to me.

When I was leaving for the evening, I took Mom back out to the nurse's station. I talked to the nurses and said something about how I protect Mom from head to toe, creating a "zone of protection" around her. The nurses liked what I was saying and laughed. I meant it. If I could create an invisible zone of protection around my mom that would protect her at all times, I would do it. In the meantime, I create my own "zone of protection" and do whatever it takes to make sure that she is always as happy, healthy, safe, secure, and peaceful as she can be.

April 29, 2012

Residents Lined Up in the Hallway After the Concert

When I went in to see Mom, she was in the social room at a music concert for the residents. I went to Mom's room first so that I could drop my stuff off before I went back to get her.

When I was heading back to the social room, I bumped into Trudy, the daughter of one of the residents whom I have known for over four years, and we greeted each other. I noticed that the aides were starting to line up the residents in the hallway entrance to the unit, signifying that the concert was over.

As I looked down the hallway, I saw that Mom was on the left side in the second or third position from the front of the line. It seemed so sad to me that the aides had to line up the residents that way before they took them fully into the unit, but I guess that this is the most efficient way of doing it. The residents seemed like young children to me, waiting for someone to come and bring them back to where they needed to go. They seemed so precious, and yet so helpless, as they were being lined up in their wheelchairs on each side of the hallway.

As I looked over at Mom, our eyes engaged. Mom waved her hand at me and had a big smile on her face. She was motioning for me to come over to her. I was glad that Mom recognized me. It was both heartwarming and heartbreaking at the same time. I'm angry and sad that Mom has this disease and is confined to a wheelchair and to a nursing home. I love her so much. I just wanted to rush over there, sweep her up in my arms, and get rid of her terrible disease. I could then take her home where she belongs, and we could live happily ever after. Just as I was getting ready to head over to Mom, Trudy said, "Go to your mom." I thanked her and said good-bye.

After greeting Mom, I asked her if she wanted to go downstairs for ice cream. Mom said, "Okay." I let the nurses know that I was going down to the café with her for about one hour.

I took Mom to the café and set her up at a table there. I got each of us a Häagen-Dazs dark-chocolate-covered chocolate ice cream bar. What a delightful decadence! I helped Mom with her ice cream. While she was eating it, I said, "It tastes good, doesn't it, Mom?" and she said, "You bet!" I love it when she says that. It's one of my favorite expressions of the many ones that she uses.

Later on, when Mom and I were back in her room, I said, "Everybody likes you, Mom." She said, "Really?" as if she didn't believe it. I replied, "Yes, you're wonderful." Mom said, "That's lovely." She's just so cute and adorable!

May 5, 2012

Home

At one point during my visit with Mom, she said, "Home." Then she said, "Please, I can't do this." Mom was saying that she wanted to go home and that she couldn't live in a nursing home anymore. When Mom said, "Please, I can't do this," she meant that she can't live with being confined to a wheelchair, in a nursing home, dependent on other people for so many things, and not able to fully enjoy her life and have the independence and quality of life that she used to have.

In that moment, I said what I normally do to comfort her. I totally understand how she feels and what she must be going through on a daily basis. It is even more pronounced because she is a mom who worked hard all her life raising four children and was married for such a long time. Home means so much to her. I wish that I could wave a magic wand and make her better again. This disease is most difficult on her. She lives with it every minute of every day. It's difficult on us, also.

May 11, 2012

Visit to Mom's Dermatologist

I accompanied Mom to an appointment with her dermatologist. I had noticed something unusual on her face a few weeks earlier. The doctor looked at it and recommended that she be taken in for a biopsy, which revealed that Mom had squamous cell carcinoma. We had to have it removed.

I seemed to be the only person catching these skin problems on her. For the previous year or so, I had noticed certain things on Mom's skin. The previous time, a skin abrasion on the upper part of her chest had also turned out to be squamous cell carcinoma. The only reason that I had noticed something then was because Mom happened to pull down on the top of her blouse. I noticed it right away and brought it to the attention of the nursing staff. The next time the doctor came by to check on Mom, she recommended that we come to her office for a biopsy, which we did, and we ended up having that spot removed because it was cancerous.

I was happy to help Mom and to bring problems to the attention of the appropriate people. However, it is the responsibility of the aides to report anything unusual on residents' bodies. They spend time with the residents and help them get changed for bed and get them prepared in the morning. They also change the residents whenever they need to be changed. In addition, they give the residents their baths or showers. It is their responsibility, along with the nursing staff, to mention anything unusual that they notice on the residents' skin. My main concern is what might happen if I don't see something on Mom because it's in an area that I can't see. I can see only those areas that are viewable when she is in her everyday clothes. I'm happy to help my mom in any way that I can. However, it shouldn't be left up to me to find these things.

As we were in the ambulette and driving to the doctor's office, Mom was looking around and noticing things. I could tell that she was happy because it was a beautiful, sunny day. Mom does get to go outside whenever they take the residents out to the back of the facility. The grounds are lovely, and there's a lot of beautiful scenery for them. However, the only time that Mom really gets off the campus is when she has to go to an off-site doctor's appointment or to the hospital, neither of which happen very often because many of the doctors have offices inside the facility. Mary and I promised Mom that we would take her out once a month when the weather got warmer and take her to Mary's place for a nice lunch.

On our way to the doctor's office, Mom said, "It's pretty." I noticed that we had just passed a nice house on a pretty piece of property, so I asked Mom if she was saying that the house was pretty. Mom said, "Yes." I said, "That's good, Mom."

When Mom was in the surgery room of the doctor's office, I told her several times about what was about to transpire. I try to help prepare Mom emotionally as much as possible for what will happen. Of course, I do it in a loving and comforting way. During the beginning of the surgery, Mom didn't react to being injected with a needle to numb the area that was being worked on. I was holding Mom's hands down so that she wouldn't interfere with the work. Mom can't help her reactions in situations like this. She doesn't understand what is being done to her; she only knows that it hurts. She reacts to the pain. At one point, Mom started to get agitated when the doctor was using a laser to burn off the skin that she had just peeled away from Mom's face. The doctor gave Mom a third injection to make sure that she didn't feel any pain. I could feel Mom's strength. She was trying to break free of my grip. Of course, I talked to Mom throughout the procedure to comfort her and to let her know that it was almost over. When I told the doctor's assistant at the front desk about it before we left, she remarked that it's good that Mom still has that fight in her. I completely agree.

When we first got into the ambulette for the return trip to the nursing home, I watched the driver get Mom into the van and safely situated. I was looking back at Mom, and she smiled and winked at me. It was so touching and adorable. It was Mom's way of telling me that she was okay and that she appreciated all that I was doing for her. God bless Mom!

May 15, 2012
Mom Gets Agitated, and I Show Up at the Right Time
I walked down the hall in Mom's unit and looked into the dining room
to see where she was seated. I started to head directly to her room so
that I could drop off my jacket and notebook. At this point, I was about
twenty feet away from the entrance to the dining room. All of a sudden,
I heard a woman's voice being raised in the room. As I listened, I realized
that it was Mom's voice. Sometimes Mom gets agitated and starts to say
things loudly. I totally understand why she would do that.

As soon as I heard her voice, I turned around and headed straight back
to the dining room. I walked in and made sure that Mom could see me. I
approached her and said, "What's the matter? What's the matter, Mom?"
At first, she had a surprised look on her face. She hadn't expected me to
show up, but I could tell that she recognized me. I started to comfort
her. I gave her a nice hug and kissed her on the cheek, and she kissed
me back. I loved it. I was especially happy to be there when she really
needed to be comforted by a loved one.

I noticed that the aides were just sitting or standing by the table near to
where my mom was seated and hadn't done anything. I feel as if some of
them do only the minimum and don't go out of their way for anyone. I
decided that I would bring it up to the nurse manager the next time that
I was there to visit. I feel strongly that either a nurse or an aide should
take a moment to go over and try to comfort and reassure an Alzheimer's
patient who is in distress. I'm sure that if it was a close relative of their
own, they would go over to that person and really try to help. Also, the
staff of the previous facility that Mom was in would comfort residents
that were in distress. This is another reason that you have to continue
to advocate on behalf of your loved one. Whenever your loved one has
to be moved to another facility, there are problems that can come up
that may not have been problems at the previous place. In fairness, there

may also be things that the new facility does better than the previous one on behalf of their residents.

People with dementia are at the mercy of the disease. They need all the love, attention, and compassion that they can get. They should always be treated with respect and dignity and be allowed to live that way at all times. If someone had a baby and the baby was crying for help, would it be okay for the parent or guardian to ignore the child and not try to help? No, it wouldn't. The same standard should always be applied to people suffering from Alzheimer's disease.

May 24, 2012
Mom Claps at Performance and Tries to Whistle
I went with Mom to the nurse's station to speak to the nurse about my mom's medication. I told the nurse that I was concerned because they were giving Mom two separate medications within an hour of her dinner time, and it was making her too sleepy to eat much of anything. The nurse said that she would check it out and let me know.

I took Mom to her room, and we started watching *The View*. During the show, the cast of *Jesus Christ Superstar* performed the title song, and I told Mom what it was that they were performing. During the performance, I told Mom that she was a superstar. She grabbed my hand and started kissing it. She was showing her appreciation. It was a sincere compliment that came straight from my heart.

After the performance was over, Mom started clapping her hands and trying to whistle. I was happy to see it. I was also pleasantly surprised that Mom was trying to whistle. It was the first time that I remember seeing her try in many years. She used to whistle by placing her thumb and index finger between her lips and whistling through them, making a loud and piercing whistle. She used that whistle to call us in for dinner when we were kids. I could hear my mom's whistle from a block away. This time, however, Mom was trying to whistle without her fingers. She probably forgot that she used to whistle using her fingers, but I was still happy to see her try. She demonstrated that she has some memory of whistling, and she can still show a strong measure of emotion when she is happy.

A little while later, I turned to Mom and said, "I love you." Mom replied, "How much?" I laughed. She's so cute! I told her that I love her so much that my love for her is infinite. Right after that, Mom said, "Let's go." It always hurts whenever she says this. I explained to her very gently and lovingly why she was there. I also told her that if I could take her back home, I would do so.

May 25, 2012
Caring for the Caregiver—Part 1
It was time to go away for a little vacation. I had scheduled a getaway for the Memorial Day weekend (Friday, May 25, to Monday, May 28) to get some much-needed time off. I had reserved a spot at the Omega Institute in Rhinebeck, New York, for their Rest and Rejuvenation (R&R) weekend program.

By the time I had finished packing that morning, filled the car with gas, added oil to my engine, and checked and adjusted the air in my tires, it was 11:47 a.m. It was the official starting time of my trip.

I was excited at the prospect of getting away from it all. As all caregivers know, you need to take care of yourself while you're on this long and arduous journey of loving and caring for a loved one with Alzheimer's disease. I was driving into upstate New York on the way up to Rhinebeck. At some point I needed to find a restroom. I had to get off at a certain exit while the situation was still under control, and I chose one that had a sign indicating that there was a restaurant nearby. I decided I might have to get something to eat there so that they didn't think that I was just there to use their restroom.

As I was driving down this long and winding road, it seemed somewhat familiar to me. I recalled going down a similar road a few years before when I attended my first R&R weekend at the Omega Institute. As I went farther down the road, I noticed that it forked off to the left and went in another direction. After the stop sign, I passed a few other landmarks. All of a sudden, I noticed a funeral home with a nice-sized parking lot on the right side. It turned out to be the exact same funeral home that I had used a few years before when I had to make a rest stop back then. How remarkable! Both times that I had to stop, I ended up picking the exact same exit off of the highway. It was a complete coincidence. I didn't remember that particular exit from the first time that I had used it. I went to the same funeral home and used the restroom there. I was so grateful to the proprietors of this funeral home. I thought that maybe I should send them a thank you card for allowing me to use their facility. If I don't send a thank you card, then maybe, when I pass away, I can have my wake held there as a way of thanking them for their hospitality. You know, you really can't make this stuff up.

After taking my restroom break, I got back on the road and headed to Omega. This would be my sixth time on their campus in Rhinebeck. I also did three additional weekends at the seminar that they hold in New York City every year.

It was about two o'clock in the afternoon when I arrived on the beautiful, 195-acre campus. I checked my bags in and went to registration. I could check into my room at 5:00 p.m. I went to the café and got some complimentary coffee that was available to the R&R participants.

After I checked into my room and got things set up, I made my way to the cafeteria for dinner. Omega serves only vegetarian meals in their cafeteria. I had forgotten that vegetarian meals could be so good. The first night, they offered a lentil meat loaf with mashed potatoes, which had chunks of potatoes in it. They also had mushroom gravy. I poured it over my lentil meat loaf and potatoes, and it was absolutely delicious! The second night, they had a tempeh Reuben dinner. I added some organic sauerkraut and shredded Swiss cheese to mine, and it came very close to tasting like an actual Reuben. It was also delicious! The third night, the cafeteria offered whole-wheat tortillas and assorted toppings. I put refried beans, salsa, cheese, black olives, and more on the top of the tortilla—another wonderful vegetarian meal. It made me feel better inside. I got such a feeling of well-being and had more energy as a result of eating all of this wonderful vegetarian food. Of course, they also had salad, other vegetables, and whole grains to choose from. After experiencing this wonderful cuisine, I decided that I had to commit to eating more vegetarian fare and to start juicing.

On Friday night, May 25, we had a greeting and orientation for the R&R participants. After that, all were invited over to the library to see a movie screening of *No Impact Man* and have a follow-up Q&A session with the main subject of the documentary. It is the true story of a man, his wife, and their little daughter trying to live in New York City for one year without electricity, refrigeration, air conditioning, eating out, toilet paper, and so on. It seemed like it was an extremely difficult thing to do. I enjoyed the lessons from the movie and the follow-up Q&A session.

May 26, 2012
Caring for the Caregiver—Part 2
Every morning, Omega offers early-morning classes in yoga, meditation, and tai chi to participants who choose to get up early and participate. This particular morning, I got up early, showered, and decided to go directly to the cafeteria for breakfast instead. After breakfast, I attend-

ed a workshop in Reiki magic group healing from 10:00 to 11:00 that morning. It was definitely relaxing.

After I had finished my lunch, I went on a guided tour of the Omega Center for Sustainable Living (OCSL). It was very interesting to see how Omega processed water on the campus in an environmentally sound way. I went to the café later for my complimentary coffee and tea.

I noticed that they offered an open twelve-step program meeting to anyone who wanted to attend, and I went out of curiosity. It was very interesting. I ended up meeting new people and making some new friends. After dinner, the musical performance for the evening was an earth harp concert. The musician had long harp wires extending along almost the entire length of the inside of the facility. I thought that it was very interesting; it made a variety of sounds. However, after about fifteen minutes, I decided that it wasn't my cup of tea unless the musician was able to play some rock-and-roll music. I left and headed to the café, where I could listen to their music being piped in and spend some time on the public computer looking at the news, sports, and so on.

May 27, 2012

Caring for the Caregiver—Part 3

I got up early in the morning and took my shower. I decided that I didn't want to do any of the early-morning classes and again headed straight to the cafeteria for breakfast.

At 10:00 a.m., I attended a session called Mettā Meditation. It was basically a meditation of loving kindness to oneself and others. It was very interesting. It's important to show yourself as much loving kindness and compassion as possible on a daily basis. Giving ourselves loving kindness and compassion can take many different forms. For me, it starts with taking good care of my basic needs. I try to eat well, get enough rest, and do what needs to be done each and every day. After that, loving kindness and compassion could involve meeting up with friends, buying myself a new book to read, going for a walk, seeing a movie, listening to music, catching up on things on the Internet, going shopping for clothes, and so on. Please believe me when I say, "You need it." The loved one that you give so much of yourself to wants you to have it. All of your other loved ones and friends want it for you. You benefit from it, your loved one will benefit from it, and the world benefits from it. It's really that important! I also believe that it's proportionate. The degree to which you take care of yourself is the degree to which you will be better in every area of your life.

After leaving that class, I bumped into a woman I had met at Omega earlier that weekend. She asked me what I was doing, and I said that I was heading back to my room for a while. She asked me if I wanted to join her in kayaking on the lake. I said that I didn't have any sunscreen on, but she told me that she was only going out for a little while. I agreed to go. She allowed me to put my personal stuff (cell phone, wallet, keys, and such) in the trunk of her car so that they wouldn't get wet while I was kayaking. I was out on the lake for about a half hour or so. I kayaked across the lake and saw the eagle's nest that the Omega staff had said was there. When I took the kayak back in, my friend let me get my personal belongings out of her trunk. I knew that I was going to be sunburned from being out there for over half an hour without any sunscreen.

After kayaking, I attended a dance/movement class. It was so much fun moving and dancing to music under the guidance of the instructor. I also found it to be very creative and stimulating. During one of the exercises, we had to pick up a scarf and use it to dance and express ourselves with, and I came up with an inspirational idea. After this class, I had lunch and then saw a guy who had been in the dance/movement class. I had originally talked to him after the class because he was wearing a Beatles shirt, discussing my love of their music and some other musicians and bands that I like. I went over in the hope that I could continue my music discussion with him. It turned out that he was a musician and a singer. I talked with him outside at a table, again exposed to direct sunlight without the benefit of sunscreen. I knew that it would just make my sunburn worse. However, I really enjoyed talking about music. At the end of our conversation, he thanked me for sharing my passion for music with him.

Later on, I went to the café and had my complimentary coffee and tea. After dinner, I went over to the concert, which involved musicians who were playing music and chanting. I stayed outside of the venue to see if I liked the music enough to go in. It started getting dark out, and the mosquitoes were getting ready for their evening meal. I knew that I would soon become the choicest part of their buffet. They have always seemed to like my blood. I decided to leave before I became an unwilling host to their feeding frenzy, and I went over to the bookstore and bought a book.

May 28, 2012

Caring for the Caregiver—Part 4

I woke up, took my shower and then decided to attend one of the early-morning exercise classes before I went over to have my breakfast. I participated in the qigong/tai chi class. It was very interesting and helpful. Afterward, I went over to the cafeteria.

A little while later, I attended the last workshop designed specifically for the R&R participants. It was called "The Tarot Within." I'm a little bit skeptical about these things. I look at tarot like I look at astrology. I find it interesting, but I'm not sure what, if any, scientific validity there is to it. However, there seems to be something quite compelling about it. For example, whenever I've read about my astrological birth sign, I've been amazed at how accurately it describes me and my personality.

Toward the end of this class, the instructor allowed each of us to pick one tarot card out of the deck of seventy-eight cards that were in a cloth bag. The instructor asked us to pick a card and cover it with both hands until she let us know that it would be okay to look at it. When the bag got to me, I searched around in it with my hand to pick the card that felt right to me. For some reason, I felt that my hands were pulsing with the card that I held in between them. It may have just been my imagination. I'm really not sure. It just felt like the card for me to pick.

The instructor advised us to say one or two words to describe our reaction to or feeling about the tarot card when we first revealed it. We were divided into groups of four people, and when I looked at my card, I said, "This stinks!" The card portrayed a person lying on a flat surface with three swords hanging over his head and one sword lying horizontally underneath. There was also a stained-glass window in the upper background of the picture. My initial thought was that it was negative and that it predicted something bad for me. The instructor allowed us to show our cards individually to her so that she could interpret what they meant. When I showed her my card, she said that it meant that I needed to rest. She also said that I needed to let go. I couldn't believe it! The women in the immediate area and I were astounded by what she said. It was an absolute bull's-eye. It wasn't what I expected her to say. However, when she said it, it felt so true and real to me. I had gone up for the weekend to rest and relax because of all the stress that I had been under, especially when it comes to caring for my mom.

It actually took me a while to unwind after I first arrived at Omega. I got there on Friday afternoon and started to feel like I was getting into the mellow vibe sometime on Saturday afternoon. I spoke to an instructor there on my final day, Monday, May 28. I told him that now that I was totally into the Omega experience, I had to go home. He laughed. Life is funny that way.

I ended up driving a woman whom I had met at Omega that weekend back to Manhattan. I live on the other side of the George Washington Bridge in New Jersey, so it wasn't a problem for me. Besides, it was nice to have some company on the ride home.

After I returned, I shared the experience of the Omega Institute weekend with the people at my weekly volunteer club meeting. I first asked the president of our club to allow me to speak about my weekend, promising that it wasn't going to be a "what I did on my summer vacation" presentation but a time to share some things that I thought would be relevant and interesting to the group. He agreed to let me speak about it during the portion of the meeting in which we share club news and have a guest speaker. One of the things that I said was that there is a difference between knowing that you need to go away and actually doing it. After I came back from this weekend, I realized how badly I had needed to get away. It took being away for the Memorial Day weekend to fully realize how much stress and pressure that I had been under. I was able to notice a positive difference in the way that I felt and in my lowered level of stress. It proved to me what a strain that I had been under without fully knowing it. I strongly encourage all caregivers to try to get away at least once per year, if possible.

May 29, 2012
Brown

As I was visiting with Mom, she pointed to my shirt and said, "Brown." I was wearing a brown T-shirt with some lettering on the front and back. I was so happy to hear Mom identify the color and say the word clearly. I love it when Mom demonstrates that she still has it. I always consider it a milestone whenever Mom says something that surprises and delights me. It also serves as a benchmark for me to see how she is faring with her illness.

June 2, 2012
Do You Like Me?
Mary and I were visiting with Mom, and Mary was sitting on Mom's left at the time. I was on Mom's right side by the window. At one point, Mom turned to me and said, "Do you like me?" I said, "Of course, Mom. I like you, and I love you." I appreciate that she can still verbalize her feelings. It hurts me to think that Mom would ever have any doubt about how much I truly love her and care about her. It's one of the more unfortunate aspects of her disease. However, I always reassure her in the moment. I also tell her that I love her many times during each visit.

Before we left for the evening, I told Mom that she makes life worth living. I meant it from the bottom of my heart. I don't know what I'll do in this world without her.

June 3, 2012
I Know What Mom Wants
Mary and I visited Mom, and I asked Mom if she wanted to go downstairs for a while. She was very happy to hear that suggestion. She motioned for me to come over and then started kissing my face. I said, "Thanks, Mom." I then said, "You see, I know what Mom wants." When we were down at the café, I bought her a strawberry shortcake ice cream, and I had a cup of coffee. It was fun to see Mom eat her ice cream. She ate all of it right off of the stick. I was so proud of her. It was just like Mom. She wouldn't let anything go to waste, especially something sweet like ice cream. Believe me when I say that if I could live off of ice cream and a lot of other things that aren't considered healthy to eat, I would. It's funny how the things that taste the best are, more often than not, some of the worst things to eat for a balanced and nutritious diet.

After leaving the café, we took Mom on a tour of the facility. We also took her to the main lobby area and looked at some magazines. She seemed to be enjoying everything. A woman showed up with her two little girls and her baby. We told her that Mom loves kids and babies, and Mom smiled at the girls. The woman was nice enough to show Mom her baby in the carriage. I really appreciated it and thanked her. Her husband showed up a few minutes later, and they went off to visit a relative. They were such a nice family.

We went back upstairs and helped Mom with her dinner. A while later, our brother John showed up. It was good to see him there. I was grateful that Mom could spend time with another one of her children.

Around eight o'clock that evening, I asked John if he was going to stay with Mom for a little while because Mary and I were leaving, but John said that he had to go back to work. Since it was a Sunday evening, I grimaced when he said that. Mom laughed when she saw my expression.

June 10, 2012
Mom Really Listens to What I Say
I went to see Mom early, and the nursing home was having a music concert for the residents. I wanted to be with Mom so we could enjoy the music together, and I took her downstairs to the concert. I told the nurses in the unit that we were going downstairs and then to the café and that I'd have Mom back within an hour or so.

When we went downstairs to the concert, the room was full. Some residents were stationed outside the room in their wheelchairs, listening from there. I stayed in that area with Mom for a few minutes. The music was okay, but I didn't think that it was interesting enough for us to stay there. So I took Mom to the café instead. I bought her a strawberry shortcake ice cream and a sandwich for myself. After Mom finished her ice cream, I went over to the table outside the café to get some refreshments that were there for the residents. I got Mom a small plate of mixed fruit and a few cookies, and I got a small bottle of water for myself. Mom enjoyed everything.

A little while later, I took Mom outside to the back area of the nursing home, where there are tables with large umbrellas that block the sun. Mom became even happier as soon as I took her outside. A beautiful smile came across her face. It was sunny and partly cloudy outside, and there was a nice breeze in the air.

I took Mom to the table where Carmella, a private aide, was sitting with the resident she works for. Carmella is originally from Jamaica, and we talked about her experience growing up there. I told Carmella about what I'd been up to recently in my life. I mentioned that I had some money saved and that I had had to sell some stock recently to pay my bills. As soon as I finished saying it, Mom said, "How much?" I laughed. Even though Mom may not say much during a conversation that I'm having with someone else, she listens to everything. She hears everything that I say. I explained to Mom that I don't have a lot of money but that if I did I would buy a big house and take her home with me. God bless Mom always!

June 23, 2012
Thank You for All That You Do for Me
I went to visit Mom earlier than I normally do. When I first saw her, she was with some of the other residents in the living room area.

Mom was eating a pastry. I could tell that she was happy to see me. I'm always happy to see her. I gave her a kiss and told her that I would be right back after I dropped my stuff off in her room. I had purchased some toiletries for her, and I had also brought a change of clothes because I was going out to a dance that evening. It felt nice to have plans for myself on a Saturday night.

I dropped my stuff off in Mom's room and went back to get her. I told her that I had to clean her up a little bit before I took her into her room. As I was cleaning off Mom's hands in the hallway, she said, "Thank you for all that you do for me." I was absolutely shocked that she was able to say that so clearly to me. Sometimes she surprises me with the things that she can still do. I was also very happy to hear what she said. I replied, "You're welcome, Mom. I'll do anything for you." A little while later, I told Mom that I love her, and she said, "I love you" back. Wow! That was a bonus! I thanked her.

When we were back in her room, Mom was saying something that I didn't understand. I told her that I was sorry. I told her that I was trying to understand her but can't always do it. Mom replied, "I know. It's okay." I gave her a hug and a kiss.

June 29, 2012
Alzheimer's Disease: What If There Was a Cure?
I talked to the top doctor at the nursing home about the possibility of giving my mom some coconut oil products to try to reduce the effects of her Alzheimer's disease. I had read about this in Mary T. Newport's book *Alzheimer's Disease: What If There Was a Cure?* This book is a true story about a medical doctor who did research and found that there is something in coconut oil that helped her husband, who has Alzheimer's disease.

I gave the nursing home a copy of the book. The doctor I had spoken with thought that what he had read in the book was very interesting and well written. He told me that there was nothing else that he could do for Mom at the time, so it would be okay for her to have coconut oil added to her diet. He knows Mom's medical condition and all the medications that she has to take. I was overjoyed to hear that news. It gave me a ray of hope in the midst of all of the darkness and despair of this disease.

June 30, 2012

Safety First!

When I first went in to see Mom, she was chewing on a piece of a paper towel that was in front of her. The nurses and the aides know that she will do this from time to time. I think that she does it because she misses chewing gum. However, the staff also knows that we are concerned about it. It is a safety issue because Mom could eventually try to swallow it. It is a potential choking hazard.

I got one of the aides, Rose, to help me extract the pieces of paper towel from Mom's mouth. I also notified the nurse on staff about it. I feel that they should keep a closer eye on Mom and all the other residents at all times whenever they are out in a public area. People with Alzheimer's disease are capable of doing things that could be unsafe for them at any time. Besides, the staff should know better than to leave a paper towel in front of my mom. They already know that she chews on them. Thank God I was there at the right moment, again, to help Mom.

July 1, 2012

Thank God I Was There Again

I went to see Mom in the morning because I had to leave early that day for another commitment. I took her down to the café and bought her a Klondike ice cream bar. When I took her back up to her room and set her up with her lunch, I found a chicken bone in her food that was an inch to an inch and a quarter long. I got rid of it right away and told the nurse on duty about it. Thank God that I was there both days for the paper towel and the chicken bone incidents. I resolved to tell the head nurse of the unit about both the next time that I was there to visit Mom.

July 17, 2012

Problem Aide Gives Me a Dirty Look

I visited Mom after having been away for almost one week. I had gotten a respiratory infection from one of the residents there who had been coughing and such. Anyway, I went to get Mom at the table to take her back to her room, but she looked at me and seemed agitated. She started to yell at me. I didn't understand why, but I know that Mom gets agitated from time to time. As I was getting her ready to go back to her room, I noticed that some of the aides were looking over at me to see what was going on. Of course, nothing was going on except that Mom was agitated. I didn't know it at the time—because the nursing staff hadn't told me—but Mom was suffering from an infection. That was what was bothering her and making her agitated.

I turned around as I was helping Mom. I had the feeling that someone was looking at me. When I turned around and looked, I saw that an aide was giving me a dirty look. I knew right away why she looked at me that way. She had been Mom's aide about a year before, and at that time, I observed that she was being a little rough in caring for my mom. I had gone to the head nurse and complained about it, and I found out a few days later that she had been written up for it. That's when the "dirty looks" campaign started. I tried to ignore it for a long time and even gave her a look a few weeks back that imitated and mocked the look that she was giving to me. Anyway, at this point, I had had it with her shenanigans. It was heartless that she would give me a dirty look while I was trying to help my mom, who was obviously distraught at the time. I mentioned her behavior at the quarterly interdisciplinary care meeting a few days later, and the staff said that they would look into it. I followed up several times to make sure that the matter was addressed, and I found out that she had been spoken to about it. That's when I noticed a change in her behavior—no more dirty looks, at least for the time being.

July 24, 2012

Why Should I Have Compassion for Her?

As I entered the dining room to get Mom, one of the other residents there was complaining but not saying anything clearly definable. Another resident started to scold her by saying, "Oh, will you stop your whining..." I defended the woman, saying, "Why don't you leave her alone. She can't help it." I then said, "Do you know that she's ninety-five years old?" I told the other resident to have some compassion for her, and she replied, "Why should I have compassion for her?" I said, "Because you should." At that point, the resident stopped berating the woman. I wished that I had told the other resident at that time, "You should have compassion for her because you wouldn't want someone talking to you like that if you were in her shoes."

August 11, 2012

Take Me

At one point while I was visiting with Mom, she started to lean out of her wheelchair and said, "Take me." She has done this a few times in the past because she wants me to take her home with me. It is absolutely heartbreaking to hear her say that. I always explain to her that I can't take her home with me now but that if I could, I would. I also tell her that in the meantime, she is in the best place that she can be. I mention to her that I live close by and that I come to see her as often as I can. I want nothing more than for Mom to be rid of this disease and living back at home, safe and sound, with her family.

August 29, 2012

Mom Falls Out of Her Wheelchair

I received a call from the nursing home saying that Mom had fallen out of her wheelchair. The nurse explained to me that Mom had been in the room where they have musical acts and entertainment for the residents, and at one point, she reached over for something. She leaned too far out of her wheelchair and fell out of it before the aides could get to her. The aides and the nurse checked Mom out for any possible pain, bruising, and so forth. At the time, Mom didn't seem to be hurt, but I found out later that no X-rays were taken.

I was very concerned about Mom, but I was grateful to hear that there was no apparent injury to her at that time. However, Mom should never have been able to fall out of her wheelchair. The staff there was negligent in not preventing it from happening.

August 31, 2012
Birthday Luncheon for Mom
We took Mom out to a nice local restaurant for her birthday lunch. We had to pay for an ambulette to pick her up and take her back to the nursing home because it would be difficult to take her in and out of my car several times and get her into and out of her wheelchair. Taking Mom in an ambulette is the safest way to go and it's definitely worth the extra money. That way, Mom can stay in her wheelchair.

We had thirteen people at the party, including Mom. We had a real nice time. Mom enjoyed her meal along with having her loved ones with her to celebrate her special day. It was nice to get Mom out of the nursing home for something other than a visit to the doctor's office or the hospital.

The guests also liked it because we had wine with the meal for anyone who wanted it. We also had a beautiful cake made and brought it with us to the restaurant. It was fun singing "Happy Birthday" to Mom and giving everyone cake after the meal. Mom also got some really nice birthday presents, which we always appreciate.

I didn't like one thing that happened toward the end of the luncheon. Mom started to get a little agitated, and a couple of people who were at our table both smiled and started to chuckle about it, as if seeing my mom suffering was something to laugh at. I didn't say anything to them at that time. However, I was very hurt and angered by it. They know that my mom has Alzheimer's disease and that she can't help it. Also, this wasn't the first time that they have behaved in a cruel and insensitive manner toward her. I decided to never invite them to any other functions or special occasions for our mom.

September 28, 2012

Mom's X-Rays Detect a Fracture

I was visiting with Mom on Friday, and the head nurse told me that Mom had been experiencing pain for the past few days. They took X-rays of her but didn't see anything at first. The doctor then requested an X-ray of Mom's pelvic area, and that one showed that she had a broken right femur. She had to be taken to the hospital immediately.

Before we left, I asked the head nurse of the unit along with the nursing supervisor if Mom's fracture had anything to do with her fall out of the wheelchair almost one month earlier. The head nurse first said that the fall had been a while ago. I pointed out that it had happened within the past month. The nursing supervisor said that Mom could have sustained a hairline fracture at the time of her fall that just got worse. I also knew that Mom has osteoarthritis, which may have not been the cause of the fracture but may have contributed to the pain.

I waited until the ambulette showed up and then escorted Mom to it. I told the driver that I would meet them at the hospital. I went to the waiting area outside of the emergency room and told the woman at the desk that I was there for my mom. She said that she'd let me know when Mom arrived.

I called my sister and told her about it, and she said that she'd meet me at the hospital. I also called and left messages for my two brothers.

Mary and I stayed with Mom the whole time that she was in the emergency room and later when she was transported up to a private room. I ended up being with Mom for twelve hours that day, including the time that I drove to the hospital and waited for her to arrive.

September 29, 2012
Doctor Reveals That the Fracture Is Worse Than the Initial X-Ray Showed

I got a call early in the morning (the morning after Mom was admitted) from the orthopedic doctor who had checked Mom's X-rays out, and he told me that Mom had a bilateral hip fracture, meaning that there was also a fracture on her left side that was almost identical to the one on her right side.

I asked the doctor if the fracture could be the result of her fall from her wheelchair, and he said that more sophisticated tests would have to be run that could determine when the fracture actually occurred. He didn't tell me that they *would* perform those tests.

On subsequent days, I talked to Mom's nurse practitioner about it. He stated that Mom's fracture was chronic, which meant that she had had the fracture for a while. I don't know how long she might have had it. I also don't know how he came to this conclusion when the orthopedic doctor couldn't determine when the fracture first occurred after seeing the same X-rays. Either way, I realized after talking to different professionals that it would be difficult to prove that Mom's bilateral hip fracture was directly related to her fall from her wheelchair.

I also requested a CT scan on Mom's hip and one more set of X-rays after that to see what changes, if any, had occurred. We took Mom to another orthopedic surgeon for a second opinion. Based on the first and second opinion and on what the head doctor of the facility said, it wasn't advisable for Mom to have surgery. The main reason for this was because Mom can't walk anymore. Also, she is eighty-five years old and has had Alzheimer's disease since at least January 2000. Mom has also had congestive heart failure on two different occasions over the past few years.

Additionally, as told to me by the doctors and the nursing supervisor, there are many inherent risks in surgery, especially with all the risk factors that my mom has. Some of the risks are blood loss, the possibility of getting anemia, the risk of infection or a pulmonary blood clot from surgery, the fact that people with Alzheimer's disease are more negatively affected by general anesthesia than other people are—it can make their dementia worse for an extended period of time—postoperative pain, and the chance of death in surgery or shortly thereafter. We had to weigh these risk factors against the possibility that surgery would be successful and make Mom's life better, even though she'd still be unable to walk. I was told at a later date that even if they did surgery, they wouldn't be able to completely fix the fractures. They could only make things a little bit more comfortable for Mom.

I also knew from talking to the doctor that the longevity of people with hip fractures in Mom's medical condition is not long. According to the doctor, most people don't survive more than one year after this injury. My understanding is that this is the case when surgery isn't recommended for or done on the patient. Unfortunately, based on the recommendation of all of the doctors, the nurse practitioner, and the nursing supervisor, we decided after much thought and consideration to not have Mom undergo surgery. We also knew that as long as Mom's pain was managed and kept under control with the proper pain management regimen, this was the best that we could do for her in this situation.

There are no easy decisions in matters like these. No matter which way you go, the decision is fraught with peril. It was still a very difficult decision to make. It seemed like any outcome would not be good. We had to choose the alternative that did the most good by doing the least harm for Mom. We ended up choosing the best path that we could with all things considered. Basically, we agreed with the medical assessment that to perform surgery could potentially do more harm than good. The best way to go was to treat Mom's injury conservatively.

A few weeks later, Mary and I went to a law firm to see if it was worth pursuing legal action due to the fact that Mom fell out of her wheelchair while in the activity room with the staff present. The lawyer said that it wouldn't be an open-and-shut case. For example, Mom already had osteoarthritis. Also, she started to experience pain a few weeks after the initial fall. The doctor whom I spoke to about Mom's bilateral hip fracture initially told me that they would have to run more sophisticated tests to determine when the fracture actually occurred. When I spoke to this doctor a few months later, I asked him about these tests. I don't remember his answer, but I know that he didn't say anything more definitive about it to me.

The lawyer went on to say that a legal case would involve our experts versus their experts and that it could drag on for a few years before it got resolved. She said that it would involve money and time on our part and that there was no guarantee that we would win. After hearing all of the information from the lawyer, Mary and I decided that it just wasn't worth it to pursue legal action.

Obviously, Mary and I are still angry about Mom's falling out of her wheelchair. I also know from personal experience that other caregivers have had their parents fall out of their wheelchairs at the same nursing home as our mom, either due to neglect on someone's part (a caregiver friend in our mom's unit told us that her mom was left alone in her room for a while and fell out of her wheelchair) or a mistake on the part of an aide (another caregiver friend told me about his mom, who is in a different unit in the nursing home and was thrown out of her wheelchair when the aide tried to bring her into her bathroom going forward and the wheelchair hit the lip of the entrance to the bathroom).

If it's not already a state or federal law, I strongly believe that residents in nursing homes, especially those residents with Alzheimer's disease or dementia, should, at a minimum, have a mandatory special wedge cushion on their wheelchairs that can prevent them from slipping forward, getting out, or falling out of their wheelchairs. It could help prevent a lot of unnecessary falls and the corresponding injuries. This is also important because many people with Alzheimer's disease or dementia tend to be elderly. Their bones are more brittle and more susceptible to injury or breakage.

January 26, 2013
Mom's Wedding Anniversary
If Dad were still alive, it would have been Mom and Dad's sixty-first wedding anniversary. They were married on January 26, 1952. When I went in to see Mom, I greeted her like I always do. I explained the significance of the date and wished her a happy anniversary.

I took Mom to her room to hang out and help her with her dinner. Sometime during the evening, Mom turned to me and said, "I'm sorry." She has said this particular thing to me on a few different occasions in the past, and I always feel bad when she does. I believe that Mom says it because she's sorry about all that I have to go through to help take care of her. She also may feel that she has let me down in some way. I told Mom that she has nothing to be sorry about. I went on to tell her that she needs help and that I'm happy to help her. I said that she spent many years of her life helping my siblings and me, and now it's our turn to help her.

I also said that I'm sorry for what she is going through. I told Mom that it's hard on us, but it's hardest on her. I said that I would always be by her side. My mom is my best friend and the best friend that anyone could ever hope for.

As I've mentioned before, being a main caregiver to my mom over all of these years (I've been directly involved since August 2007) has taken its toll on me. However, in spite of all of the uncertainty, stress, and anxiety that comes with it, I will never give up and will do whatever is necessary to help my mom.

January 27, 2013

I Find Mom Positioned at an Uncomfortable Angle in Her Wheelchair

As I was first entering Mom's unit to get her and take her to her room, she started to yell out in an agitated way. Carmella, the personal aide of one of the residents in Mom's unit, started laughing. She thought that Mom was yelling at me as soon as she saw me come into the dining room. I told her that Mom was yelling out just as I was first walking in, before she even noticed me. I instinctively knew that Mom was yelling because something was bothering her.

I went right over to Mom to comfort her. She started to relax immediately when she knew it was me. I noticed that Mom was lying at an uncomfortable angle in the special wheelchair she had gotten after her hip fractures were identified. Part of her upper body and head were leaning out over the top left side of the wheelchair.

I took Mom to her room. I tried to hug her upper body and move her more into the middle of the wheelchair, but Mom was at such an angle that it wasn't possible to do so. I went and told the nurse Jose that I needed someone right away to help me reposition Mom in her wheelchair. Jose said that he would get Mom's aide to help me, so I went back to Mom's room. A few minutes later, Mom started yelling out again. I tried to determine what was bothering her by asking her questions like, "Are you uncomfortable?" and "Are you in pain?" but Mom wasn't answering me. I went back out to ask Jose where the aide was. He found my mom's aide, Catherine, and as she was heading to Mom's room, I saw two other aides, Robert and George, who offered to help.

The three of them went into Mom's room to reposition her in her special wheelchair. Because of Mom's injury, they had to use the lift to get her into the air and then put her back into the proper position. They closed the door to my mom's room before they started, and I went across the hall to use the restroom. When I was in the restroom, I heard Mom let out a scream. I felt bad, but I know that she does this from time to time. She may have screamed because she was afraid when they lifted her out of the wheelchair on the lift in order to properly reposition her.

After I exited the restroom, I waited for them to finish helping Mom. They opened the door to her room and asked me to check it out. I walked in and saw Mom positioned directly in the middle of the wheelchair with pillows on each side of her body and a big pillow behind her head. I said, "It's perfect!" Not only that, but Mom was lying in her wheelchair with her eyes closed. She was very comfortable and seemed to be enjoying complete peace and relaxation. She looked like she was sleeping.

I thanked all three of the aides several times. I went back out to Jose and explained that Mom had been agitated because her position in the wheelchair, along with her injury, was causing her pain.

A little while later, I went back out to retrieve Mom's dinner tray. As I was getting it, Catherine started telling me something along the lines that Mom always yells even when they're helping her, even if there's no reason for it. She was laughing as she was telling me. I told her, "Mom has a bilateral hip fracture," but Catherine kept talking as if she didn't hear anything I said. She said more of the same and laughed about it again. I think that she was laughing because her perception was that Mom yells even if they're not hurting her. I explained to her again, "Mom has a bilateral hip fracture."

I know that she didn't have bad intentions when she said this to me. It's just that the aides sometimes need to be reminded that it's not okay to laugh at things like that. They need to be reminded to be sensitive to what is really going on for both the resident and the caregiver.

Since this happened on a Sunday, I waited until the next morning to call and tell Ava, the new head nurse of the unit, about the whole situation. Ava had recently replaced Tammy after Tammy left for another job. When I spoke to Ava on Monday morning, I first described the situation with Mom being positioned in an awkward manner in her wheelchair. Ava said this may have been because the aides who worked on the weekends were not the regular aides and may not have known exactly what to do with Mom. I asked her to make sure that all staff on every shift knows how to take care of Mom, and she said that she would do it. I'm glad that Ava was honest with me. I was also surprised and upset that the weekend aides either didn't know or weren't told about taking special precautions regarding my mom and her bilateral hip fracture. It was evident that Mom was in a special wheelchair (designed like a lounge chair that people lay on in the backyard). She was in that chair because of her injury. Doesn't anyone notice these things or care enough to ask why Mom is in a special wheelchair? I guess if it were their mom, it would be important enough to find out why she was in a different wheelchair and how she should be handled with the utmost care accordingly. I never want my mom to suffer at all. She should never suffer as a result of someone's incompetence, lack of caring, or the nursing home's not having an effective communication system that relays important, updated care information about residents to all shifts, seven days a week. Otherwise, in the event that it's not already established, a nursing home's electronic patient system must include updated patient information with an area that highlights important changes so that everyone can see it and access it no matter what shift they're working on.

I also mentioned to Ava that Catherine had been laughing when she was telling me about how Mom yells no matter what they do. I told Ava what I had twice said to Catherine. I said that Catherine doesn't know why Mom is yelling at any given time. Mom could be yelling because she's experiencing some pain, she might be afraid that they may drop her when she's being lifted by the hoist, she may not understand what they're doing to her—especially if they don't explain things to her ahead of time—she may be acting out of modesty because she doesn't know if they're going to change her, and so on. I also told Ava that Catherine wouldn't have been laughing if it were her mom instead of mine. I said that I don't like people laughing at my mom, and Ava understood. She told me that they were working on changing the views of the aide staff there. While many of the aides in my mom's unit are excellent, some of them can be insensitive not only to the patient but also to the family caregiver. They become desensitized to their working environment. I also think it's partly attributable to a cultural attitude. Ava promised me that they were working on getting the staff to change their views. I thanked her for her assistance and for her understanding about how strongly I feel about this issue.

February 2, 2013

I Want a Better Life

I visited with Mom and heard that she was trying to say something to me. I was able to put it together because I know my mom. I've developed a heightened ability to communicate with her. I said, "Did you say, 'I want a better life'?" She smiled at me and said, "How did you know?" I told Mom that I know her. I also told her that I want her to have a better life too, that I understand how she feels, and that I'm doing everything that I can to help her out.

It's so unfortunate what our mom goes through on a daily basis. I still try to reconcile within myself and with God as to why someone as wonderful as her would have to suffer like this. She has done so much good for so many people. She has always been a giving person. While I understand that many people get chronic diseases and other medical problems as they age, I still don't understand (and maybe never will) why my mom's golden years are being stolen by this disease and her bilateral hip fracture.

May 22, 2013

Disagreement with an Aide While Defending My Mom against Another Resident—Part 1

I had just come in to see Mom. She was in the dining room along with the other residents of her unit. I'm not sure why, but Mom got a little agitated and started to raise her voice. I was able to comfort her. A minute or so later, a resident of the unit whose back was to Mom at the time (she was sitting at the table about ten or fifteen feet away) got out of her chair, came over, and started talking to Mom. At first, I wasn't sure why she got up from the table. She and Mom were talking to each other for a minute or two in a conversational tone of voice. I couldn't really understand what either of them was saying, and I'm not sure whether or not they understood each other. Just before the woman turned around to go back to her table, she started to raise her voice to Mom and point her finger at her. I knew right then that she was trying to scold my mom for raising her voice when she got agitated.

I jumped into action. I said to the other woman before she sat back down, "Don't you talk to my mom like that!" The woman turned back around and responded to me clearly by saying something along the lines that she'll talk to her any way that she wanted to. I replied, "Oh, no, you won't! You don't talk to my mom like that!" All of a sudden, Frances, one of the aides, jumped in. She said to me, "She can't help it" in defense of the other woman. I replied, "I understand that, but I'm going to stick up for my mom." Frances repeated herself, and I repeated exactly what I had said. I'm pretty sure that we went back and forth the same way one more time. Then, surprisingly—I guess because she had to "win" the argument— she said to me something like, "Would you want someone to speak up to your mom like that?" I was caught off guard, but I replied that it would be okay if that was the case. However, I gave that response reflexively. My honest response would have been, "I understand that this other woman may not understand exactly what she's doing, even though she is higher functioning than my mom. However, you need to understand that I'm always, always going to defend my mom whenever I feel that she's been attacked or treated unfairly. You would do the same thing for your mom." Besides, I know my mom. She is a really nice person and would never scold or try to tell anyone off for talking too loudly.

I was angry with the aide for trying to make me understand her point of view while simultaneously showing no concern whatsoever for mine. In fact, her last comment to me was hostile and inappropriate. She should know better than that, especially since she knows my mom and because she's a mom herself.

A little while after this incident, I spoke to Ava, the head nurse of the unit, about it. I told her that I was angry at Frances for her attitude and that she didn't care about anything that I had to say on my mom's behalf. She only cared about making her point of view and winning the argument.

May 23, 2013

Disagreement with an Aide While Defending My Mom against Another Resident—Part 2

While I was visiting with Mom for a while, I noticed that she needed to be changed. I asked the nurse for an aide to help her. Frances, the aide with whom I had had the argument the day before, offered to help out. Also, another aide came by to help. They closed the door to Mom's room and changed her for me. When they came out, I thanked both of them several times. I always thank the aides, the nurses, and the housekeeping staff for anything that they do for my mom.

The other aide left the room. Frances was still in the room with Mom but was getting ready to leave. All of a sudden, with me standing right there in front of her, Frances lifted Mom's left arm up and poked her hard in her left side. I'm pretty sure that Mom let out a little yelp. I don't remember Mom's reaction exactly because everything happened so fast and so unexpectedly. However, I know that she poked Mom hard. It wasn't playful at all. It was mean and cowardly. I responded immediately by rushing over to Frances and saying, "Hey, don't do that!" and I pinched her on her left side. Then, I tried to make nice with Frances after that because I was afraid that she might do something else to my mom when I wasn't there. I mean, she poked my mom in a hostile way right in front of me. I knew that she was retaliating against me for speaking to the head nurse about the disagreement that we had had the day before. I also saw her action as a way of trying to intimidate me, in essence saying, "If I'm crazy enough to do this right in front of you, think of what I can do to hurt your mom when you're not here." To make matters worse, about ten or fifteen minutes after this happened, I distinctly heard Frances's voice about fifteen to twenty feet down the hall from my mom's room saying, "Do you know what I just did . . ." to some of her aide friends. Unfortunately, I couldn't hear the rest of what she was saying. I'm 99 percent sure that she was talking about the stunt that she had just pulled on my mom. Either way, she should be ashamed of herself for what she did.

May 24, 2013

Disagreement with an Aide While Defending My Mom against Another Resident—Part 3

I was driving up to the Omega Institute in Rhinebeck, New York, for another Rest and Rejuvenation weekend there. I really needed it. Those weekends have really been the only times that I have gotten away for the past two or three years for an extended stay away from home.

As I was driving north to Omega, I knew that I had to call and speak to Ava again about what had happened between Frances and me. I told her the entire rest of the story, including the part after Mom was changed and Frances lifted up Mom's left arm and poked her hard in the side. I forgot to tell her then what Frances said about ten to fifteen minutes later to her aide friends. I told Ava about that comment at a later date and mentioned to her that I had forgotten to tell her about it the last time that we talked.

During this same conversation, I went on to tell Ava that I'll always defend my mom no matter what. I told her that Frances would do the same for her mom. I also said that it doesn't matter how tough some-one is—when it comes down to my mom, I'll defend her in any given situation, and I won't back down from anyone.

I'll always be there for my mom. I have a holy and sacred bond with her. I am completely devoted to her and committed to helping her in every way possible. I won't allow anyone to bother her in any way or to get in the way of my doing what's right for her. No one should ever do anything inappropriate to my mom or anything that violates the faith and trust that I place in them in caring for her.

June 1, 2013

I Like You

I was visiting Mom and helping her with her dinner. There were times during the meal when Mom was saying things to me that I couldn't fully understand. In those situations, I usually tell Mom that I can't understand what she's trying to tell me, but I'm doing the best that I can. I also tell her that I'm taking care of everything that I can for her. At one point, Mom just came out and said, "I like you" to me in a very distinct manner. I said, "Aw, I like you too, Mom. I like you, and I love you." I went on to say that I appreciated her saying that to me and that it must have been hard for her to do that. She's the best!

June 13, 2013

Reading Mom's Body Language

I was visiting with Mom, and I asked her if she loved me. Sometimes I ask her because I like to be reassured. It's always nice to hear Mom say it. Obviously, we can't communicate like we used to. As soon as I asked Mom this question, she looked right up at me, smiled, and nodded her head. The expression on her face along with her body language told me everything. She gave me the warmest and most wonderful smile. It hit me square in my heart. I knew right away that Mom really loves me and really appreciates me. It means everything in the world to me.

When I was leaving Mom for the day and bringing her back out to the area by the nurse's station, I was saying good-bye to her for the evening. It's the most difficult part of any visit because I never want to leave her side. Mom was looking down and not looking at me. It made me feel even worse than I normally feel. I knew from her body language that she didn't want me to go. Mom didn't want me to leave, and neither did I. She may have also been preparing herself for my leaving by not looking up at me.

August 18, 2013
Mom Clearly Says "I Love You"
I was helping Mom with her dinner. All of a sudden, she turned to me and said in a very clear voice "I love you." It came out of nowhere. I wasn't expecting it. I was really touched by her kindness and thoughtfulness. I knew that it was difficult for her to say it to me so clearly at this point in her battle with Alzheimer's disease. I told her that I love her, too. I got up and kissed her on her right cheek. Then, I kissed her four or five times on her forehead. I'm so lucky to have her in my life.

13

How I Communicate with Mom

WHEN SOMEONE YOU LOVE has Alzheimer's disease, her ability to communicate slowly but steadily declines as the disease progresses. My ability to understand and communicate with my mom is heightened because, first and foremost, I'm her son and I've always been very close to her. It also comes from all of the many hours that I've spent visiting her while she has lived in a nursing home, my knowledge of Alzheimer's disease and how it limits people, along with all the emotional work that I've done for myself as part of my commitment to self-awareness and self-improvement. My emotional work has opened me up even more to people and has helped me to listen better, keep an open mind, be present and be as nonjudgmental and accepting as I can be. When I'm not distracted by negative thoughts or issues from my past, it enables me to be as alive, open, and present as possible.

The question that I get most often from people is, "Does she recognize you?" My answer is that it depends on the situation. The highest recognition level for Mom would be in the morning after she has gotten up and had her breakfast. This also is dependent on whether she had a good night's sleep the night before and is feeling well.

Otherwise, there are several different factors that can affect Mom's recognition of me when I first show up for the day. Some of these include whether she's feeling well or not, if she's tired or has just woken up from a nap, or if she is distracted by something that is going on in her unit when I happen to walk in. In those instances when Mom doesn't recognize me right away, she may look at me and try to figure out who I am. I believe that in many instances she initially recognizes me as someone she knows but can't put it all together in that moment. Other times, she will look at me and say, "Mine?" to verify that I am one of her children. Sometimes she'll say, "Who are you?" However, in the worst-case situation, it usually lasts no more than one to two minutes. When Mom makes the connection, she'll smile, wink at me, or give me another facial expression of recognition.

One of the key things that I have learned is to listen closely to what Mom is saying and to be as proactive as possible. For example, I know that people with Alzheimer's disease lose the ability to think abstractly. If you ask them what is bothering them, they may not be able to give you an answer. On the other hand, if I say, "Are you hungry, Mom?" I might get an emphatic, "Yes!"

The acronym HALT, which stands for Hungry, Angry, Lonely, Tired, is important to remember when dealing with someone who has Alzheimer's disease. I can ask Mom if she is experiencing any of those feelings, and she may answer yes to one of them. Another one that I started using as of 2011 is, "Mom, are you scared?" She has given an affirmative answer to this question many times. Mom will sometimes say, "I'm scared" or "I can't take it!" in response to my prompting.

Also, Mom doesn't like loud noises or a lot of commotion going on around her. Sometimes when she is exposed to a high level of noise or commotion, she starts to get agitated. Discovering what is really bothering Mom is the key to solving many of the communication issues that come up. People with Alzheimer's suffer emotionally because they can't express themselves the way that they used to. They feel trapped by their disease. Also, they're not back at home with their loved ones. People with advanced Alzheimer's disease also suffer physically because they can't get around and exercise like they used to. They can't get up and go out to do things outside the house like they did before the onset of the disease.

I remember something that happened on Mother's Day 2011. My sister, my younger brother, his daughter, and I were visiting Mom to celebrate Mother's Day. We had lunch in the café. We then took Mom back to her room to talk and to watch some TV. My brother was talking about something for a while. All of a sudden, Mom said something out loud that was very hard for us to understand. I listened to everything that she said. I picked up on the key words that I could identify along with recognizing her emotions and the context of the moment. I said, "Mom wants us to talk to her, right, Mom?" Mom said, "Yes!" My younger brother was amazed. He asked me how I knew what Mom had said. I said that I spend a lot of time with her, so I have learned how to pick up on the key words in her statements. I was able to figure out what she was saying. I felt like I had hit a home run in Yankee Stadium during the World Series knowing that I have developed an enhanced ability to understand and communicate with my mom.

Regarding being proactive with Mom, there are occasions when she says something to me and I don't really understand what she is saying. However, especially in the instances when I can tell that she is concerned about something, I always try to be proactive in my response to her. For example, if Mom says, "He said this and he said . . . ," I will attempt a proactive response to let her know that everything is okay. I might say, "Mom, I'm not sure what you're trying to tell me, but I'm trying to understand. Please don't worry about anything. I'm taking care of everything for you. I'm making sure that you get the best care possible. I make sure that no one bothers you and that you are safe. I know that you live here now. If I can make money and become able to afford to buy a home and bring you back home with me, I will do it. In the meantime, I'm taking care of everything for you. You don't have to worry about anything." Usually when I say something along these lines, Mom says something like, "Okay," which makes me feel that I was able to relieve her of whatever was bothering her. Of course, everything is in the moment. I may have to say a similar thing to her later that same day or on another visit.

Mary and I recently discovered that Mom tends to act a certain way when she is feeling scared. She will start by talking out loud in a way that is hard to understand. Sometimes she sounds as if she is going to cry while she is talking. When Mom did this recently, Mary went over and asked her if she was scared, and she said she was. Mary told her to not be scared and comforted her in the moment. Now, when Mom talks like this, we ask her right away if she is scared. So far, Mom has said yes each time. This is extremely helpful to us in understanding Mom and what she is going through and in helping her get through it.

Like I have stated before, I live in Mom's world; she doesn't live in mine. It's like I'm surfing out in the ocean. If I follow the waves and go with the flow, I'll be okay. I'll get back safely to the shore. If I fight the wave or go against the flow, I'll get thrown off of my surfboard and tossed into the rolling and turbulent ocean. Mom is always my guide. I let her lead the way.

Learning to communicate effectively with my mom is like learning a new language in which there are no words. It is a combination of things. It takes knowing that Alzheimer's patients can't think abstractly after a certain point in their illness. You also have to know the person, know or try to find out what is bothering them, and know the context of the situation. Furthermore, it is important to understand their body language and what they are trying to communicate through their eyes. By doing these things, I am usually better able to piece together what Mom is trying to tell me. By being proactive, I can usually come up with the right answer whenever the situation calls for it.

I also believe that Alzheimer's patients at a more advanced stage of their disease try not to speak a lot of the time because they know that they can't communicate like they used to. They feel embarrassed and ashamed by it, even though they shouldn't. It's not their fault. However, I understand why they feel this way and how they can feel powerless and helpless in certain instances.

I am an emotionally sensitive person who naturally feels compassion and empathy for other people. I give most of the credit for developing this part of myself to my mom and the way she was always so compassionate with her family, her relatives, and the people in our community. A lot of my feelings of compassion and empathy for people come from her. This has given me an advantage in my ability to communicate effectively with my mom. I may be partial when I say this because she is my mom, but she is absolutely the most loving and compassionate person I have ever met in my entire life.

As often as I've been with my mom since she was placed into the nursing home environment, I have come to realize that Alzheimer's patients are really like delicate flowers. They need water, nutrients, sunshine, care, love, and attention not only to survive but to thrive and to bloom. For example, the day that we celebrated Mom's eighty-fourth birthday, she stayed so alert, energized, responsive, and happy, even after ten o'clock that evening, because her family was spending most of her special day with her. We were with her until late into the evening. It made a big difference in how she felt about her day and in how she responded to us. It also made a big difference to us. All of us really love being with Mom.

People with Alzheimer's disease live a rich and vibrant life under the surface. It is like a coral reef hidden in the ocean. If you dive underneath the water and swim up to it, you will see an amazing and intricate structure of coral with beautiful tropical fish swimming in and out of it. It is surrounded by all of the natural beauty that goes along with being a coral reef. This coral reef is something that can't be seen from the shore; it is hidden underneath the surface. This is how many people with Alzheimer's disease live on a daily basis. They have a beauty and richness that is hidden just under the surface. It isn't easy to see or notice. You have to go into their world on a very intimate and caring level to see it. Once you do, you have to be willing to stay there as long as possible. It takes a lot of patience, love, understanding and compassion to do so. They really do want to communicate so strongly with the people outside of their world. However, in many cases, they just can't communicate with us the way that they used to.

Unfortunately, some people don't know as much as they think they do about people with Alzheimer's disease. It can sometimes even be a mystery to those of us who have a lot of experience in dealing with it. For example, Mary had stopped by to visit a friend whom she hadn't seen in a while. At some point, the woman asked Mary how our mom was doing, and Mary gave her an update. The woman stated several times, "That's not your mom." Mary was offended. Even though this woman was trying to help, her words were not helpful to us. We know our mom well enough and have spent thousands of hours with her during her stay in different nursing homes. We know our mom is still there, even though communicating with her has become more challenging. After Mary's visit was over, she decided to write this woman a letter to let her know how she felt. Mary asked me to review it before she mailed it out. I made some editorial changes, and Mary sent it.

I told Mary after she mailed the letter about the old saying that says, "You can't get milk and bread from a hardware store." In other words, don't expect people who haven't been that sensitive, compassionate, or empathetic with you in the past to all of a sudden change and become people with whom you would want to share such personal information and feel comfortable and confident in doing so. This woman had demonstrated this to my sister in the past. I know because my sister had complained to me about it. For whatever reason, some individuals are either unable or unwilling to express compassion in the way that people would reasonably expect of them.

There are many misconceptions about Alzheimer's disease. For example, one of the statements that people have made to me is that the patient isn't affected by it, only the caregivers. They say that those who have it don't *know* that they have it. This is not true. My mom has said to me numerous times since November 2007 that she can't stand it, she wants to go home, she wants to walk, she wants to feel more useful, she is scared, and so forth.

Although science has uncovered many things about the brain and how it works, there is still a lot more that we don't know at this time. The brain is a very complex organ, which is one reason that scientists haven't discovered a cure for Alzheimer's disease or a medication that people can take now to avoid developing it. Another example about the complexity of our brains is that people with Alzheimer's disease can surprise us from time to time with their abilities and what they say. I have heard it from the nursing staff in my mom's unit, and I have experienced it firsthand with my mom.

14

*Fight for Awareness,
Sensitivity, Funding,
and a Cure*

I AM TRULY PASSIONATE about advocating on behalf of those people who have Alzheimer's disease because my mom has it and I am her main caregiver.

A lot of information is now coming out about Alzheimer's disease and all of its ramifications. We must fight for awareness of what the patients and their caregivers go through on a daily basis. There must be more sensitivity and compassion in dealing not only with those with Alzheimer's disease but also with their family members. Part of my advocacy will also be on behalf of greater funding for Alzheimer's disease to help bring about a cure as soon as possible for this terrifying and deadly disease.

When your loved one is affected by Alzheimer's disease, you get it. You truly understand the devastating impact that the disease has on them and on you. Whenever I see a family member visiting a loved one who has Alzheimer's disease, we have an unspoken understanding with each other. It's a shared experience that can only be fully understood when you actually go through it yourself.

I know a lot of well-meaning people who will sometimes give me their opinions on Alzheimer's disease, its symptoms, and how to deal with a person who has it. In some cases, they may know someone who has it or a family member who is married to someone with the disease. I do appreciate the input and the feedback. I know that it comes from a good place. However, if their assessment comes across as inaccurate or insensitive to the situation, I may tell them that they don't really understand the disease and its impact until they have experienced it firsthand. Although they may know some things, they still don't know as much as they think they do.

I don't like it or appreciate it when someone says, "It's only going to get worse." Believe it or not, I've actually had a person who leads an Alzheimer's caregiver support group say this to me. Other people have also said it. I know that this is a progressive disease. I know that it's an uphill battle both for Mom and for us. It's just unnecessary to say this to me. It's not helpful at all to remind me of what we're facing. It just makes me feel worse. Besides, I don't think that they would want the same thing said to them if they were dealing with it.

I also have had some experiences with a friend of my sister Mary and me. I shared with her some personal experiences that I had while being a caregiver to my mom in some really difficult situations, and she laughed out loud on at least two separate occasions. The last time she did that, my sister and I had been invited to her house for dinner. At the dinner table, I shared a personal story of something that happened when Mom was in the hospital that was upsetting to me, and she laughed out loud. I told her that I was being serious and that it wasn't funny to me. I wish that I had said, "Why would you laugh at something that is troubling to me?" I know that sometimes people laugh at something that might seem funny because they're listening to the content and not to the context of the story. For example, there have been times when I've been visiting with my mom for an hour or two and then she turns to me and asks me why I'm there. Even though there's an incongruity, it's because of Mom's disease. It's not funny. It's not something to laugh at. Also, if it was happening to their loved ones or to themselves, they wouldn't think it was funny at all.

I also really don't like it when people make jokes about Alzheimer's disease. For example, there have been several occasions when a member of a volunteer group that I'm involved with have made jokes about it. In fact, as I mentioned earlier, one person from this group made an Alzheimer's related joke in front of our guest speaker that day, who is a representative of the Alzheimer's Association. Unbelievable! Unfortunately, it's not funny, especially when you are either living with this disease or are helping a loved one who has it. I can't believe that someone would try to make a joke about Alzheimer's disease, especially directly to a representative of the Alzheimer's Association!

People may joke about Alzheimer's disease for various reasons. People joke about it because it makes them feel uneasy or they're afraid of getting it. More than likely, they can't relate to it because they aren't personally affected by it, or they don't have a loved one who has it. If they were in that particular situation and still made jokes about it, I'd say that they should have their own heads checked out. Also, Alzheimer's disease is in the brain. It's not something that people can see, like a physical disability. However, people with Alzheimer's disease are disabled, also. They have a chronic disease. Since you wouldn't joke about someone with a physical disability, then you should never joke about someone with Alzheimer's disease. People also may joke about it because it's an easy target. Unfortunately, it still seems acceptable to some people to make jokes about memory loss in the conversation of someone discussing Alzheimer's disease. Part of my mission is to educate and sensitize people as to why they're saying what they're saying and why it shouldn't be acceptable for them to say it, also.

Believe it or not, most of us have already experienced what it's like to have dementia. Have you ever parked your car at a mall and then come out later and discovered that you didn't remember where you had parked? Have you ever left your house and driven off, only to realize that you left something important back at home? Have you bumped into someone whom you haven't seen in a while and not been able to remember his or her name? Have you ever awoken in the morning and not remembered what day it was? Have you ever tried to remember something and been unable to make the connection as to what was actually said to you, where it was said, when it was said, and who said it (in a sense, trying to connect the dots of a specific past event with the assistance of your short- or long-term memory)? I am sure that there are many other examples of temporary memory loss that you can relate to from your daily life. How do you feel when these and other memory lapse-related events happen to you? Think about it. Really take the time and think about it. Hopefully, it will help to sensitize you even more to the daily plight of people with Alzheimer's disease.

I ask people to put themselves in my mom's shoes. How must it be for her every day? She has to deal with this crushing loneliness and fear. She is disconnected from her normal life, where she could be in her own home and surrounded by the love and care of her family. She has been thrust into an unfamiliar environment. She is surrounded by people she doesn't know and who aren't her family. She isn't able to perform the activities of everyday living that most people take for granted. She wonders sometimes if she has done something wrong, as if she is being punished. I know this because she has expressed this sentiment to me in the past. In those instances, I always reassure her. I tell her that she hasn't done anything wrong and that she's living there so she can get the nursing care that she needs. She must wonder if her family even knows that she's there or if they even care. She doesn't know if we'll ever come to see her again or if she'll ever go back home to stay. She can't access the many memories of her wonderful life like she used to. When something happens during the day that would require her to access her short—or long-term memory, she probably won't be able to access it, especially her short-term memory. Some of her memories aren't based in our current reality. For example, she doesn't realize that she is thinking and communicating in the present tense about a relative who has already passed away. This is common for people with Alzheimer's disease.

It would be a good idea sometime to sit down, close your eyes, and perform a visualization exercise. If you want to record what I've written in this paragraph as a guide or add some personal words of your own and play it back during your meditation, please do it. Also, if some guided meditation or soothing music in the background will assist you, by all means, take advantage of it. Once all of your preparation is complete and you are ready, you're in a relaxing place and in a meditative state of mind, it's time to start. Begin by thinking about someone whom you loved growing up and you know loved you. This is the most important person in your life. This is a person whom you love with all your heart. Think about all that this person means to you. Think about all that he or she has done for you. Consider all of the hard work, sacrifice, devotion, and love given on your behalf. Think about how this person took care of you, loved you, guided you, comforted you, and protected you. This person always made sure that you got what you needed. Think about all the good times and the wonderful memories that you shared over many years. Now imagine that this person has become stricken with Alzheimer's disease and starting to lose his or her short-term memory. His or her long-term memory is being affected, also. He or she can't function as well as before. Your loved one is doing the best that he or she can. However, this person is really frightened inside and terrified about what he or she knows is happening. At this point, your loved one has an awareness of the disease. He or she knows that it's progressive and that there is no cure.

How would you feel about Alzheimer's disease then? How much of a commitment would you be willing or able to make to help your loved one in this time of need? Would you be in it for the duration? Would you try to do as much as possible? Would you stand for your loved one the way that he or she stood for you? It's definitely something worth meditating on and thinking about. If you are able to perform this exercise in an earnest and sincere way, it should give you some insight into what it's really like being a caregiver to a loved one with Alzheimer's disease. It might even give you a window into what it could be like to come down with this disease yourself.

15

My Address to Congress

FOR THE PURPOSES OF this book, I imagined myself having the opportunity to address the US Congress about the daily plight of people suffering from Alzheimer's disease and the consequences for them and for their loved ones.

My address to Congress would be as follows.

Mr. Speaker, Mr. Vice President, members of Congress, and fellow citizens, it is truly an honor and a privilege to be here today. I am here to speak to you about the emotional impact of Alzheimer's disease.

In each of our hearts and minds lie great memories. We remember and cherish the experiences of our childhoods through our early adult lives with the people who took care of us, nurtured us, and helped us to make our way in this world.

In my case, these people were my mom and dad. They were both raised during the Great Depression. They were part of what has been called the

Greatest Generation of Americans. I came to understand their generation from all of the stories that my parents told me about growing up during the Great Depression, World War II, and the postwar years. I've also read a lot about this unique period of time in our nation's history. Not only did they survive the Great Depression, but they all came together to fight a common enemy during World War II. It was the Golden Age of Radio. The big band era held sway with its music, and the accompanying dance styles were popular all over the country.

Things seemed simpler back then. People related to one another with more respect and consideration. It was very important to have manners and to treat your elders with respect. They had strong values and ethics. They knew the difference between right and wrong. They worked hard. They believed in America. They really loved our country. All the good that they did and all that they stood for are what I refer to as "timeless values." It doesn't matter what the day and age is, these values are and will always be important in life.

Mom and Dad sacrificed so much for our family. They raised four children. They worked very hard their entire lives, believed in God, and loved our country. My Dad was a US Army veteran of World War II. He served in postwar occupied Japan. My mom was also a very proud and patriotic American. I remember how much they both loved and cherished our country and its freedom.

One of the many things that I remember from growing up was Mom going shopping for clothing. She always tried to buy clothing and items that were made in the USA. There were occasions when Mom would shop for some time just to make sure that all the things that she purchased were made here. As the years went by, it became more and more difficult to find things that were still manufactured in America.

Unfortunately, when my dad's cancer returned in August 2007, he passed away within two months. My mom has been confined to nursing homes since August 2007, with the exception of being home with us for only two weeks after Dad passed away. It is unimaginable to me that all of this could happen in such a short period of time. I understand that families go through their share of tragedy and that our parents will eventually pass away. However, I don't understand how two really good, hard-working people who loved God and country and who made so many personal sacrifices could end up this way. Dying quickly and painfully from cancer and progressively declining from Alzheimer's disease is no way to have to spend your golden years.

Regarding Alzheimer's disease, I speak not only for my mom but for all the other people who have been stricken with the disease. I'm also here to represent all the caregivers who give all that they can every day on behalf of their loved ones.

Like anything else in life, you really know on a deep and profound level how devastating this disease is when it strikes home. It's personal then. We hear a lot about heart disease and heart attacks. Alzheimer's disease is an attack on the brain. It is a brain attack for which there is no known cure. Today's medications for Alzheimer's disease only slow down the progression of the disease.

Take a moment to imagine what it feels like to be in my mom's shoes. Mom and Dad raised four children and worked very hard to make sure that we had what we needed. My mom kept very busy throughout her life raising her family at home, taking jobs outside the house from time to time, volunteering for different charitable organizations, helping out neighbors in need, going to church, and so forth. Mom also loved to walk. She used to walk a lot around town. She didn't have a car and never learned to drive. If she had to go some distance, she would either get a ride from Dad or one of her children or she would take a bus.

When my mom got Alzheimer's disease, her memory started slipping slowly but surely. The disease has progressed to the point where she can no longer walk. She is now confined to a wheelchair. She lives in a nursing home and has trouble communicating like she used to.

Mom wants to go home. She doesn't remember that Dad passed away. Many times she will ask for her husband, dad, mom, grandma, or grandpa. People with Alzheimer's disease lose the ability to think abstractly. Sometimes when Mom gets agitated, I have to ask her specific questions to find out what's wrong. I may ask her if she's scared. When she says yes, I feel very bad about it. I always try to comfort her the best way that I can. However, I'm grateful that she can still tell me that she is scared. She may not always be able to do that in the future. Alzheimer's patients live in a silent world. Although they can still communicate at a level commensurate with the severity of their disease, they often keep quiet because they can't communicate like they used to. I believe that this is because they're not able to or they're too ashamed to try.

Put yourself in their shoes. What must it be like to know that you're slowly but surely losing your memory and your ability to perform activities of daily living? You end up losing the ability to walk. You can't communicate as well as you used to, or you can't speak at all. It's difficult for other people, including your loved ones, to understand what you're saying. You need assistance with almost everything. You're no longer in your own home, and you're living with strangers. You don't get to see your family every day. You start to lose the ability to immediately recognize your loved ones. You know that you're declining, and you know that there's not much that you can do to either stop it or slow it down.

Alzheimer's is a progressive disease that debilitates the individual over time. It robs them of their precious memories; diminishes their natural gifts and abilities; produces recurring feelings of abandonment, fear, anxiety, hurt, anger, frustration, along with other corresponding feelings; has a profound effect on their human dignity and spirit; and, ultimately, breaks their heart and the hearts of all of their loved ones. It prevents them from fully engaging in life and enjoying a normal, happy, and productive lifestyle. It's unimaginable to me how painful it must be for them each and every day.

How many people die while in nursing homes from neglect or from a broken heart? Our loved ones need our constant visits, our demonstrations of love and caring, our commitment, and our companionship. They are counting on us to help them in every way necessary, especially concerning the level and quality of care that they get inside the nursing home.

What about the rights of seniors with dementia in nursing homes? They should always be treated with understanding, love, compassion, kindness, gentility, patience, dignity, and respect. Unfortunately, from what I've seen and what I've heard from other caregivers, this is not always the case.

Alzheimer's disease is a national tragedy. It affects both the patient and the entire family. It is an unwelcome intruder to the beauty and innocence of life. It robs people of their ability to take care of themselves, to live a full life, and to live out their golden years with a sense of well-being, dignity and contentment.

I am hoping and praying for a cure for this disease. If I were Superman, the main superpower I would choose would be to cure people of Alzheimer's disease. I would fly all over the United States and the world to heal all the people who suffer from it. My outfit would be purple because purple is the color of the Alzheimer's Association. The front of my shirt would have a big *C* on it, standing for *Champion*. I am a champion on behalf of all people, especially my wonderful mom, who suffer from this disease. I am also a champion for the community of loved ones and caregivers.

I ask the good members of Congress, especially those of you who are fortunate enough to not have to deal with Alzheimer's disease on a personal level, to look deep inside of you. How would you feel if this were to happen to you or to your loved one? If it were to happen, what would you do about it?

Some of you may know what I go through on a daily basis. No matter what your circumstances are, funding for a cure for Alzheimer's disease is a national priority. It will also build more awareness and sensitivity to people with Alzheimer's and their caregivers. As you know, Alzheimer's disease is a tremendous burden on our health care system. It's incredibly difficult emotionally on the patients and their families. We need a cure for Alzheimer's disease as soon as possible. We can't wait any longer. It's that important.

I ask that you consider what I'm saying here with an open heart and an open mind. We owe Alzheimer's patients the best collective effort that our country can make toward fighting this disease. This is the least we can do for so many people from the Greatest Generation of Americans who suffer from it, along with others who have this disease. They have all done so much for our country. Now it's our turn to do as much as we can for them.

I strongly believe that our main focus should be on our fellow Americans and our national problems. When we focus on solving our own problems first, we can take even more of a leadership role in helping to solve the world's problems. It's not only common sense, but it is also wise, compassionate, and visionary governance.

Solving the intricacies and complexities of the mind and making it work for us, not against us, is our final frontier. We can cure Alzheimer's disease. We can find cures for other diseases of the mind. We can learn how our minds really operate and get them to work even better. We can learn to love one another and to forgive more. We can learn how to communicate better and more compassionately with one another. We can all live in peace and harmony.

There comes a time in everyone's life when you have to make a stand, to stand for something that's really important. That time came for me the day that I found out that my mom has Alzheimer's disease. My heart breaks each and every day for her. The time has come for us to stand up and be heard. I ask each and every one of you to stand powerfully with me. They need your help, and so do I.

We have to work together to eradicate this horrible disease. We can do it. We're Americans. That's what we do. From every area of our great country, we must raise our voices in unison to orchestrate a great chorus of action that inspires us to reach even higher and to do more. I look forward to a more passionate commitment to change the landscape of Alzheimer's disease. Let's demonstrate our love for them the way that they showed their love of us.

I will continue to advocate powerfully and effectively on behalf of those who can no longer speak or advocate for themselves. It's the right thing to do. That's why I do it. It's my calling.

When I was a young boy, I used to like to lie on the grass and look up at the beautiful clouds rolling by. It was all peaches and cream back then. Now when I go outside and look up at the sky, I can still see the beautiful clouds dancing by in all their glory. I also see the promise of a new day when we finally rid the world of this dreadful and debilitating disease.

Finding a cure for Alzheimer's disease along with better treatments for the people who already have it must become our national priority right now. We can't wait any longer. Every day that we wait for a cure is one less day for my Mom. Let's all roll up our sleeves and work together to make Alzheimer's disease a thing of the past. Imagine a world without Alzheimer's.

Thank you.

16

Why It Hurts So Much

IMAGINE WHAT IT FEELS like to know that your mom is living in a nursing home because you can't afford to have her at home. It's also a tremendous burden to take care of your loved one at home, even with the assistance of a live-in aide.

Now imagine what it feels like to see your mom slowly progress in this disease. In the beginning, she could still function at a fairly high level. Eventually, her memory worsens, she can't walk anymore, and she can't communicate like she used to. She is trapped in her own body. It has to be so frightening and frustrating for her every day.

I know in my heart that my mom deserves so much better than this, especially in her golden years. To have to live out the remaining years of her life with Alzheimer's disease, or any other chronic disease, doesn't make any sense to me. As I've said before, she worked very hard her whole life for our family and for the community, just being the wonderful person that she is. Now she is confined to a wheelchair and unable to walk, unable to communicate as effectively as she once did, and dependent upon others to assist her with her daily activities of living.

I would never wish this disease on anyone. The greatest risk factor in getting Alzheimer's disease is increasing age. Another troubling aspect of this disease is that there is no cure at this time. There are only medications that can slow down its progression.

Not only does this disease affect our mom in so many different ways, it also affects our family. My life really isn't the same anymore because I am my Mom's main caregiver. It feels as if I'm just surviving every day. It's very difficult for me to live a life with unlimited possibilities when my mom is in her condition and confined to a nursing home. I worry about her every day, seven days a week. I don't take any days off. I spend a lot of time doing things on her behalf and visiting her. Even if I were to go away for a week-long vacation, I would still be thinking and worrying about my mom every day, like I always do. Although I know that eventually a day will come when my mom passes away, and I will have to face up to it the best that I can, it is the knowledge of it and the daily anticipation of its occurrence that is so anxiety-producing and stressful.

In the midst of everything, I have to continue to take care of myself and try to maintain balance in my life. With all of my current responsibilities, sometimes I'm not sure that I'll ever be truly happy again. I work at it every day. It's harder for me to find joy in everyday living while my mom's care and overall well-being is on my mind.

I know that things can happen to our parents when they get older. How many parents actually die peacefully in their sleep of old age? After we found out that my dad's cancer had come back, he passed away two months later. He had just turned eighty years old. It is tremendously unfair to both of our parents and to our family that things happened this way. I still don't understand why Mom and Dad, who were both loving, strong, responsible, caring, and devoted people, could end up suffering from these diseases. It's so unfair.

I wish that through my prayers, I could achieve a miracle and cure my mom. Sometimes I wish that when I'm visiting my mom, all it would take is a kiss from me on her forehead to take away this disease and make her all better again.

This disease is hardest on my mom. She has to live with it every minute of every day. There is no time off for her. After my mom, it is hardest on her children. It is especially hard on me and my sister because we are Mom's primary caregivers. I am responsible for all her paperwork. I'm intimately involved in every aspect of her care. My sister and I have power of attorney and the advanced health care directive for her. I make sure that Mom is getting the best care possible. I advocate for her at the nursing home whenever it's necessary.

I feel as if I live every day trapped in a nightmare. There are times when I experience feelings of anger, frustration, resentment, despair, and hopelessness. It's as if there's a dark cloud attached to me by a long, invisible cord. It follows me wherever I go. It is constantly hanging over me.

My mom's condition affects me even more on an individual basis because she's all that I've got in this world. I'm not married. I don't have any children of my own. Although I have a close relationship with my siblings, it's just not the same as the relationship that I have with Mom. First and foremost, she's my mom. She will always be the most important person in the world to me. She is the strongest and most significant link to me and to my past. She is absolutely my best friend and the best friend that I could ever want or hope for in life. She's my hero in every sense of the word. She shows me every day by her example how to live life with courage, dignity, and grace while she is dealing with some of the most extraordinary medical, social, emotional, and spiritual challenges. It's truly amazing to me how strong she is under her circumstances. Both my mom and my dad have taught me many valuable lessons. They have shown me the proper way to conduct myself in this world and how to best live my life.

The most important thing is to help my mom in every way possible while trying to live my own life in the best way that I can. I know that Mom would want that for me.

17

*Is There Any Joy
in All of This?*

THIS CHAPTER WAS INSPIRED by a conversation that I had with a woman
in a class that I took in New York City in June 2011. I was scheduled
to read to the class from the introduction of my book. Our seminar
leader said that I had only one minute to read. I asked her if I could
speak for three to four minutes, but she said that she could only give me
one minute. I ended up reading excerpts from the book's introduction
for two to three minutes. When I had finished reading, the whole class
applauded. In fact, approximately thirty or more people actually stood
up and applauded. I was very touched by and grateful for their response.

The woman who had inspired this chapter actually missed my reading
that evening because she had arrived to the class later on. After the class
ended, she asked me to read from my introduction, so I read her some
excerpts. She seemed to get a lot out of it. After looking over my table of
contents, she recommended that I add a chapter on joy. I thought that
it was an interesting perspective and worth considering.

When I reflect on it, there is joy to be found, even under the circumstances. For example, I feel happiness and joy whenever I see my mom. I'm also happy when she recognizes me right away and shows her love and affection for me by giving me a hug and kisses on my cheek.

It's a joy whenever I see that Mom is happy and enjoying herself. I love it when I see Mom laughing at something that's happening in the nursing home or something that she's watching on TV. She has a wonderful laugh and the greatest smile in the world. I feel joy when I see her eating her meal and really enjoying it. I also love it when Mom comes up with one of her famous expressions or says something funny to me. I'm happy after Mom has been changed and put to bed for the evening. She seems so happy then. She is not only my mother, but she is my best friend. My mom is the best friend that I could ever have or ever even hope for in life. As they say in the movie *Forrest Gump*, Mom and I are like peas and carrots.

The hardest part of the joy with Mom is when I have to say good-bye for the day or evening. I never want to leave her side. I wish that I could be with her every day for as long as possible.

If I could ever make enough money, I would buy a house and take Mom home. I would have a live-in aide to help us take care of her. I would spend the rest of the time that Mom has with us making sure that she got the best of everything. I would make sure that she was always as happy, healthy, and content as she could be.

There is a certain level of contentment in knowing that I'm doing the very best that I can for her. We feel that this particular nursing home is the best place that she could possibly be outside of being at home with her family.

It's also good for Mom to be around a lot of people and to be involved in activities that help keep her connected. The food seems to be of good quality and nutritious, and the nurses and aides are generally very good. Also, many doctors are on staff there and have their own offices in the facility. I know that my mom gets very good care overall, and knowing these things helps me to cope better with her situation.

An example of how joy was created involved an idea that I came up with for Mom's birthday in 2011. A few months before her birthday, I was thinking about what gift to get her, and I came up with the idea for an updated family portrait of her children. At that time, we had two family portraits in Mom's room. One of them was a portrait of her four children that was taken back in 1982. The other portrait was of my mom and dad that was taken for their fiftieth wedding anniversary.

I thought that an updated portrait of Mom's children would be a great gift to her. Not only would it be a more recent picture of us, but it would also help to keep Mom's memory fresh regarding how we look today. After a week or two went by, I came up with an even better idea. Why not include Mom in the portrait? This would really help her memory because she would see herself together with her children.

I discussed it with my siblings, and they all thought that it was a great idea. My sister got an additional idea from her friend's husband. Instead of having Mom in her wheelchair in the portrait, we could transfer her from the wheelchair into a chair suitable for a family portrait. Having Mom sitting in a nice chair and not in her wheelchair would make our portrait even better.

We had to wait a while to get the final product after the pictures were taken and updates were made. It came in a beautiful frame and was covered by glass. It turned out to be a wonderful portrait, a great thing for Mom to look at in her room, and a wonderful keepsake for our family. I was so happy that we were able to get it completed for Mom. It is now displayed prominently in her room.

I have discovered more joy in the world for myself just by noticing Mom's reactions to the smallest things in life that people may not notice. For example, she gets joy whenever she sees a baby on a TV commercial or in a TV show or movie. She shows so much joy and appreciation for her family whenever we visit her. It's apparent because she lights up when she sees us coming in to visit her. She also listens very closely to conversation and takes everything in from her surrounding environment. I can tell this by things that she's said to me and by her facial expressions and body language. It demonstrates to me that even with her medical condition and her physical, mental, and emotional limitations, she still appreciates her life and being able to live it every day. It's a real testament to her inner strength, beauty, dignity, and courage.

18

Final Thoughts

ANYONE WHO SERVES AS a caregiver for a loved one who suffers from Alzheimer's disease understands exactly what I go through on a daily basis. It is a shared understanding of the fear, anxiety, and grief that is our constant and unwanted companion. People with this disease and their caregivers understand better than anyone else. They live with it every day.

As I've stated before, Alzheimer's disease is hardest on the people who suffer from it. Mom has to live with this disease twenty-four hours a day, seven days a week, every day of every year. She doesn't get any days off. Likewise, this disease also affects our entire family. I don't get any days off, either. I worry about my mom each and every day, year in and year out.

Since my mom and dad did so much for me in my life, I am happy to help them in any way that I can. I continue to help my mom in every way possible to fight this disease and to live her life as fully as possible. Although it wears me down from time to time, I am completely committed to being there for her and helping her as much as possible.

I will use all of my individual strengths and abilities to help my mom and to be a powerful and effective advocate on her behalf. I want to be an important and resonant voice for people with Alzheimer's and dementia. They can't speak effectively enough for themselves anymore. In some cases, they can't speak at all. I will continue to fight for a cure and for more funding, awareness, sensitivity, and compassion.

I will always be on the front lines, fighting for my mom and the other people who are afflicted. I join this fight along with the other caregivers who give their hearts, bodies, minds, and spirits to the cause.

This is a cause that we can all rally around. Alzheimer's disease affects everyone, regardless of their background, education, or social status. We have paved many new frontiers in the fight against heart disease and cancer. Alzheimer's disease is an attack on the brain. There is so much more that we need to know about it, about how the brain works, and about how to not only prevent the onset of this disease but discover a cure for the people who already have it.

If the people who have Alzheimer's disease could speak to us about what they're going through, what would they say? The time to help them is now. We needed them for a certain period of our lives. Now they need us. I can't imagine anyone not wanting to do all that they can do for a loved one in this situation.

To be honest with you, I never thought or imagined that my life would turn out this way. I am truly grateful for everything that I have in life. However, having to deal with losing my dad so quickly to cancer and seeing my mom progress with her disease has been very painful and difficult.

Alzheimer's disease can happen to anyone. It seems like it isn't real, like this really isn't happening to my mom. Unfortunately, it is. It is unbelievable that my mom has this disease and that it will be with her until she passes. Her loving family is powerless over certain aspects of this disease. However, I empower myself to help my mom in every way that I can. This is one of the many reasons for this book.

I have been intimately involved as the main caregiver for my Mom since August 2007. Before that, although I would help out whenever necessary, it was mainly my dad and sister who took care of Mom because they all lived together then. I have always been concerned about my mom's health and well-being, especially when I first learned about the onset of her disease.

This has been my mom's fight since January 2000. This is my fight, too. I would never let anyone pick on my mom when I was growing up, and I won't allow it now.

As a result of what happened to Dad and what is happening to Mom, along with all of my responsibility in these matters, I have become the man that I've always wanted to be. There is a saying—"Whatever doesn't kill you makes you stronger." I used to really dislike this saying. I didn't think that it was true. That being said, it made a lot more sense to me after I had to go through the gauntlet of family tragedies and problems that presented itself to me, seemingly all at once. It was a real ordeal and a tremendous burden on me. I'm still not sure how I survived this period of my life when it felt like I was carrying the whole world on my shoulders. Of course, I didn't want things to happen this way. During this incredible and unforgettable journey, I responded to all of the circumstances the best that I could. I did a lot of really good things for our family. I probably made a few mistakes along the way, but if I did, they were unintentional. That being said, with all that I've done and all that there is still to do, I feel as if I can never do enough for my mom.

Another thing that has come clearly into focus is how precious life truly is. To me, life is lived best when it is lived simply. I treat people the way that I want to be treated, and I always try to do the right thing. I stay focused on what's really important in life and what needs to be accomplished every day and every week. I try to maintain a sense of balance. I stay away from people who are not good or kind in their behavior toward me.

My day works best when I do the most important things first and still allow time to be flexible, if needed. It also works better when I'm conscientious in the use of my time. Sometimes, I have to take some time out for myself. I have discovered that the degree to which I take care of myself is the same degree to which I can take care of my mom, my family, and the world.

If I could have one wish in life, it would be that I would take away my mom's Alzheimer's disease and make her all better again. I want Mom to be like she would have been twenty or thirty years ago, before there were any traces of this disease.

I long for the good old days when I could go over and visit Mom and Dad at their house. We would have great conversations and meals, laugh, and really enjoy being together. I also miss the days when I was still living at home with Mom and Dad. I miss all the comforts and joys of being home. I miss lying down on my bed on a lazy Sunday afternoon during the summer, enjoying the cacophony of sounds. I remember the sound of lawn mowers cutting the grass, the train running through town, airplanes flying overhead, the voices of the kids and the adults, a dog barking, and so on. It all sounded like a perfect symphony of life. Unfortunately, those days are long gone. However, I will always want my mom back home. She belongs at home with her family.

These days, Mom lies in her special wheelchair, patiently waiting for her prince to arrive and eliminate this terrible disease from her brain and rescue her from the nursing home. I have this dream, like the dramatic end to a great movie, where I run into my mom's arms, kissing and hugging her and crying tears of joy because her Alzheimer's disease is completely gone and she's back to normal. I tell her that we're taking her home where she belongs.

I wonder how Mom must feel when she is alone there each day, whether she is watching TV or being entertained by the staff in the dining room. There are times when she will fall asleep while she is with the other residents. I hate the idea of Mom being alone and not having anyone from her family being with her. This is one of the many reasons that I go to visit her up to four times a week.

It's like Mom is being punished for a crime that she didn't commit. She is innocent. She hasn't done anything wrong. I want to get her out of her prison. I want to free her from the constraints that Alzheimer's disease has put on her.

I know that the people who never had the opportunity to meet my mom would absolutely love her. It's ironic that so many people have discovered how truly wonderful my mom is as a *result* of her having Alzheimer's disease and living in a nursing home. I've frequently heard the staff say how kind, gentle, and loving she is. A nurse at a previous facility told me that she was amazed at how wise my mom is. I have always known these things about her. She has a way of saying things in such a kind, gentle, and loving way that really gets to the heart of the matter. It is one of her many amazing gifts. She also has the most wonderful soul in the world. She has an amazing awareness about herself and her surroundings, even after the onset of her disease. I believe that this is a function of her soul, her fighting spirit, and her will to live and to love. I also feel that this disease has made some of her wonderful qualities become even more pronounced. For example, Mom takes joy in the smallest of things. She sees joy and wonderment in aspects of everyday life that many people may not notice at all. Just seeing her smile at me when I first arrive really makes my day.

I have always believed in my heart that my mom is too good for this world. She is filled with so much love, kindness, gentility, and compassion for other people. She has such an unbelievable amount of goodness in her. Maybe I'm being partial because she's my mom, but she has the most goodness and the most wonderful qualities inside her of anyone I've ever known in my entire life. She's the most amazing and remarkable person in the world to me. I'm totally in awe of her.

I feel lucky and grateful for my mom and that I still have her in my life. I never want to let her down. She has always been there for me; now it's my time to be there for her. With this book, I choose now as the time to honor her life.

Thank you, Mom, for always being there for me. Thank you for your love, caring, guidance, and wisdom. Thank you for being you. If I always do what you want me to do, I know that I'll be the person that I'm meant to be in this world. I will continue to make a positive difference in your life and the lives of others. I can only hope to be as good and wonderful a person as you. If everyone in the world were even half as good as you, the world would have a lot fewer problems and a lot more love, understanding, and compassion.

Sometimes I think back to the day that I graduated from college. My entire family was there to congratulate me and to join me in celebrating this special accomplishment. I think about what a beautiful day it was and how much my family means to me. I also think about my legacy. What am I here on earth to accomplish? I feel that my calling now is to advocate powerfully and effectively on behalf of people with Alzheimer's disease and their loved ones who serve as caregivers.

No matter what happens, I will always be there for Mom. I will be a stand for her. I will also stand as a champion and advocate for awareness and a cure for Alzheimer's disease. I stand for all the other patients and their loved ones who deal with this disease on an intimate level every day.

Mom, I love you with all my heart. I have always loved you, and I will always love you. I will always love, respect, and honor you in every way possible. I will always be by your side, and I will never leave you. You will never be alone as you deal with this disease. I will do the very best that I can to help you and to make Alzheimer's disease a thing of the past. I choose now as the time to be a light and a leader in the Alzheimer's movement.

I will also make sure that Mom always remembers me and knows in her heart that I'm doing the very best that I can for her while she is still alive.

So, I continue on this remarkable and incredible journey with my Mom. Mom, please know that I will always be by your side no matter what, fighting the good fight and never, ever giving up. I will always protect you and provide you with unlimited love, caring, support, compassion, comfort, and joy. It's the least that I can do.

You know, it really wasn't supposed to be this way.

Epilogue

OUR BEAUTIFUL AND WONDERFUL Mom, Dorothy, unfortunately passed away from Alzheimer's disease on September 26th, 2015. As I told my sister and brother later that day, "this is the worst day of my life." I will always feel that way. She is forever my angel. The greatest feelings of being loved, cherished and appreciated always emanated directly from her to me.

Mom fought the good fight to the very end. I remember her winking at me several times during her struggle over that 10-day period before her passing. God bless her. She was really suffering. Amazingly, she still wanted to reassure and comfort me during her ordeal.

As Mom's primary caregivers, I know in my heart that my sister and I did the very best we could. Although there were some mistakes made along the way, they were honest mistakes. All of our decisions were based on love, respect, compassion, and devotion.

The suffering and anguish that Mom and Dad went through were probably the hardest things in their lives. It was hard on all of us, too. In spite of that, in one way this experience was beneficial for me. It gave me the opportunity to give all of my love, care, and gratitude back to my parents throughout their difficult journey.

I look back on my caregiving years and wish that I could do it again. Although we all have a certain lifespan, I would love to spend more time with Mom and Dad. If there is any good here, they're not suffering anymore and are both resting in peace together in heaven.

There is life after death

When I went to bed the evening of Mom's passing on September 26th, 2015, I said my prayers and intentions out loud, as I always do, with a special emphasis on Mom. After my prayers were completed, I had an out loud conversation with God. I was in a lot of emotional pain. I was grieving the loss of my Mom and the best friend I will ever have in my life. I told God that I was very hurt and angry that someone as beautiful and wonderful as our Mom could suffer so much for so long a period of time, especially in the last 10 days of her life. At one point, I was raising my voice in my bedroom. No one could hear me because the walls are concrete and very soundproof. I asked how God could allow this to happen. During my outburst of anger, I was also crying. I went to sleep after I had said my piece and had gotten some things off my chest.

The next evening, September 27th, 2015 was like any other evening. Of course, I said my prayers with special intentions for Mom and Dad. I fell asleep. Around 3:45 am on the morning of September 28th, 2015, I heard a woman's voice in my bedroom. It wasn't my Mom's voice but the voice of a middle-aged woman. It sounded very crisp and clear like it was a recorded message. The voice announced "Dorothy" out loud. It woke me up out of my deep sleep.

At this point, I was very tired but unable to fall back to sleep. And then, approximately 45 minutes later, it happened. Around 4:30 am, I could see a faint white mist coming towards me. I knew right away that it was Mom coming to visit me. I closed my eyes. As I lay in bed, a field of energy gradually enveloped my entire body from my feet up to my neck. I couldn't move but I wasn't frightened, either. I felt very calm and peaceful. When I tried to open my eyes, I couldn't open them all the way without squinting. What I saw then was truly extraordinary. I saw an image of Mom's face smiling at me. It was literally a few inches away from my face looking directly down at me. I remember mostly blue dots along with some red dots in the image. They seemed pixelated to me, which certainly made for a greater impact. I saw a few other colors, too. It was very bright. The predominant color was blue. It seemed like her image was there for at least 10 seconds or more and then it faded away.

I was still enveloped in the energy field around my body. Suddenly, I felt a bolt of energy from my Mom become focused as it shot right through my chest and into my heart. I let out an audible gasp as it entered my body. When it happened the first time, I felt a surge of overwhelming love coming into me so powerful that it seemed like my eyes would pop out of my head. It was an energy of love that was much stronger than I ever thought was possible. The power and magnitude of Mom's love in this moment was well beyond anything that I ever felt or experienced in life. This focused burst of energy going through my chest and into my heart happened at least two more times during this first spirit visit from Mom. All of this time, the energy field was still wrapped around me.

This event seemed to transpire over the course of several minutes. I also remember shaking my head back and forth during it and crying out "I'm sorry Mom. I'm sorry for all that you went through. I'm so sorry about what happened, etc."

At the end of it, the energy started to slowly dissipate. This supernatural experience was easily the most important, amazing and spectacular moment of my life. It proved to me that there really is life after death.

Around 6:30 am that same morning, I was awakened by the sensation of someone tickling my stomach. I woke up. I knew it was Mom being loving and playful with me. Then, I heard the blinds in the living room make a musical wind chime noise as Mom's spirit was brushing against them before leaving the area.

I have also experienced other spirit visits from Mom. They mostly occurred in the first few months after her passing. Most of the time it included a faint white mist or cloud coming towards me. On several different occasions, I felt Mom's energy again shoot through my chest and into my heart. I gasped each time this happened. This proves to me that Mom and I have an unbreakable bond. By reaching out to me this way, Mom demonstrated that her love for me transcended her passing. I'm so grateful and proud of her for communicating with me this way and in many other ways.

For those people who might find this story unbelievable, I'm telling you that I was fully awake during every spirit visit. As I mentioned previously, during my first spirit visit from Mom I was awakened twice, approximately two hours apart. I would swear this truth on a stack of bibles. I would gladly take a lie detector test, if one were requested to prove that it's 100% true. I know that I would pass any type of test because it really happened. I was incredibly happy to hear from Mom after her passing. She was telling me that she made it to heaven all right and that she was safe, happy and free, which means everything in the world to me. I believe her spirit came to comfort me in my grieving, pain and loss. She wanted to let me know how much she loves me and loves all that I was able to do for her.

Needless to say, I loved my Mom and Dad very much and would do anything for them. It was truly an honor to serve them. It has been said that boys are closer to their moms. This was true in my case. As I mentioned before, Mom was home with her children most of the time that we were growing up. She did take jobs outside the home from time to time, but it happened more often when we were older and into our teenage years. She did a lot of volunteer community, religious and charity work, even when we were young children. She also helped out many of our neighbors in their time of need with food or a helping hand.

I've thought about the intensity of my love and devotion to Mom for a long time. I came to the conclusion, right or wrong, that it would be really cruel and inhumane for our sacred connection to end after her passing. I can't imagine that there was such an incredible bond between us and that it would just end suddenly. That would mean I would never see Mom and Dad ever again, even after I pass away. I don't believe that based on my religious upbringing, on my belief in God, and the many signs that I've received from both Mom and Dad since they passed away. I do believe that there is a place called Heaven. I know that if it exists, that Mom and Dad are always and forever together there.

A few years before our Mom passed away, I remember a woman in my Mom's unit who also had Alzheimer's disease. During the time of our conversation, she was on a higher functioning level where we could have a normal conversation. I was telling her about Mom. She then went into a discussion of being a Mom that was so remarkable. She was saying things like "there's nothing like the love of your Mom. She loves you more than you can ever imagine. Her love is the best love in the world. She will do anything for her children. There's nothing that compares in this world to the love of a mother." She literally went on for about 5 minutes or so. I was astounded by her clarity and ability to describe what a mom's love truly is. I only wish at that time that I had recorded her talking about it. It was so heartfelt and touching.

The significance of the number 117

Shortly after our Mom passed away, I remember telling my sister and brother to look out for signs. We had already received signs from Dad after he passed away in 2007.

The number 117 has a special significance to us. This was the street number of our house growing up in Dumont, New Jersey.

The most prominent example of 117 that I can think of was when I was taking two online caregiving classes through Caregiving.com. I completed them in November 2016. As part of the final certification process, all of the students were required to fly to Chicago and perform a 45-minute presentation on their area of expertise.

I stayed there at the hotel in Chicago for three days and two nights. As I was checking out, the young lady at the front desk asked about my stay. I told her that everything went well. She asked me if I could complete a survey of the hotel through tripadvisor.com. I told her that I would do so after my return.

Subsequently, I arrived at Chicago O'Hare Airport for my flight back home. I was waiting at my gate and talking to a woman there. I told her about caregiving to my Mom and why I was there in Chicago. As we were talking, a young male airport employee brought an elderly man in a wheelchair to our gate. This gentleman was also returning to New Jersey on the same flight. All of a sudden, I noticed the side of his wheelchair. It had the number 117 on it! This was the only wheelchair in all of Chicago O'Hare Airport that would have had that specific number on it.

Approximately one-and-a-half weeks after returning home, I completed the tripadvisor.com survey, as promised. About one week or so after submitting my completed survey, I received an email back from tripadvisor.com. When I read it, it stated that 117 people had read my review! One hundred seventeen people on the nose! It wasn't 116 people or 118 people. These two incidents were more than just a lucky coincidence to me. I believe it was a message from Mom showing her love and approval of me and what I had accomplished in Chicago.

There have also been other prominent times when the number 117 showed up on either a retail store receipt, a license plate number, the side of a police car or bus, etc. I know there are some people who would discount it by saying that I'm looking for the number 117 to appear. I do notice it under different circumstances. Most of the time, I believe that it's a sign from above. It has happened often enough under quite noteworthy conditions.

What I've learned as a family caregiver

I've learned many lessons as a family caregiver. I have tried to be as inclusive and concise as possible in my list below. These items are not necessarily all listed in order of importance.

- *You must give your loved one hope!* This will definitely make them happier, healthier and encourage them to stay hopeful, alive and alert for as long as possible. Visit them as often as you can. Vary the times that you show up during the day and/or evening. This way the staff will understand that you can show up at any time. Be on as good terms as possible with all of the staff. This is not just good common sense. You must ensure they're always giving your loved one the best care and treatment possible, regardless of whether or not you are present.
- Regarding additional supplementation and nutrition, always check and get their nursing home doctor's and staff dietician's approval for any supplements and/or food or drink items that you may want to give them. For example, as many people know,

grapefruit and grapefruit juice can interact adversely with certain medications. Also, if you want to add something like an Omega 3 supplement to their daily regimen, you must get approval from their nursing home doctor before you can do that. Always check first and get all of the necessary medical and staff dietician approvals before adding any supplements and/or food or drink items to their diet.

- Be present and focused at all times to whatever is going on, especially to the most important matters.

- Always be aware of your surroundings whenever you're in the nursing home. You are there first and foremost to love, comfort, protect and serve your loved one. But you must also protect yourself. There are people there who also have either Alzheimer's disease or another form of dementia. Some of them have the potential to act out in a violent or antisocial manner. It's not their fault. It's because of their disease and because they are in an unfamiliar environment. It's understandable they would have feelings of being abandoned. They may also feel afraid, hurt, angry, sad, resentful, confused, lonely, frustrated, anxious, depressed, despondent, etc. regarding their current life situation and circumstances. Unfortunately, they may even feel they're being punished for something that they did, even though it isn't true.

- Please remember that our senior citizens have feelings, too. This is always important to keep in mind regarding those who have Alzheimer's disease, including those people with early onset of this disease. Just because someone is getting older, their feelings don't age.

- Be organized and stay on top of all paperwork and documentation. I recommend either keeping a written journal, an online journal and/or a detailed record of events in case there are any problems within the nursing home or anywhere else where healthcare is provided. In the event that you ever need it, you will be happy and content in the knowledge that you have already documented it.

- Both art and music therapy have proven beneficial to people with Alzheimer's disease. Art therapy can stimulate the brain and boost cognitive function. It can help bring back memories and temporarily improve the language ability of those patients who sometimes struggle with speech. It brings a unique creativity and happiness to people suffering from this disease. Likewise, music therapy offers benefits like stimulating many parts of the brain simultaneously. Among other benefits, it can also improve their mood and enhance their memory. It is best to let them listen to music that they have a positive emotional connection with. Your nursing home may have established programs for art and music therapy. If they do, they should be able to help your loved one and to demonstrate its effectiveness while you are present.

- Aromatherapy can also be used as a treatment to help them. Studies have shown the beneficial effects on cognitive function for people suffering from Alzheimer's disease.

- Dogs and other trained pets can be a welcome guest to someone with Alzheimer's disease. First, please make sure that your loved one can handle a visit from a trained dog along with their trainer. It's probably a good idea to be there for at least the first few times to make sure that everything goes well. A pets' presence can help reduce the effects of Alzheimer's disease. For example, it helps with anxiety and loneliness.

- I understand that there are other therapeutic treatments available to people with Alzheimer's disease. You must make sure that whatever method you would like to try, that first you get approval from the appropriate medical staff in charge of your loved one.

- Instead of telling your loved one stories about them and their family, it is a much better idea to show them family photographs while you tell a story. At some point in their journey a loved one may not understand when asked if they remember "your brother Paul" or "your sister Diane." They may not have an image of them in their mind. It's more beneficial for everyone involved to show them in a photograph together like "here's a picture of you with your brother Paul and your sister Diane." They will understand better when you point out familiar people to them (ex. close family and friends) that can come from family photographs or albums.

- There are times when items will be taken from their room. For example, most personal items, like a teddy bear, can be taken from your loved one's room by another person in the unit who has Alzheimer's disease or another form of dementia. They don't understand that it's not their room and that it doesn't belong to them. A good countermeasure is to mark these items with your loved one's name or initials and to install a hidden security camera, as detailed in the next bulleted item. If the personal item is found in another resident's room, it will be easy to recover it with your identification already on it.

- It's a very good idea to have a hidden security camera in your loved one's room to help ensure that they are always safe and secure. Please note that state laws can differ on this issue. There's a real concern about a patient's privacy versus their need to have that extra level of protection. Installing a security camera is just in case there are any problems, including the possibility that either an aide or another resident could assault them while they're alone in their room. God forbid that this were to ever happen, but it's extremely unfortunate that it can occur. This is a real case of where *it's better to be safe than sorry*.

- Love is the force that drives you through all of the ups, downs and unexpected turns. Remember to always be as loving, patient and compassionate as possible both with and on behalf of your loved one. They need you now more than ever. So, it's your time to step up and do the right thing for them. We counted on them helping us to grow up properly, now they are counting on us to take good care of them in their declining years of life.

- Know that all of the time you spend with your loved one is time well spent and time that can never be replaced. You will always be grateful that you devoted yourself to spending this quality time both with them and on their behalf.

- When your loved ones have eventually passed on, if you did the best that you could do, you will have few or no regrets about the caregiving years.

- Remember to take good care of yourself, too. *It's been my personal experience that you can neglect yourself for certain periods of time and still be a loving and effective caregiver.* However, I believe the overall quality of your time spent with and working for your loved one is best accomplished by striving to maintain a healthy balance in life. Set aside some down time for yourself as a caregiver doing whatever it is that you like or need to do. If you will be away for several days, a weekend, or even a week; make sure family members are there to cover for you and are always able to contact you while you're away, if necessary.

Some Final Observations

One of the many things that I learned from Mom and Dad growing up is that there is a certain nobility and majesty to life. Mom and Dad were noble, moral, ethical and spiritual people. Being alive isn't just about making money, paying bills, and surviving. Life is also about being a good and kind person and always trying to do the right thing. It's important to carry ourselves with as much love, grace, dignity, humility and gratitude as possible, in spite of the many obstacles that life can throw at us.

I want to be able to look back on my life, view everything that happened, and know that I always did the best that I could do. I've made my share of mistakes. However, I'm committed to learning from everything. I want to transform my life experiences into something far greater than just taking care of myself every day. I want to be grateful for everything, especially the things that help me to live with more love, courage, and dignity every day. I want to become a being of light and love. I want to be a leader on behalf of Alzheimer's disease who advocates with true strength, passion and effectiveness. I want to make a significant, positive and lasting difference for this cause. I absolutely want to leave this world a better place for having lived in it.

And finally, I hope and pray that when my time comes to pass on, that I will be together forever in heaven with my Mom and Dad.